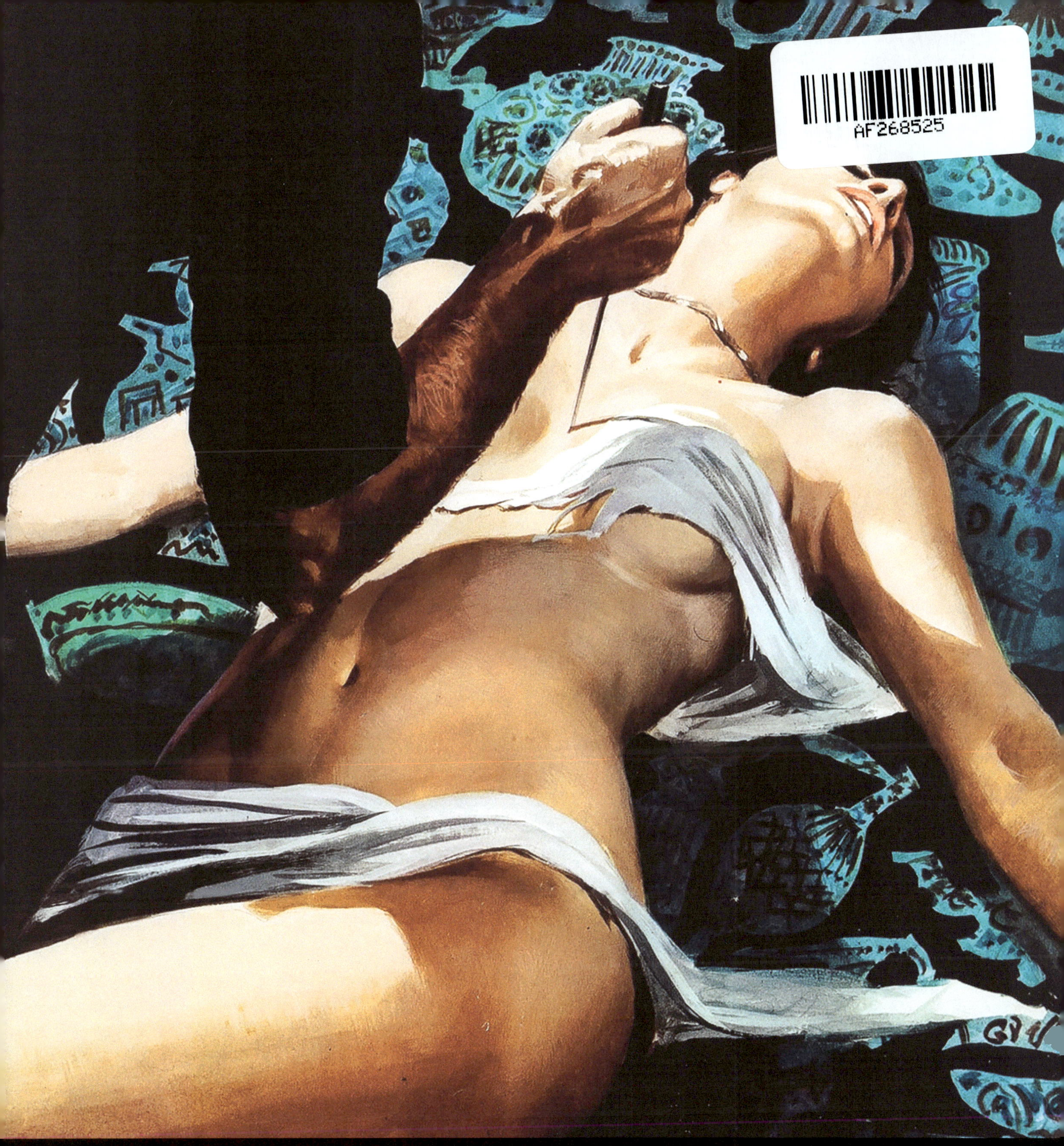

CRYPT OF CARNAL TERRORS

100 ARTWORKS FOR ITALIAN HORROR & GIALLO FILM POSTERS

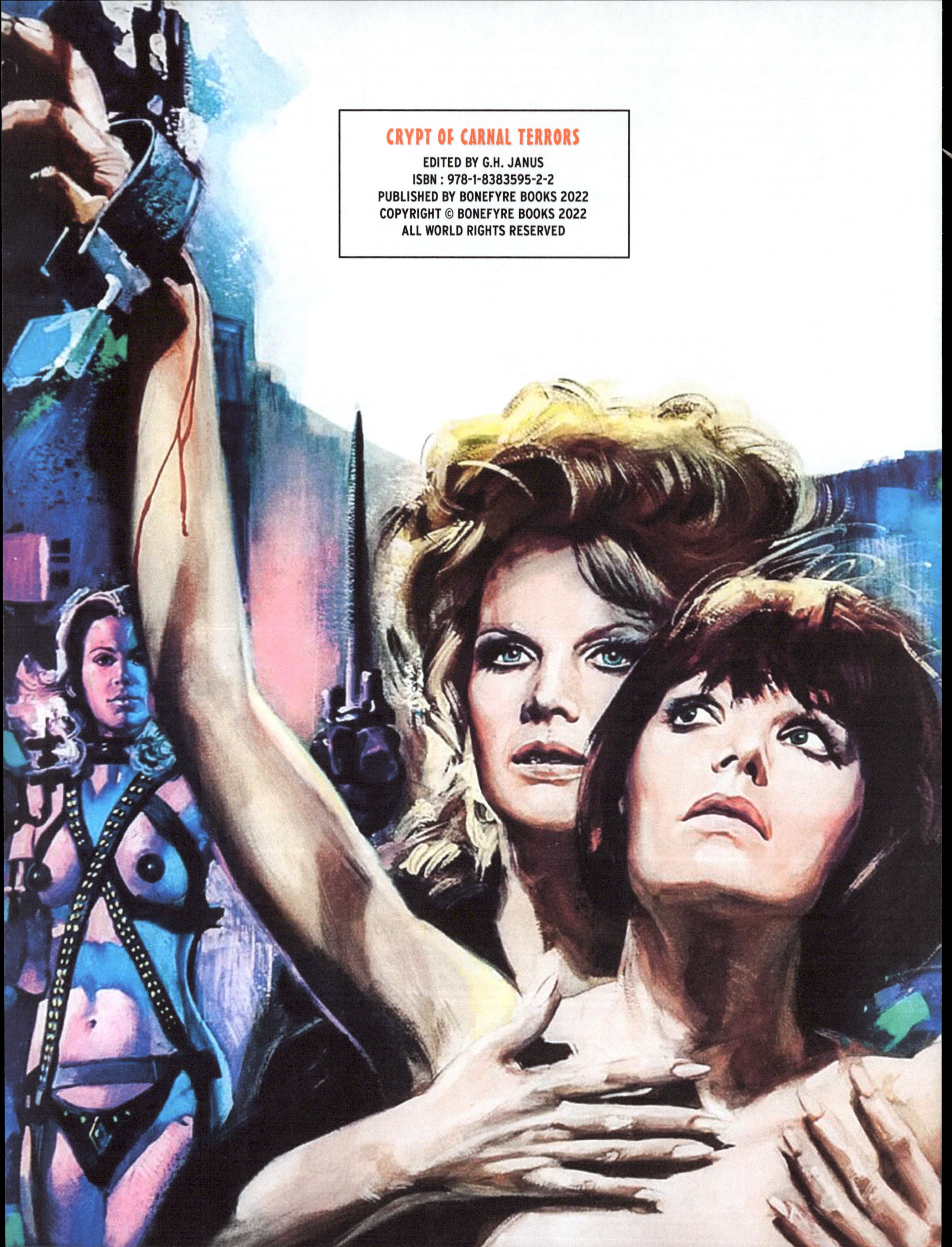
CRYPT OF CARNAL TERRORS
EDITED BY G.H. JANUS
ISBN : 978-1-8383595-2-2
PUBLISHED BY BONEFYRE BOOKS 2022
COPYRIGHT © BONEFYRE BOOKS 2022
ALL WORLD RIGHTS RESERVED

CONTENTS

LA VERITÀ SECONDO SATANA (1972) — 1
BABA YAGA (1973) — 2
DER HENKER VON LONDON (1963) — 4
CIRCUS OF FEAR (1966) — 5
DIE GRUFT MIT DEM RÄTSELSCHLOSS (1964) — 6
DER MÖNCH MIT DER PEITSCHE (1967) — 7
DAS INDISCHE TUCH (1963) — 8
DER BUCKLIGE VON SOHO (1966) — 9
DER HUND VON BLACKWOOD CASTLE (1968) — 10
DIE BLAUE HAND (1967) — 11
DER GORILLA VON SOHO (1968) — 12, 13
IM BANNE DES UNHEIMLICHEN (1968) — 14, 15
DER MANN MIT DEM GLASAUGE (1968) — 16
DIE WEISSE SPINNE (1963) — 17
BLOOD OF THE VAMPIRE (1958) — 18
I VAMPIRI (1957) — 19
LA MASCHERA DEL DEMONIO (1960) — 20
L'ORRIBILE SEGRETO DEL DR. HICHCOCK (1962) — 21
DANZA MACABRA (1964) — 22
THE SHE BEAST (1966) — 23
FRANKENSTEIN 1970 (1958) — 24
HORRORS OF THE BLACK MUSEUM (1959) — 25
HOUSE OF USHER (1960) — 26
THE PREMATURE BURIAL (1962) — 27
METEMPSYCO (1963) — 28
THE TERROR (1963) — 29
IL BOIA SCARLATTO (1965) — 30
HORROR (1963) — 31
MATANGO (1963) — 32
THE NIGHT CALLER (1965) — 33
TWICE-TOLD TALES (1963) — 34
KAIDAN SEMUSHI OTOKO (1965) — 35
CURSE OF THE MUMMY'S TOMB (1964) — 36
FRANKENSTEIN CREATED WOMAN (1967) — 37
DIE SCHLANGENGRUBE UND DAS PENDEL (1967) — 38, 39
THE BLOOD BEAST TERROR (1968) — 40
NIGHT OF THE LIVING DEAD (1968) — 41
THE OBLONG BOX (1969) — 42
AND NOW THE SCREAMING STARTS (1973) — 43
CRY OF THE BANSHEE (1970) — 44
BLOOD ON SATAN'S CLAW (1971) — 45
THE ABOMINABLE DR. PHIBES (1971) — 46
LA NOCHE DE WALPURGIS (1971) — 47
TALES FROM THE CRYPT (1972) — 48
GLI ORRORI DEL CASTELLO DI NORIMBERGA (1972) — 49
LE DEMONE (1972) — 50
DEMONS OF THE MIND (1972) — 51
THE SCARS OF DRACULA (1969) — 52
EL CONDE DRACULA (1970) — 53
HOUSE OF DARK SHADOWS (1970) — 54
COUNT YORGA, VAMPIRE (1970) — 55
THE VAMPIRE LOVERS (1970) — 56
LUST FOR A VAMPIRE (1971) — 57
BLOOD FOR DRACULA (1974) — 58
DRACULA (1974) — 59
LADY FRANKENSTEIN (1971) — 60, 61
TERROR! IL CASTELLO DELLE DONNE MALEDETTE (1974) — 62, 63
LA ORGÍA NOCTURNA DE LOS VAMPIROS (1973) — 64
LA LUPA MANNARA (1976) — 65
IL SESSO DE LA STREGA (1973) — 66
JACK EL DESTRIPADOR DE LONDRES (1972) — 67
LA REBELIÓN DE LAS MUERTAS (1973) — 68
THE SPECTRE OF EDGAR ALLAN POE (1974) — 69
BLUE SUNSHINE (1977) — 70
SHIVERS (1975) — 71
LA BIMBA DI SATANA (1982) — 72
AENIGMA (1987) — 73
DIABOLIQUE (1955) — 74
PEEPING TOM (1959) — 75
THE STRANGLER (1964) — 76
THEATRE OF DEATH (1965) — 77
JACK THE RIPPER (1976) — 78
PICTURE MOMMY DEAD (1966) — 79
LA LAMA NEL CORPO (1966) — 80
OPERAZIONE PAURA (1966) — 81
KRIMINAL (1966) — 82
SATANIK (1968) — 83
L'UCCELLO DALLE PIUME DI CRISTALLO (1970) — 84
IL GATTO A NOVE CODE (1971) — 85
5 BAMBOLE PER LA LUNA D'AGOSTO (1970) — 86
LA GATTA IN CALORE (1972) — 87
LA TARANTOLA DAL VENTRE NERO (1971) — 88
LA NOTTE CHE EVELYN USCÌ DALLA TOMBA (1971) — 89
LA CORTA NOTTE DELLE BAMBOLE DI VETRO (1971) — 90
PERCHÉ QUELLE STRANE GOCCE DI SANGUE SUL CORPO DI JENNIFER? (1971) — 91
ALLA RICERCA DEL PIACERE (1972) — 92
LE AMANTI DEL MOSTRO (1974) — 93
CHI L'HA VISTA MORIRE? (1972) — 94
MIO CARO ASSASSINO (1972) — 95
I SPIT ON YOUR GRAVE (1978) — 96
LO SQUARTATORE DI NEW YORK (1982) — 97
DER FROSCH MIT DER MASKE (1959) — 98
DER WÜRGER VON SCHLOSS BLACKMOOR (1963) — 99
THE SPIRAL STAIRCASE (1946) — 100
SON OF FRANKENSTEIN (1938) — 101
HOUSE OF DRACULA (1945) — 102
FRANKENSTEIN MEETS THE WOLFMAN (1943) — 103

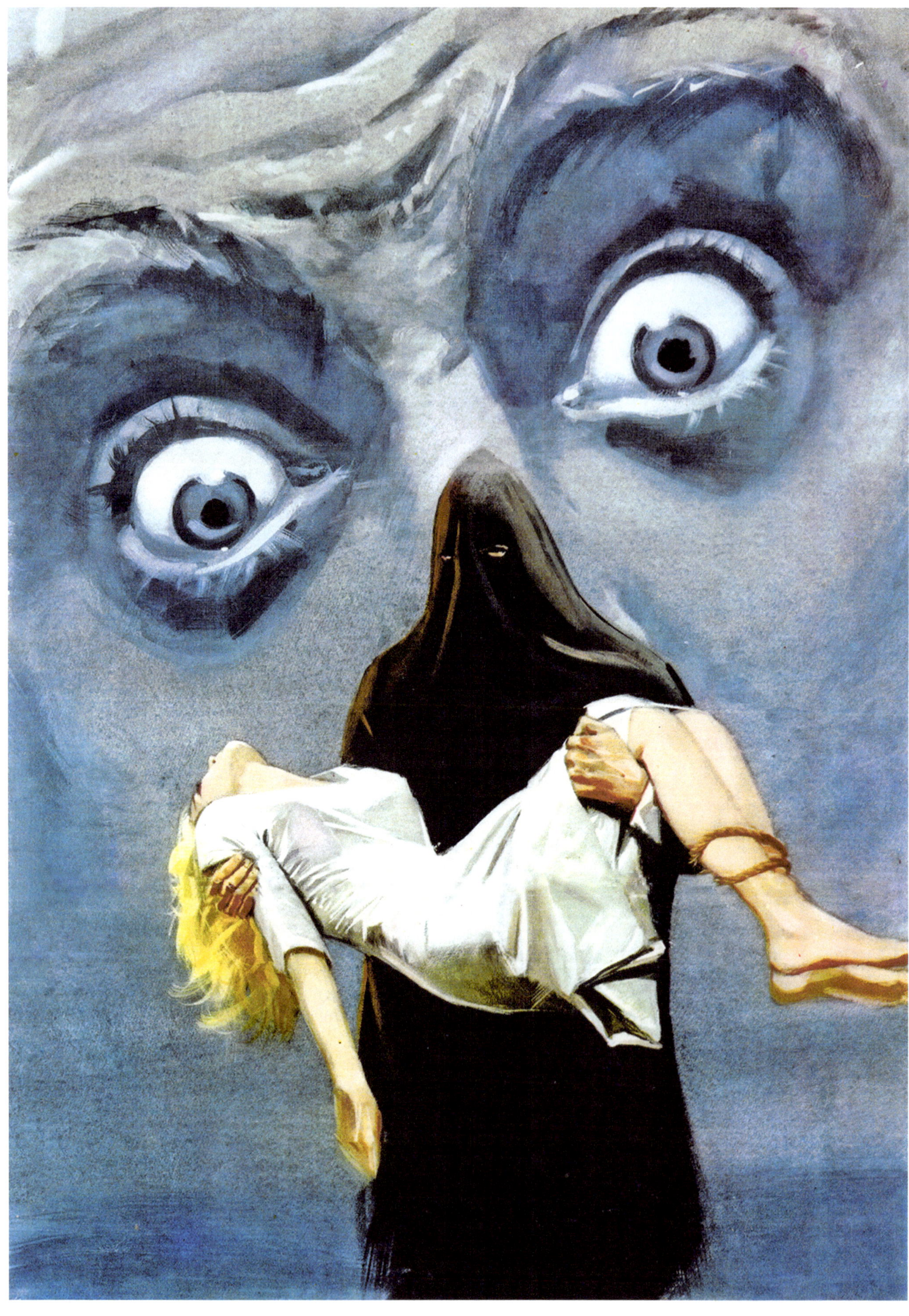

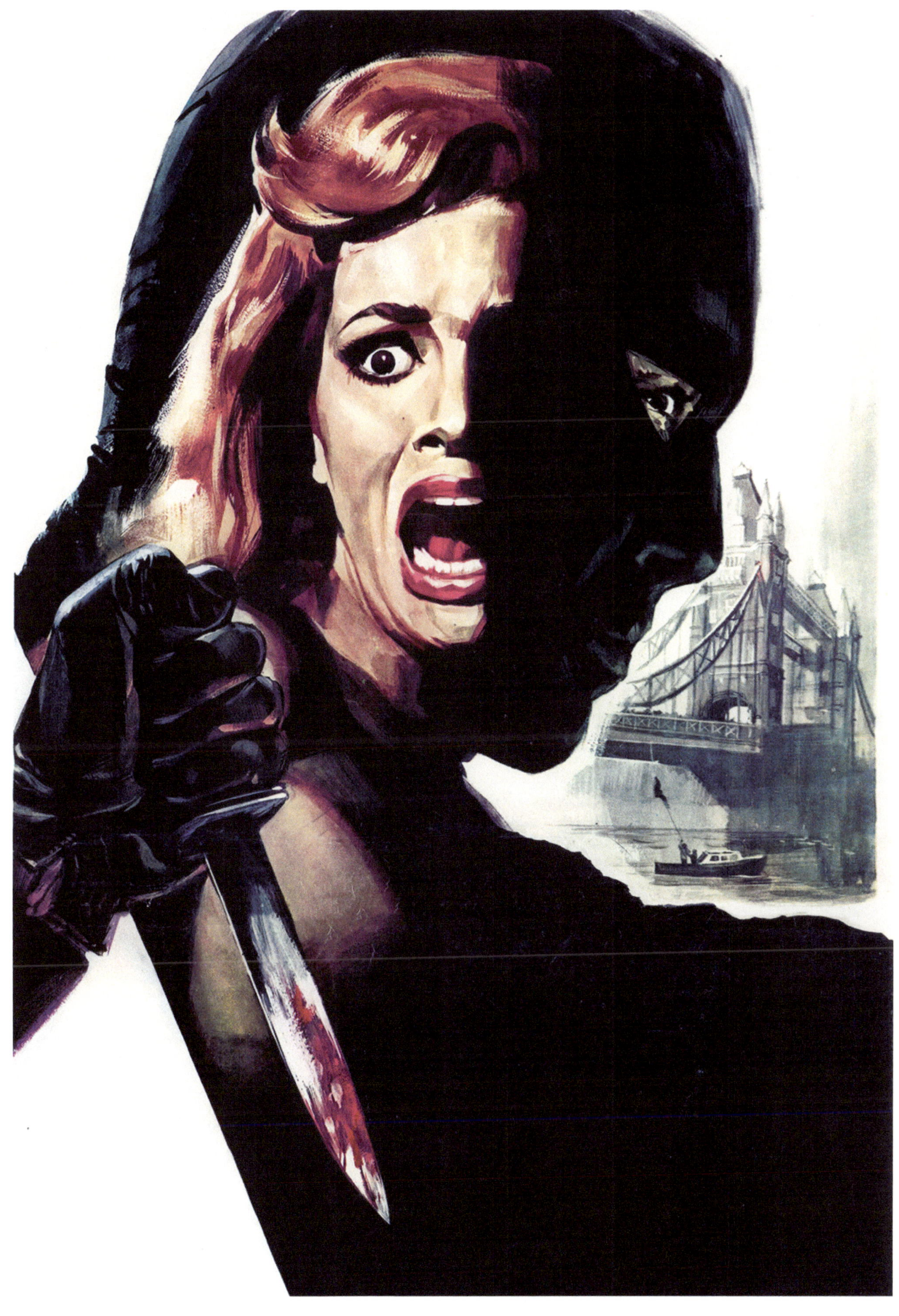

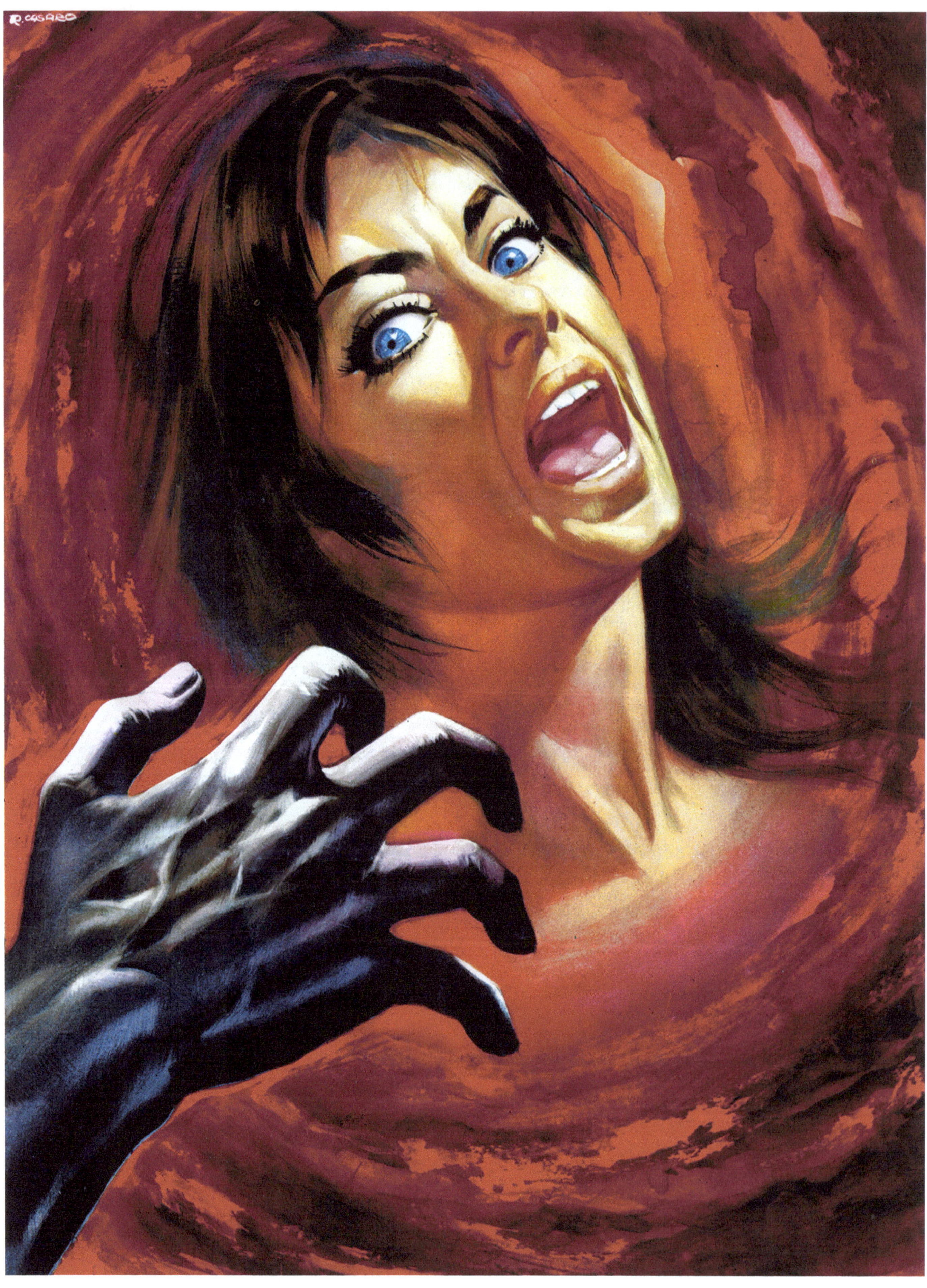

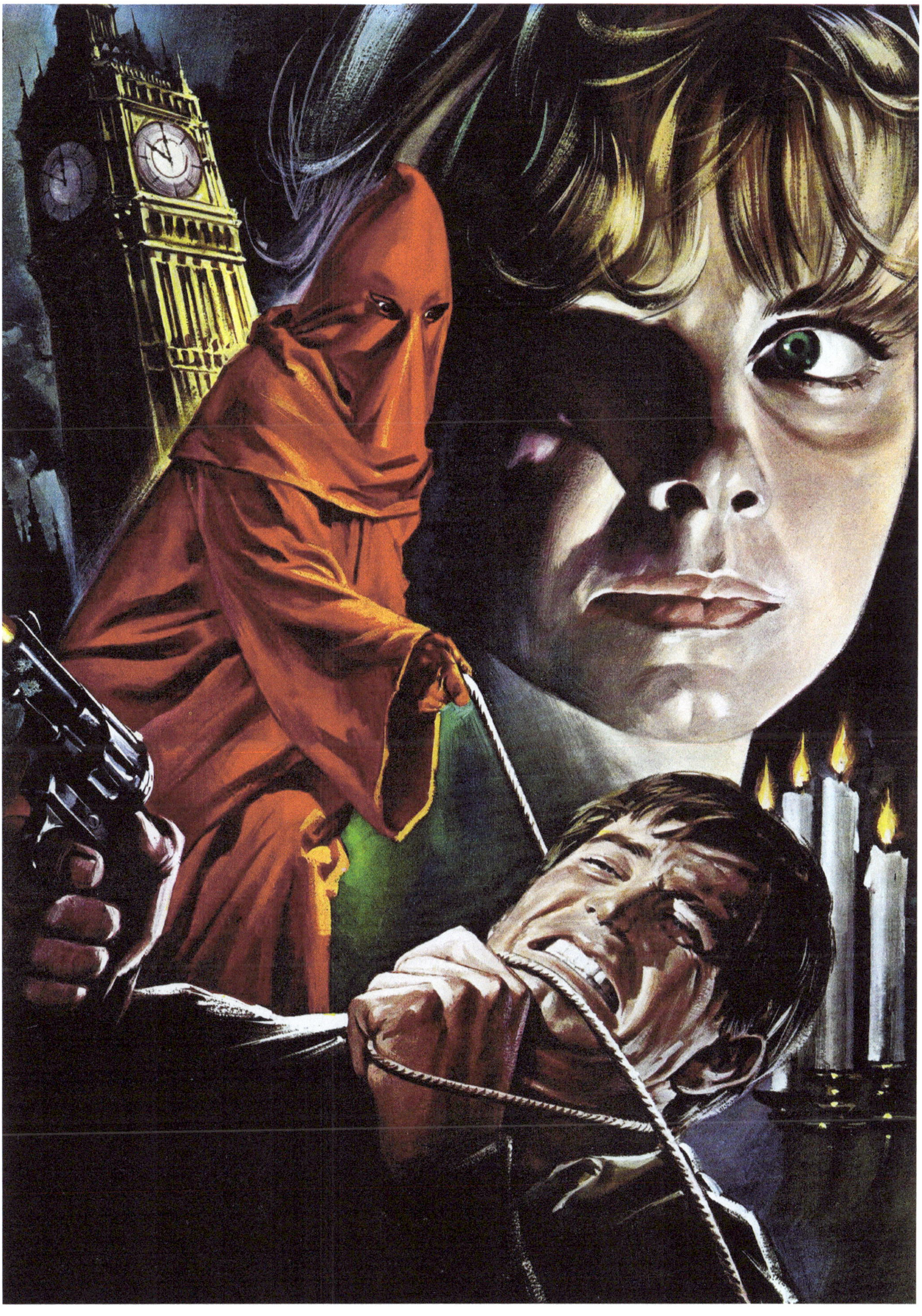

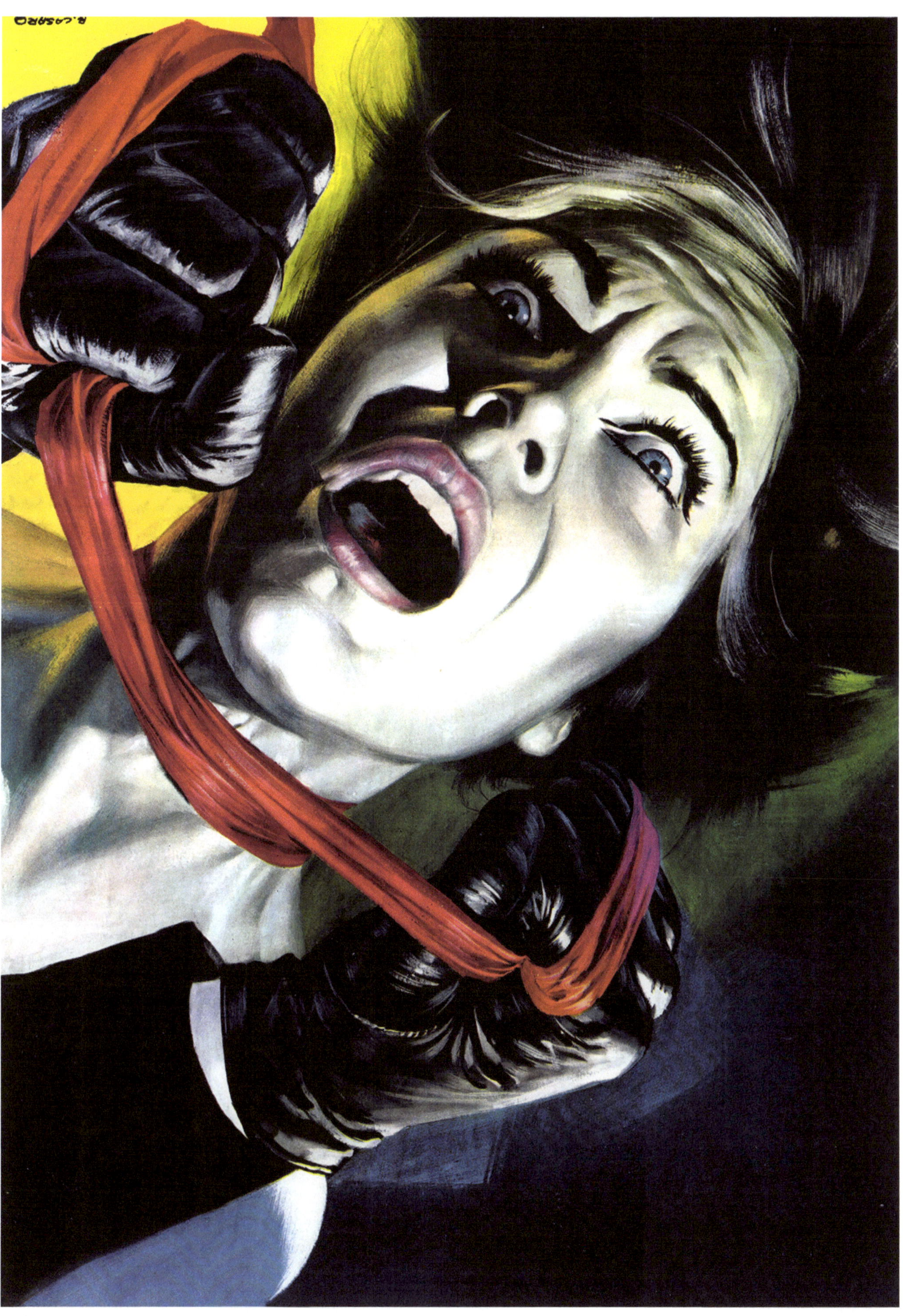

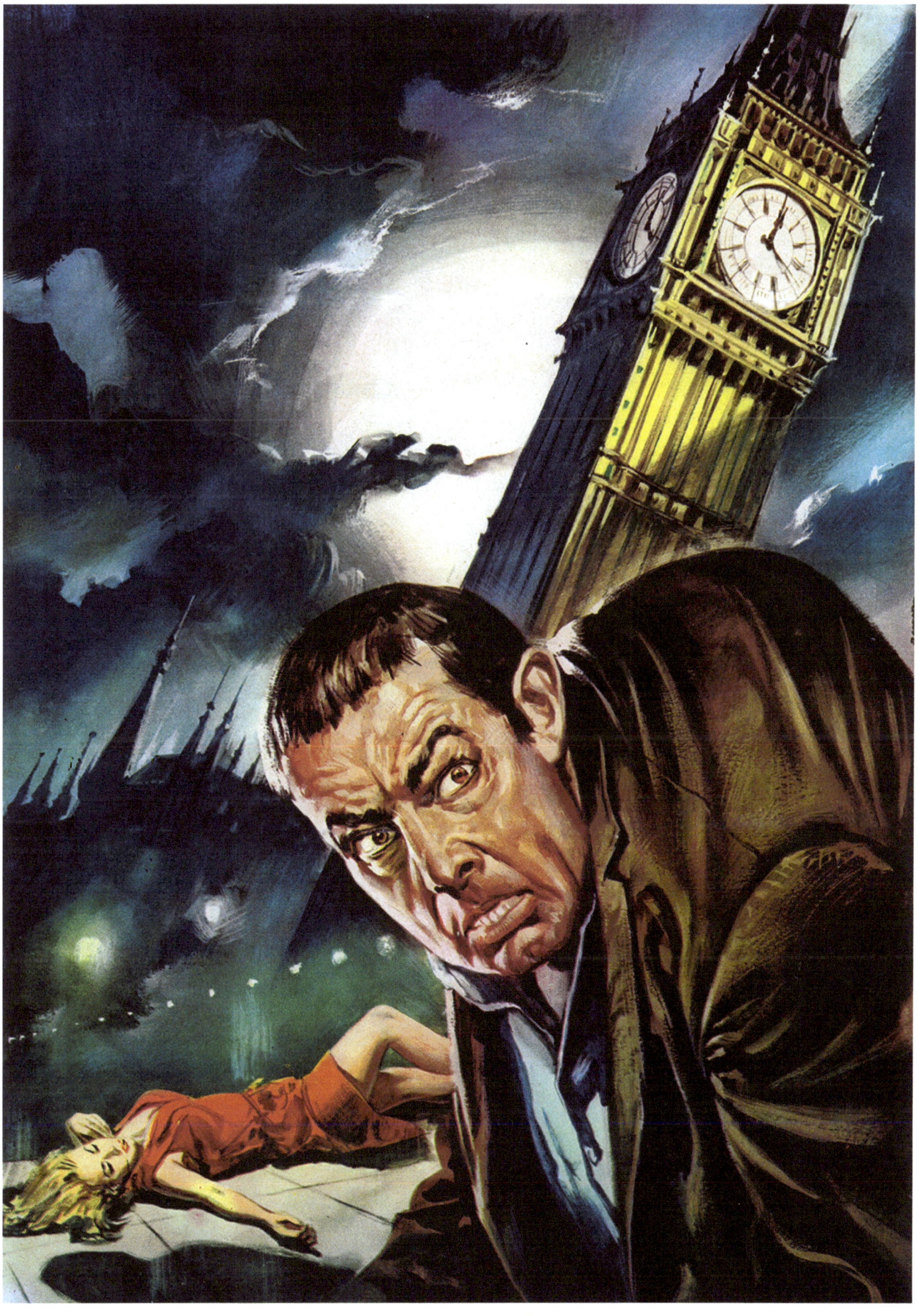

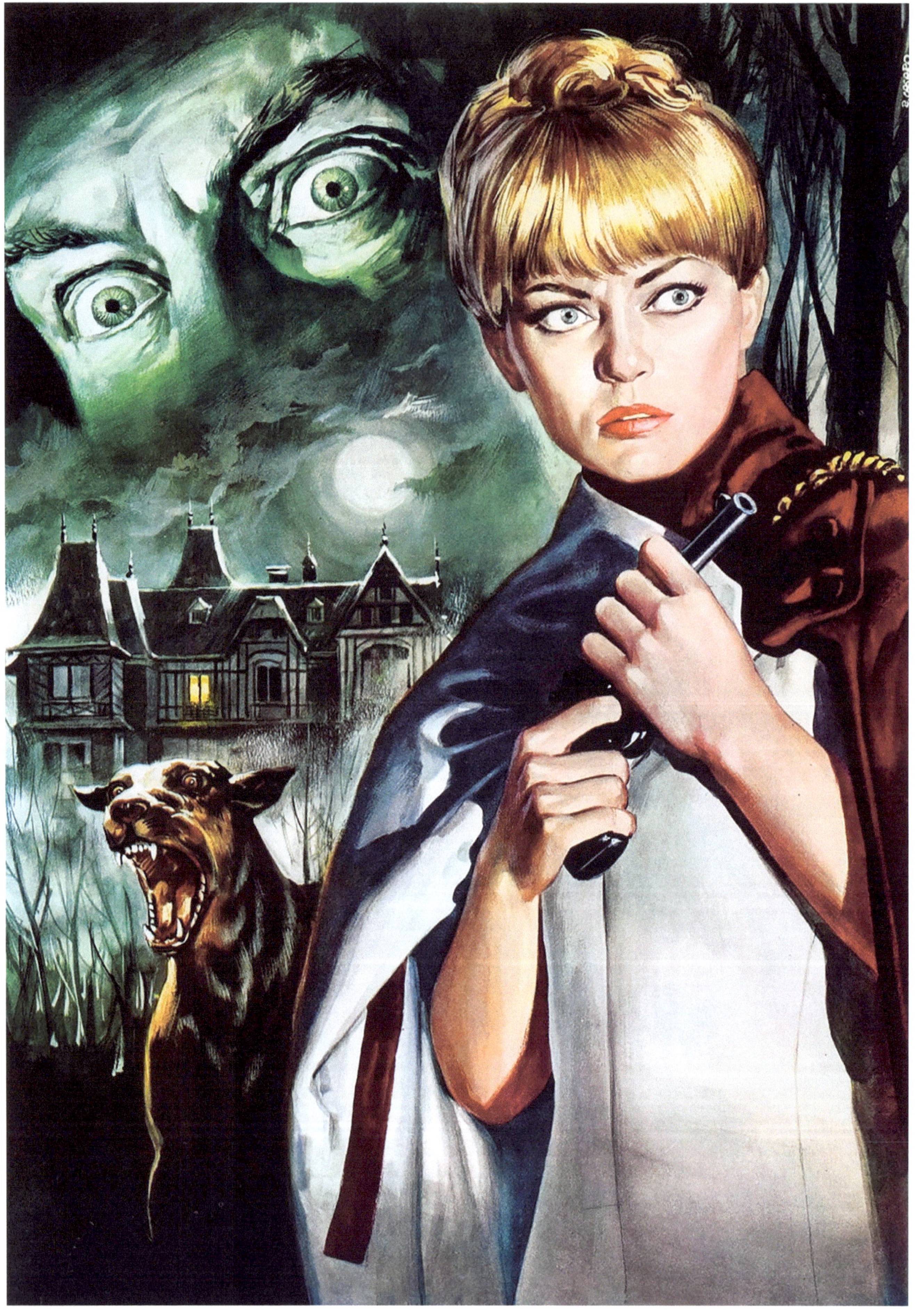

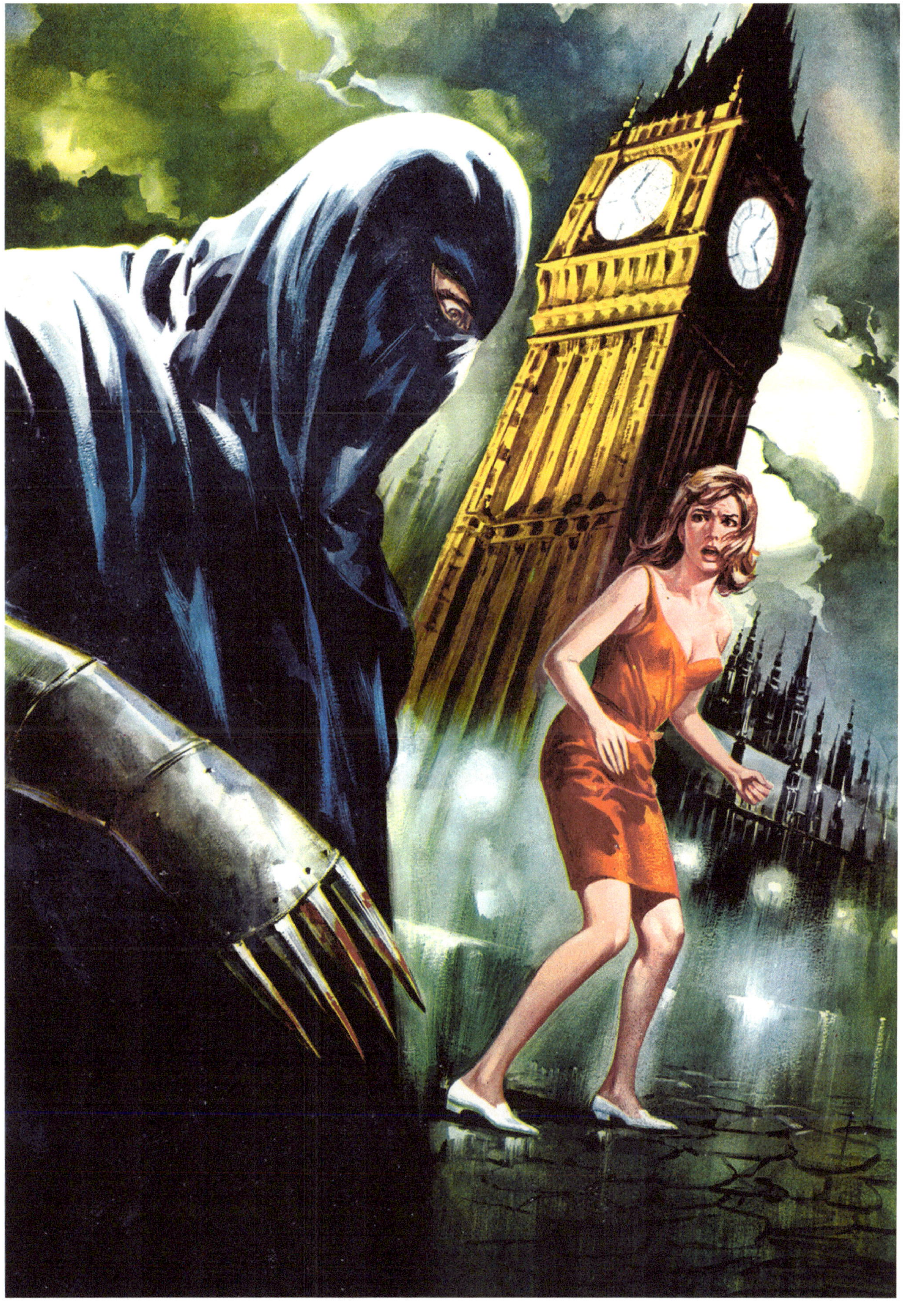

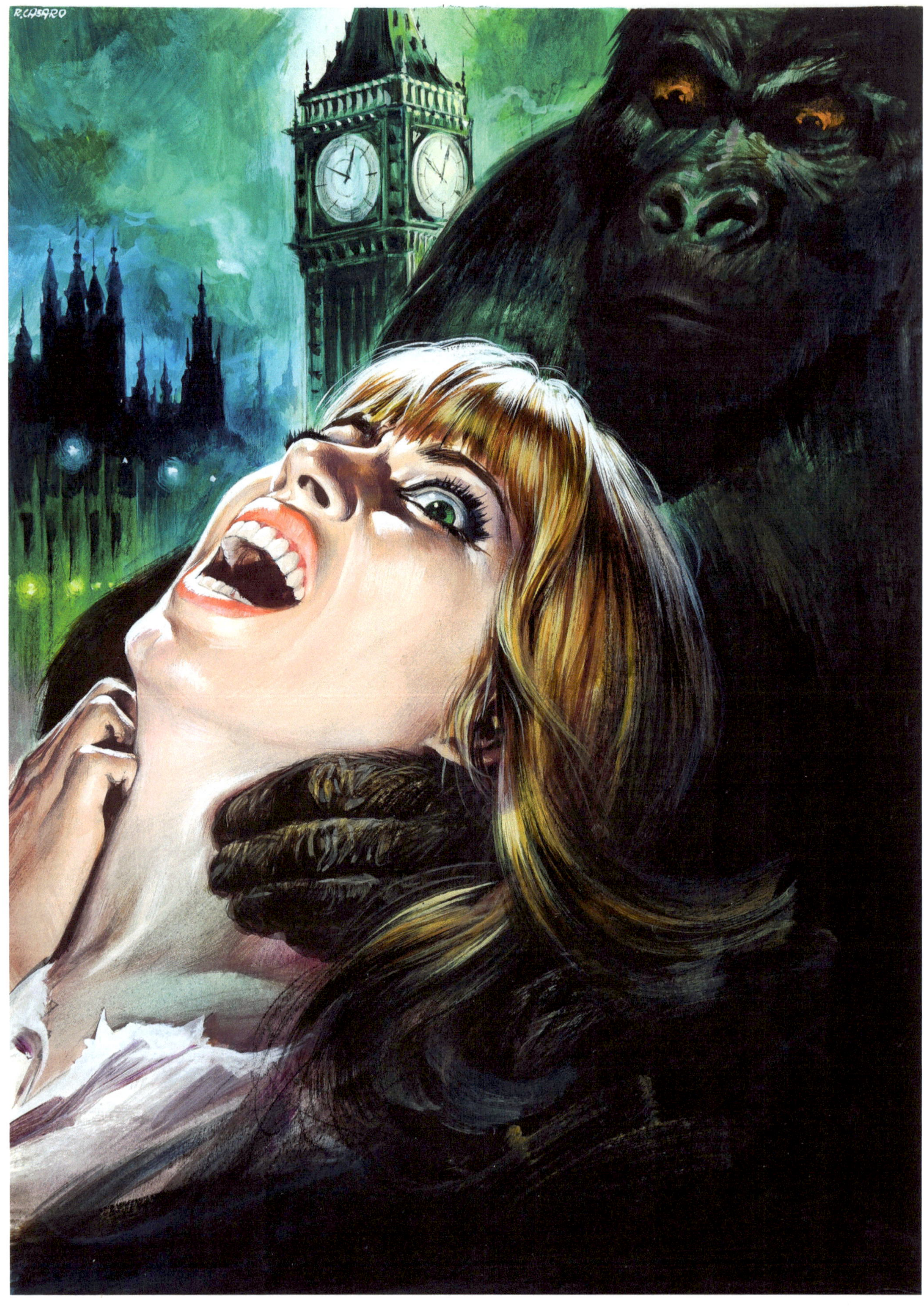

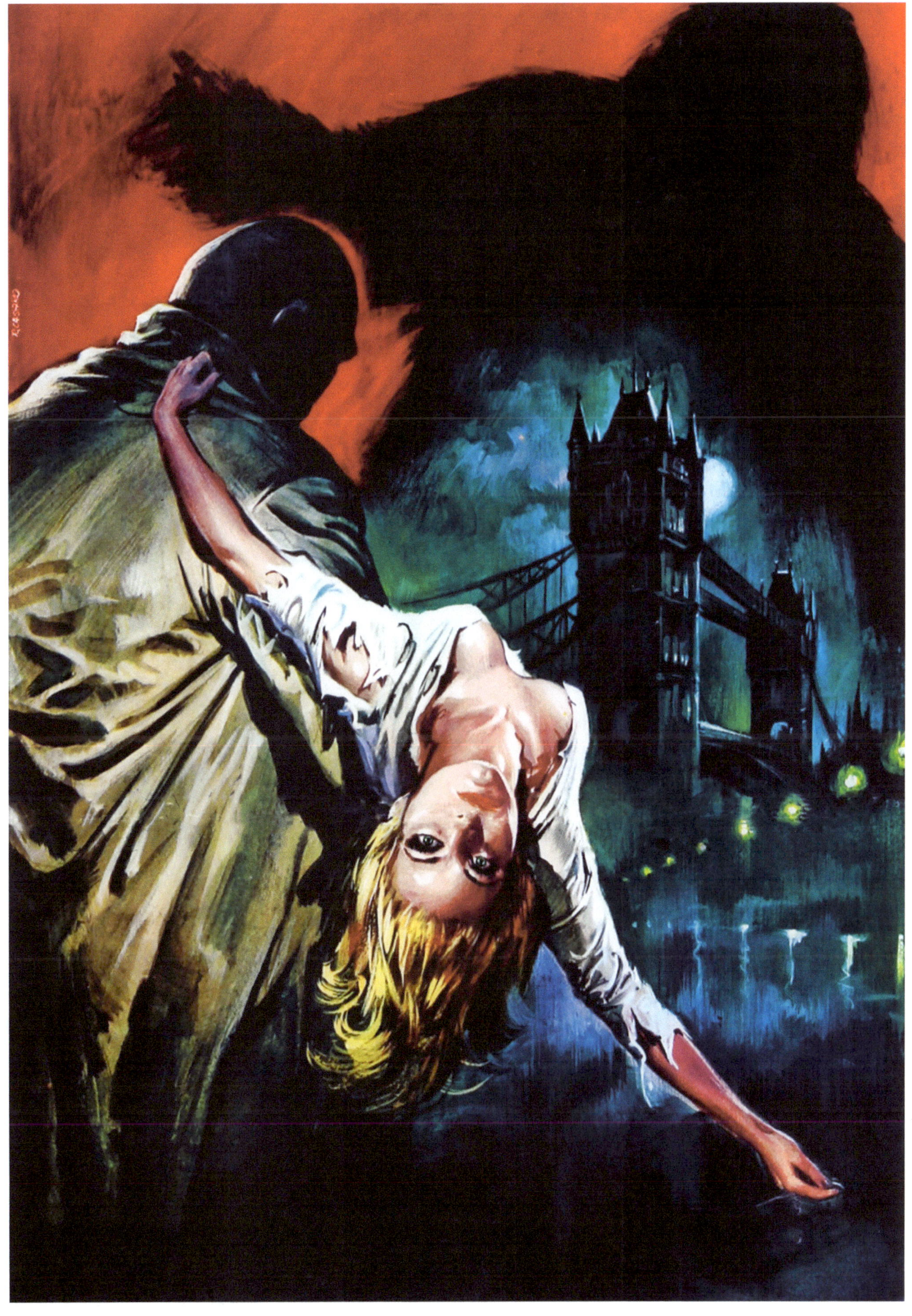

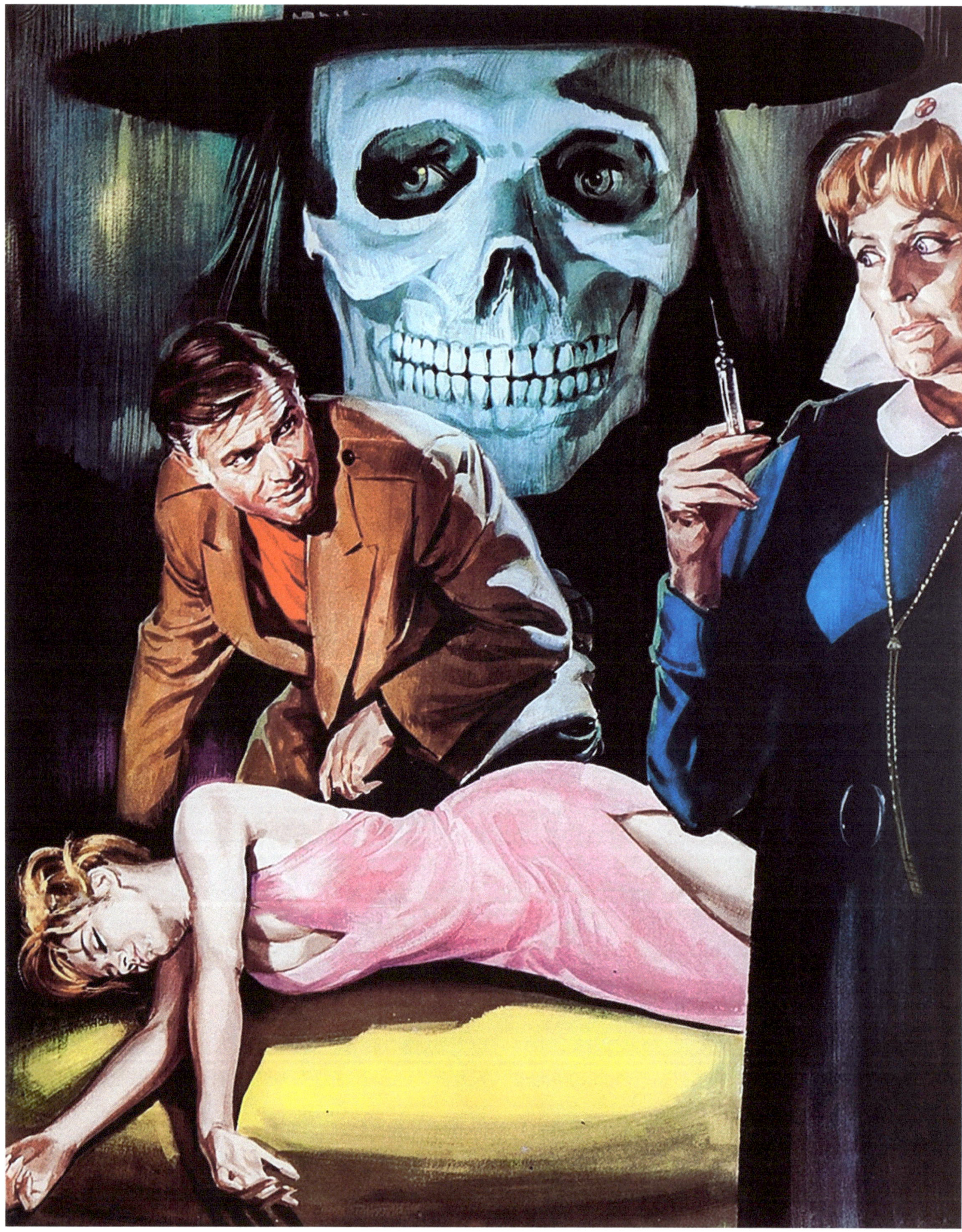

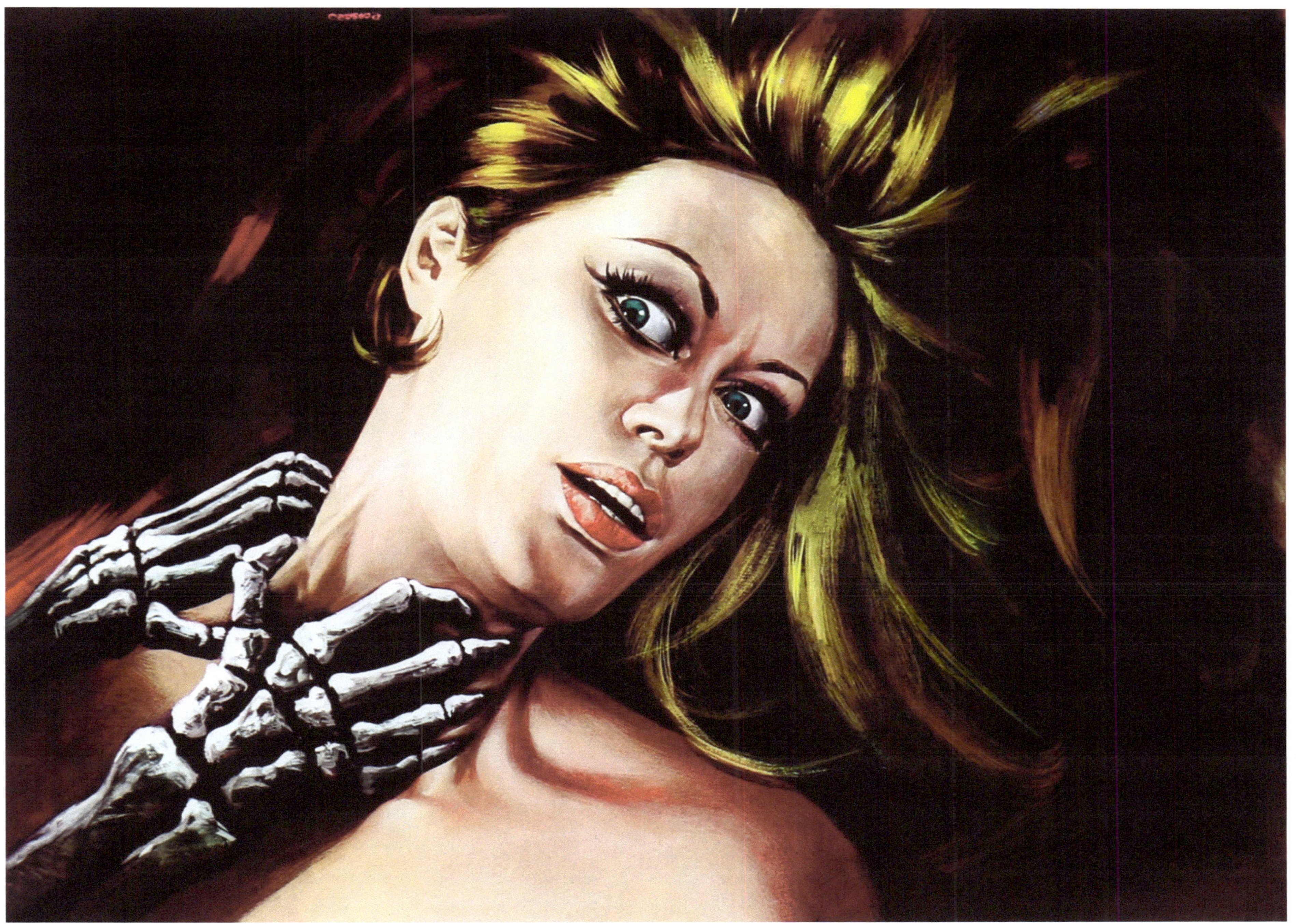

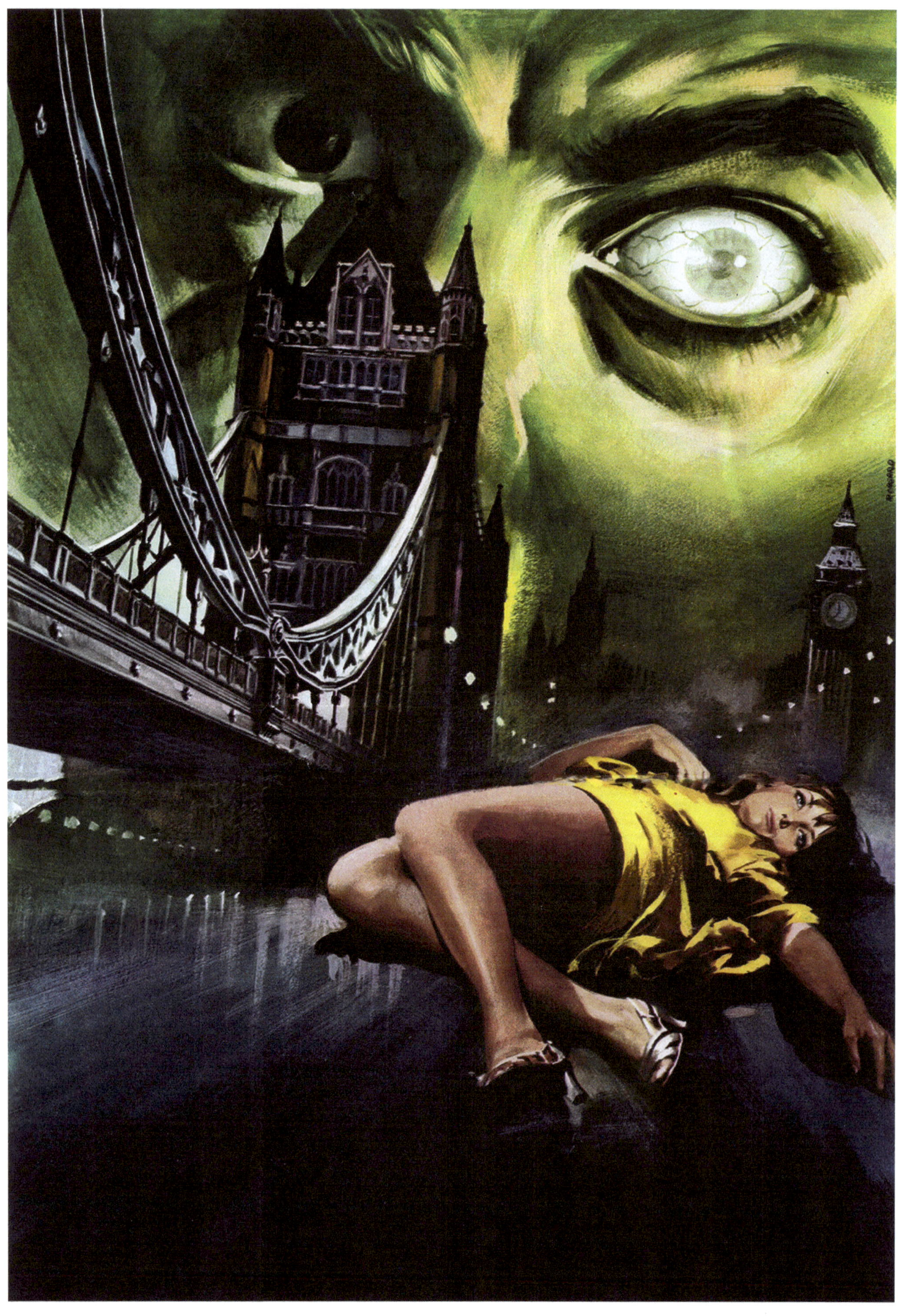

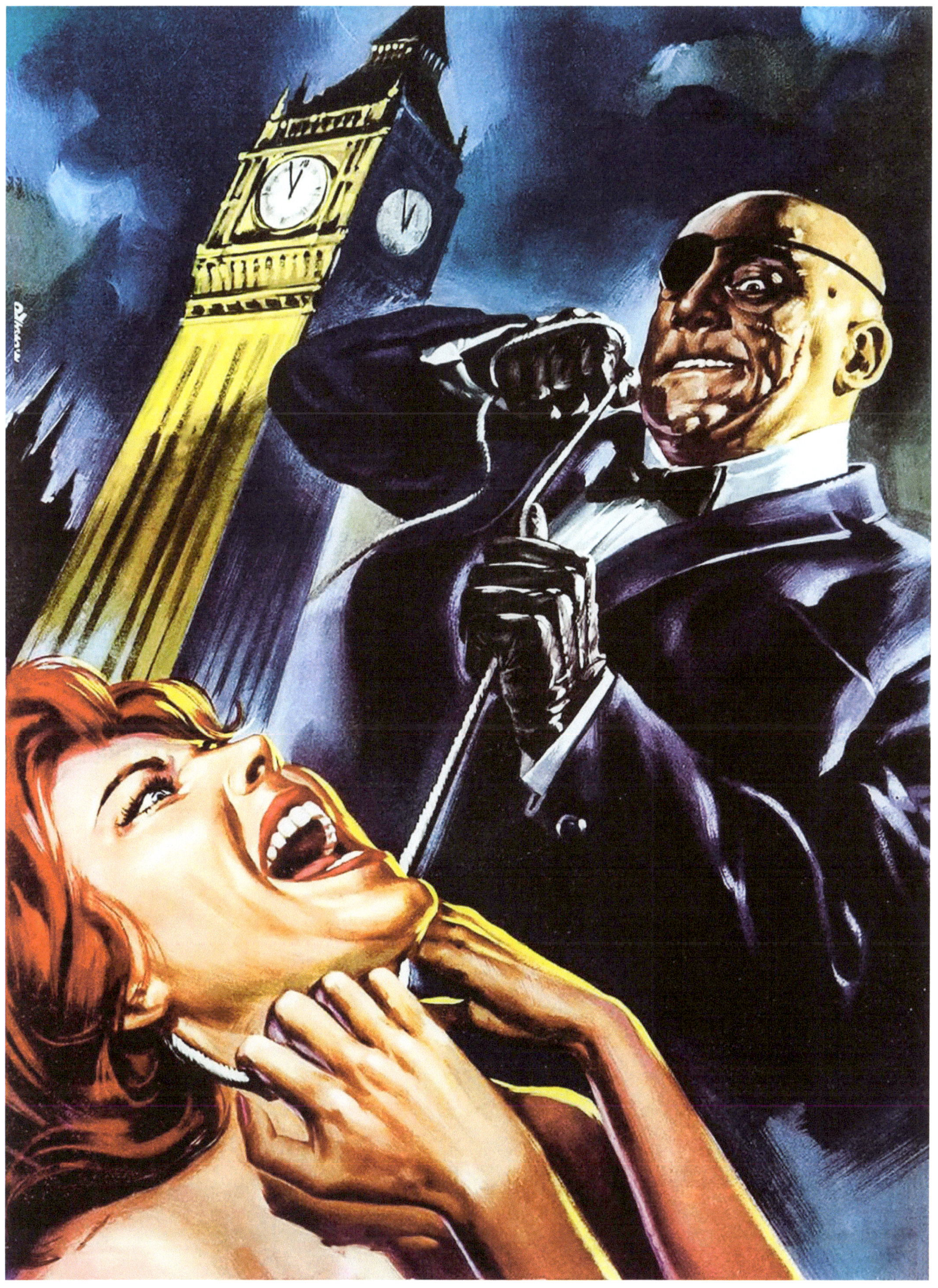

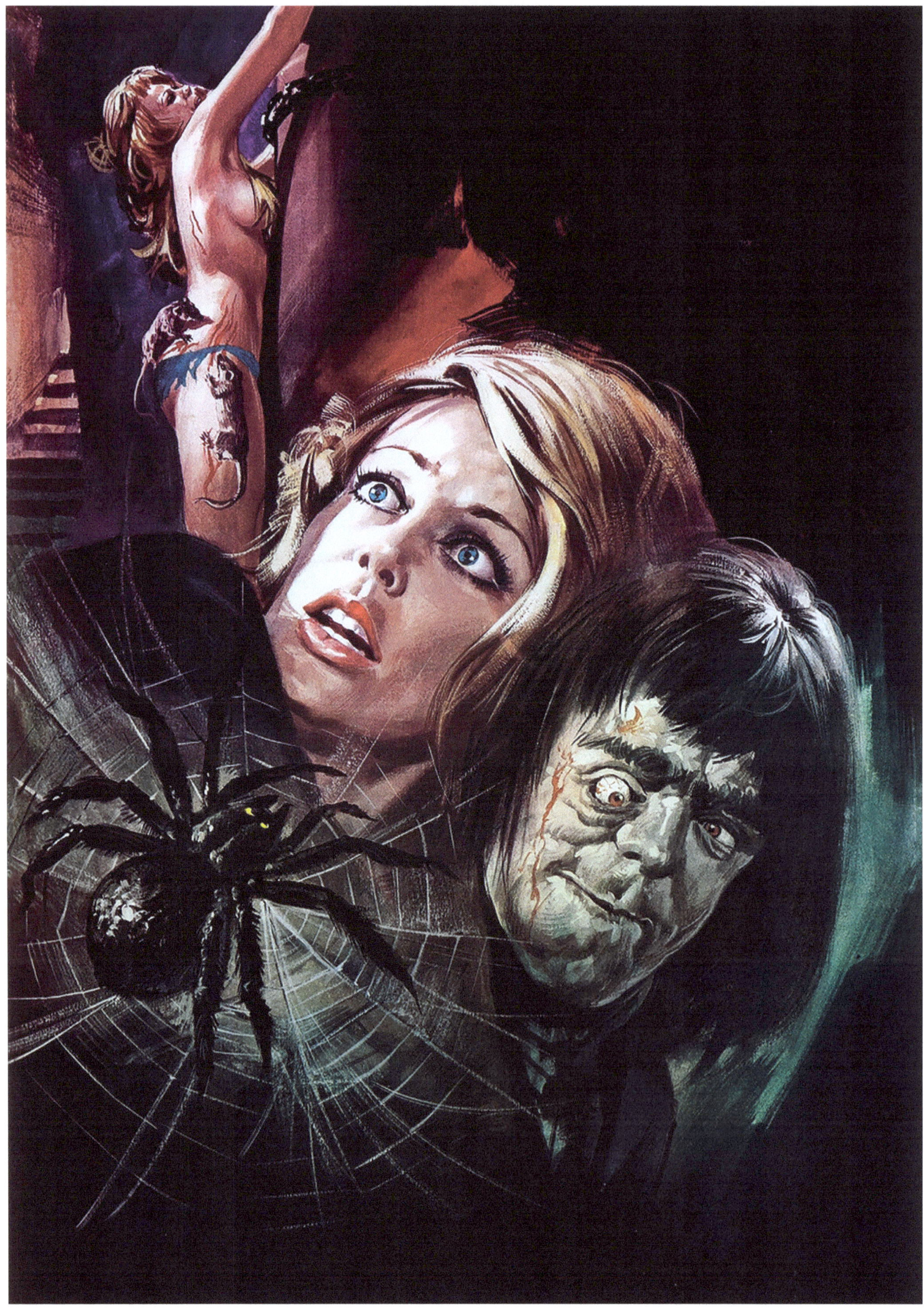

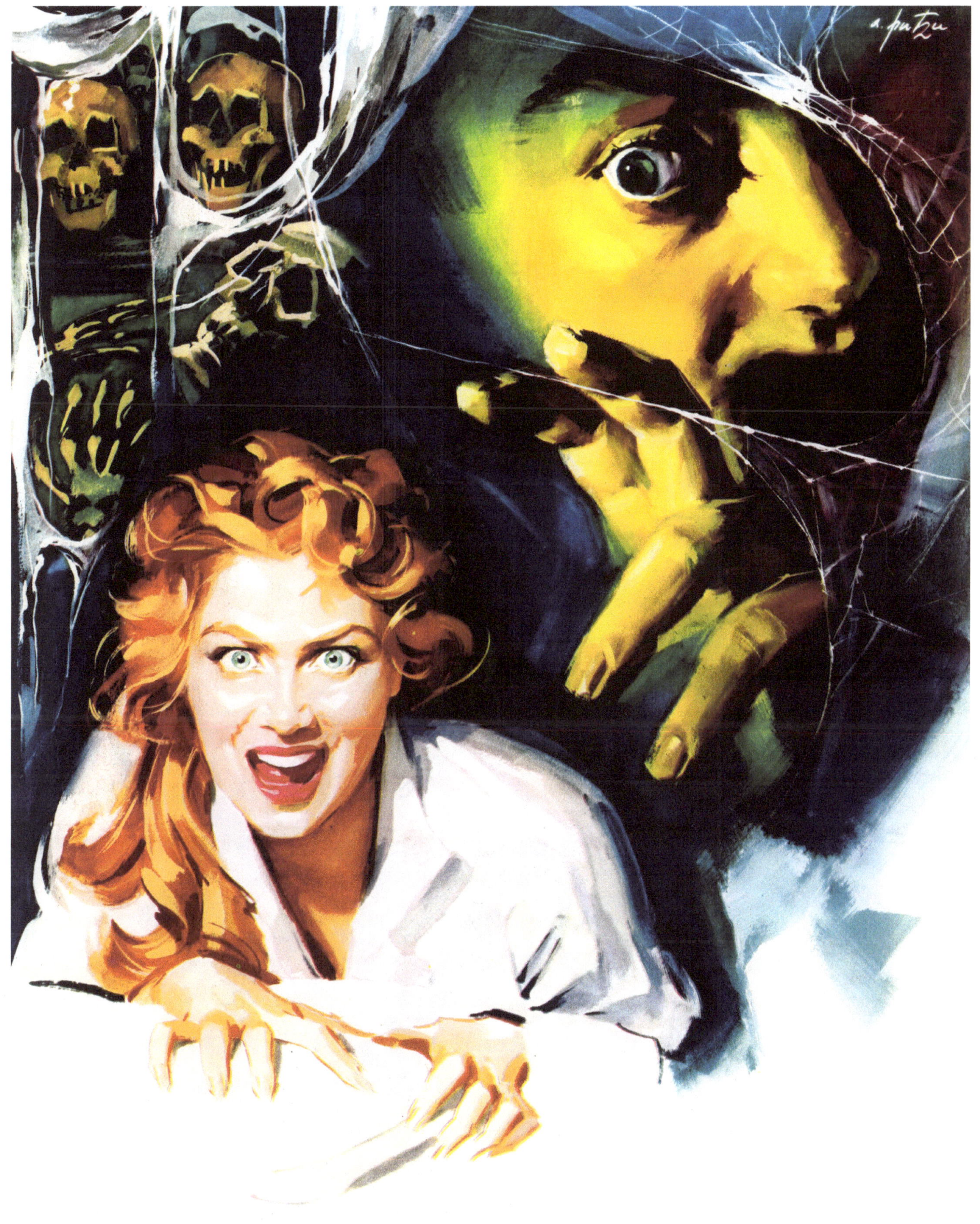

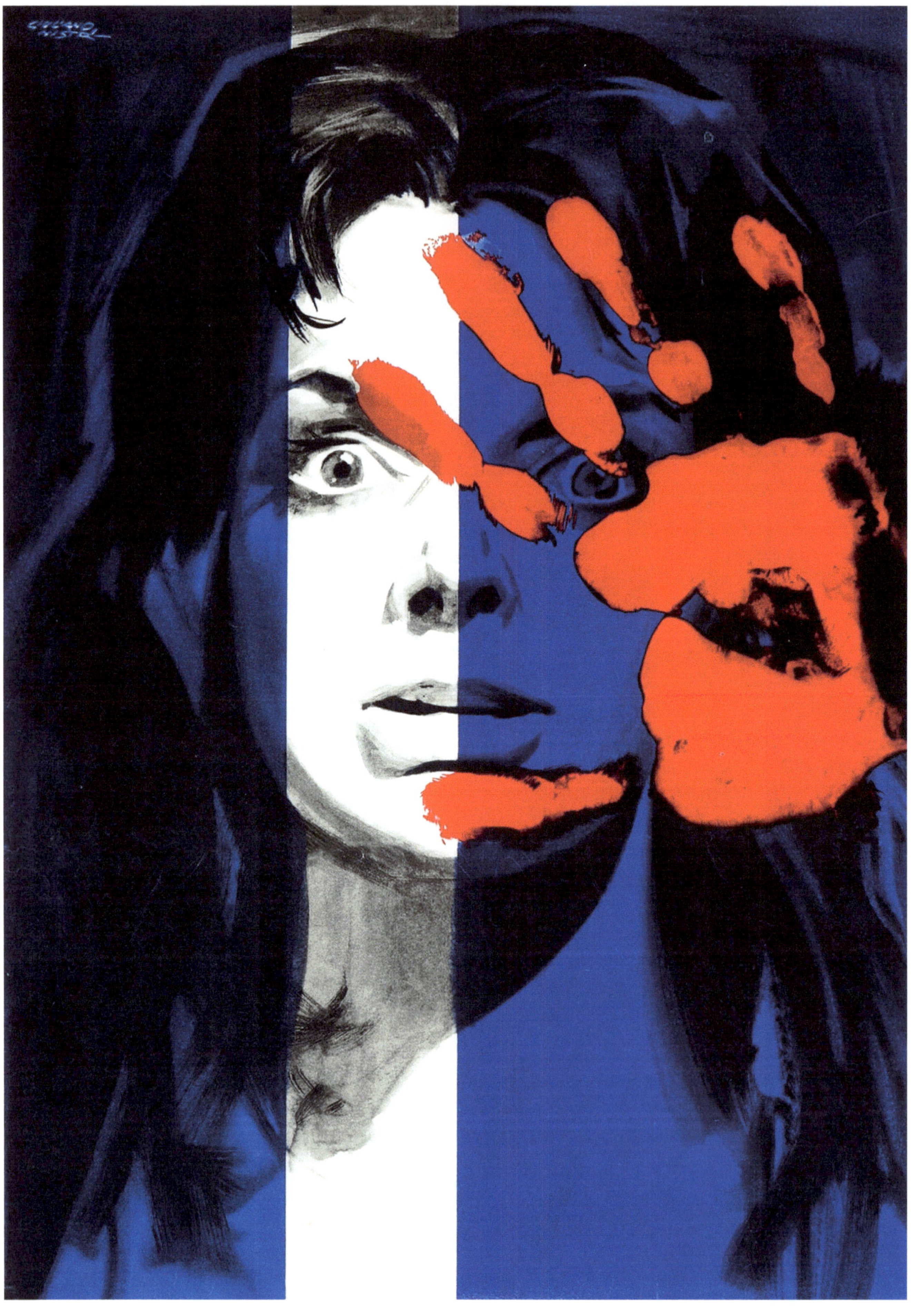

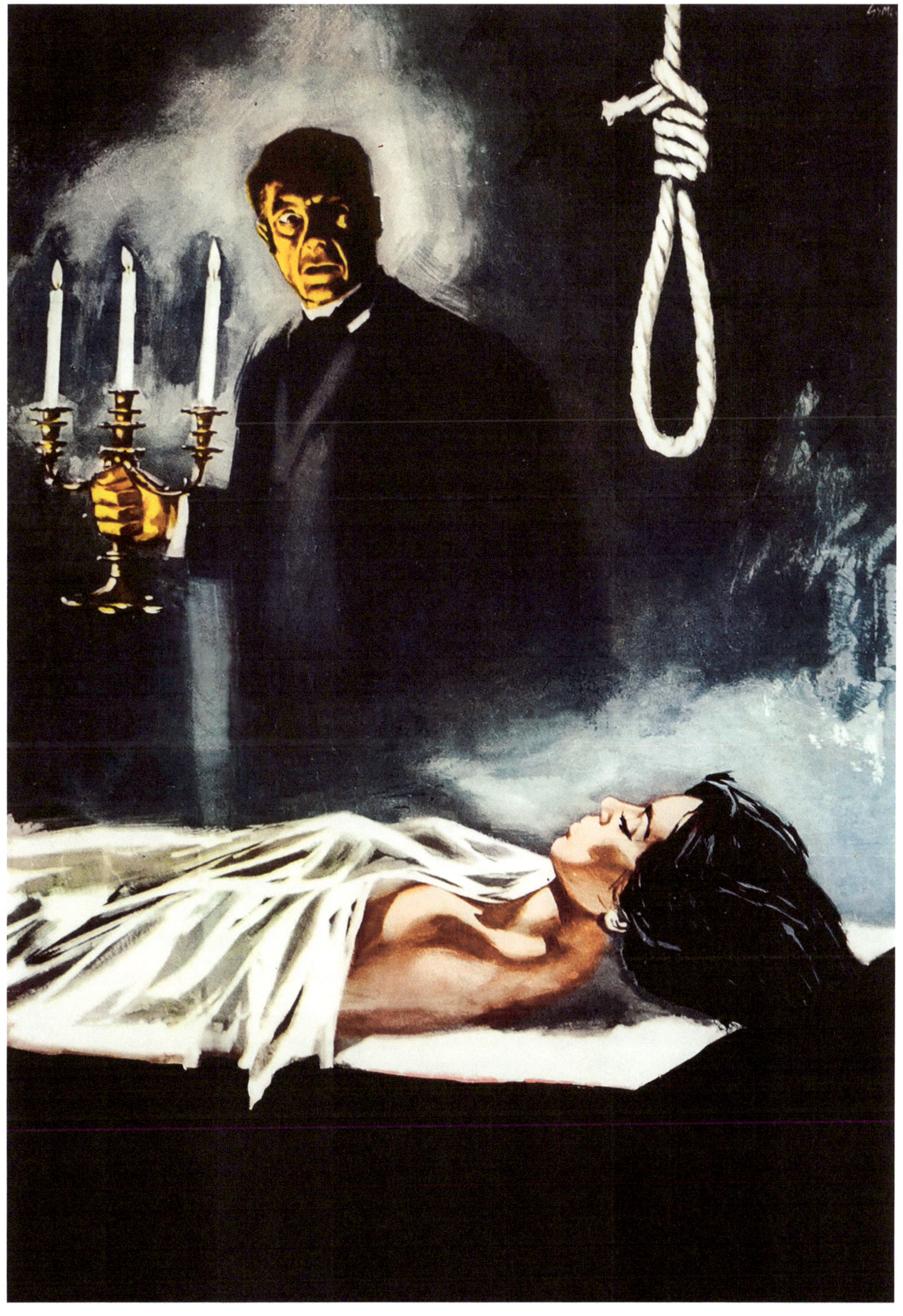

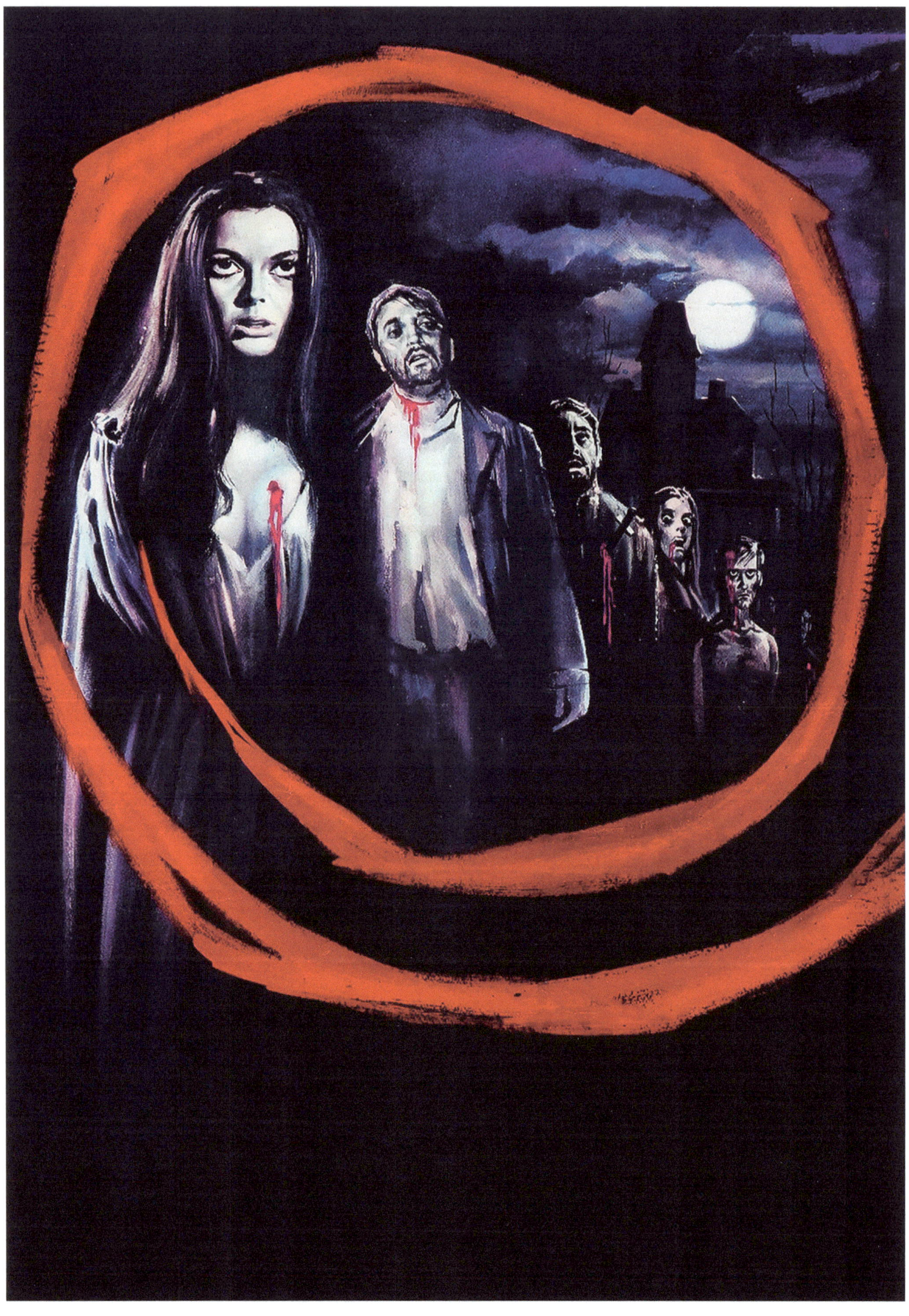

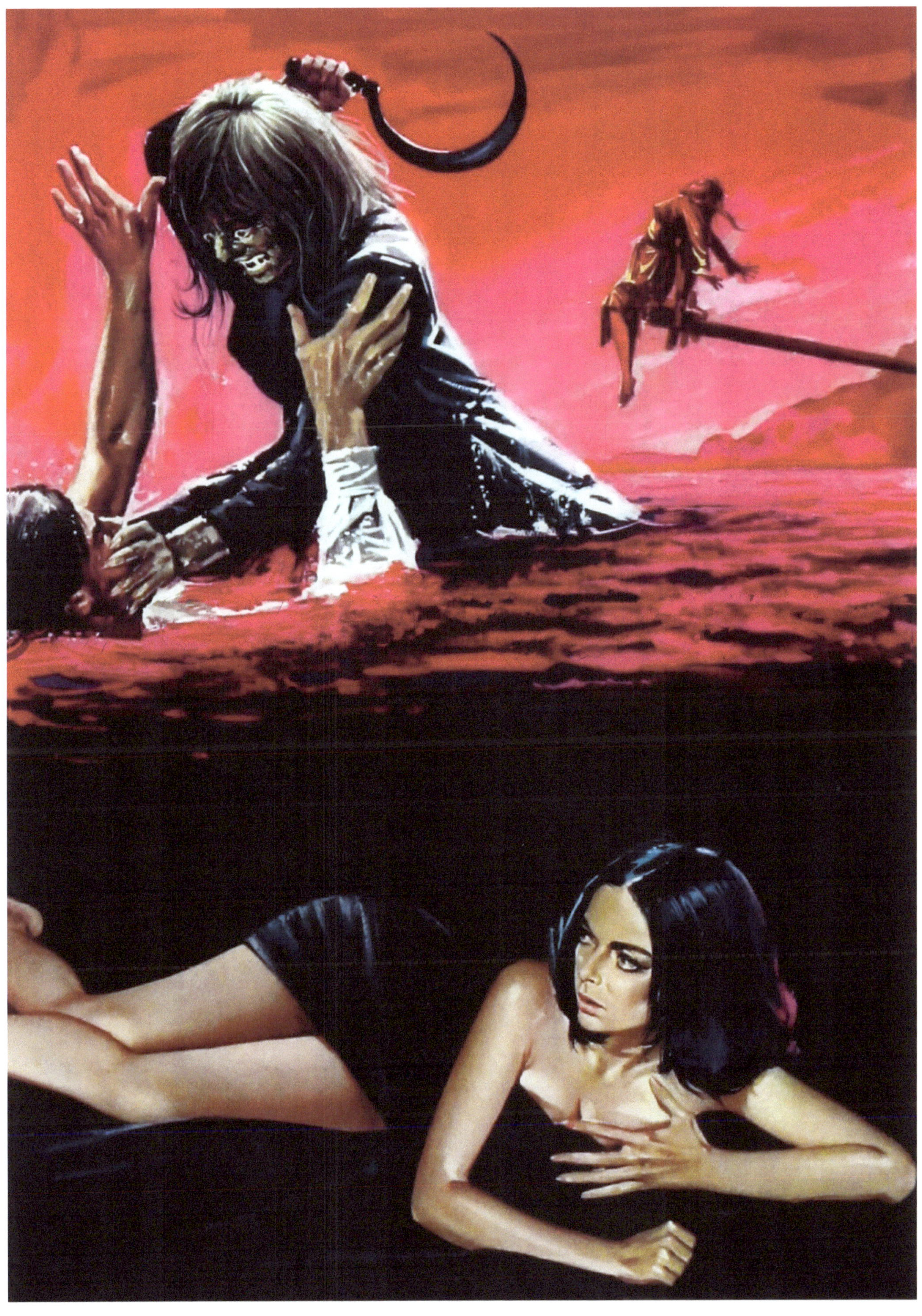

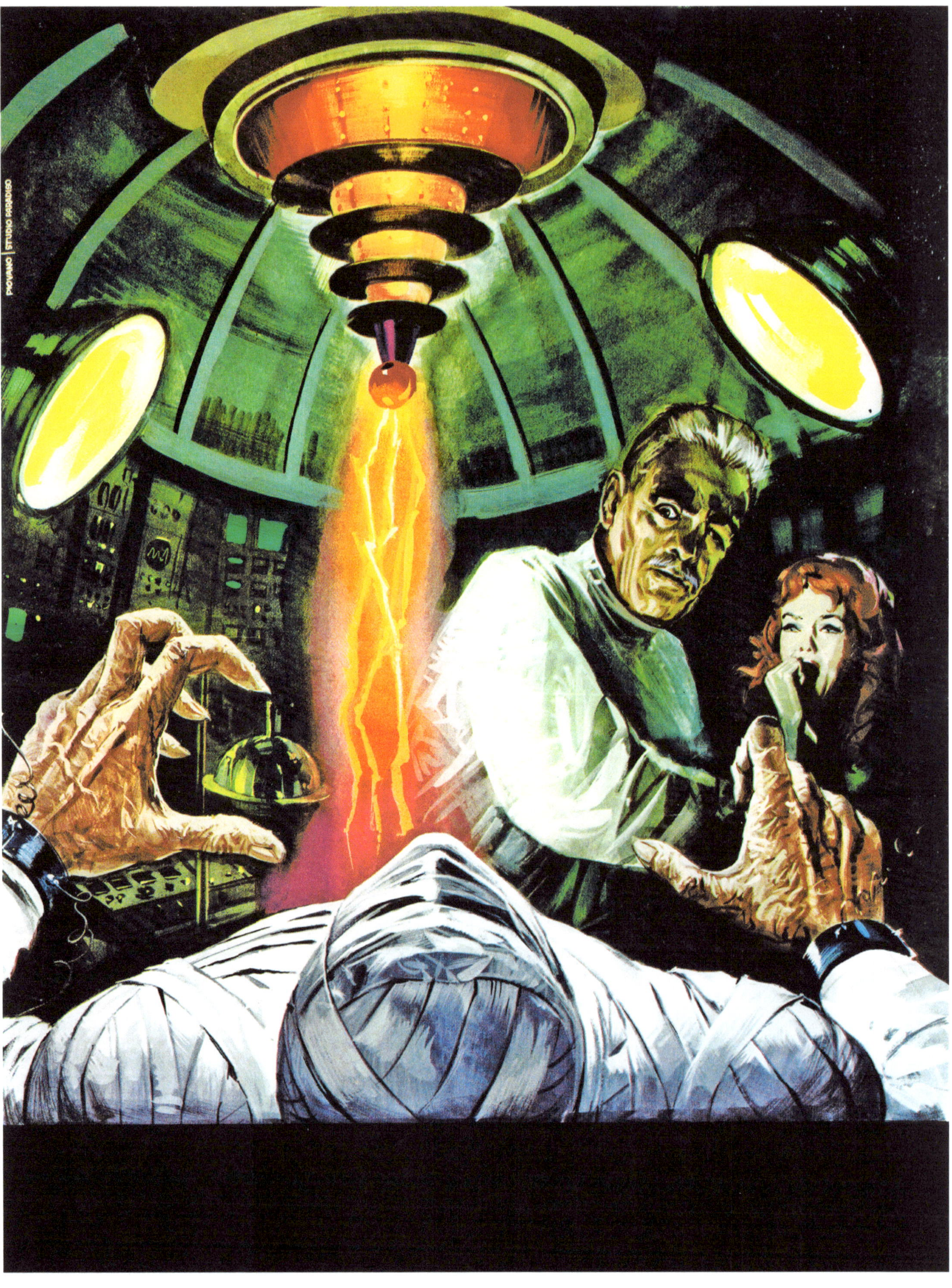
PIOVANO | STUDIO PARADISO

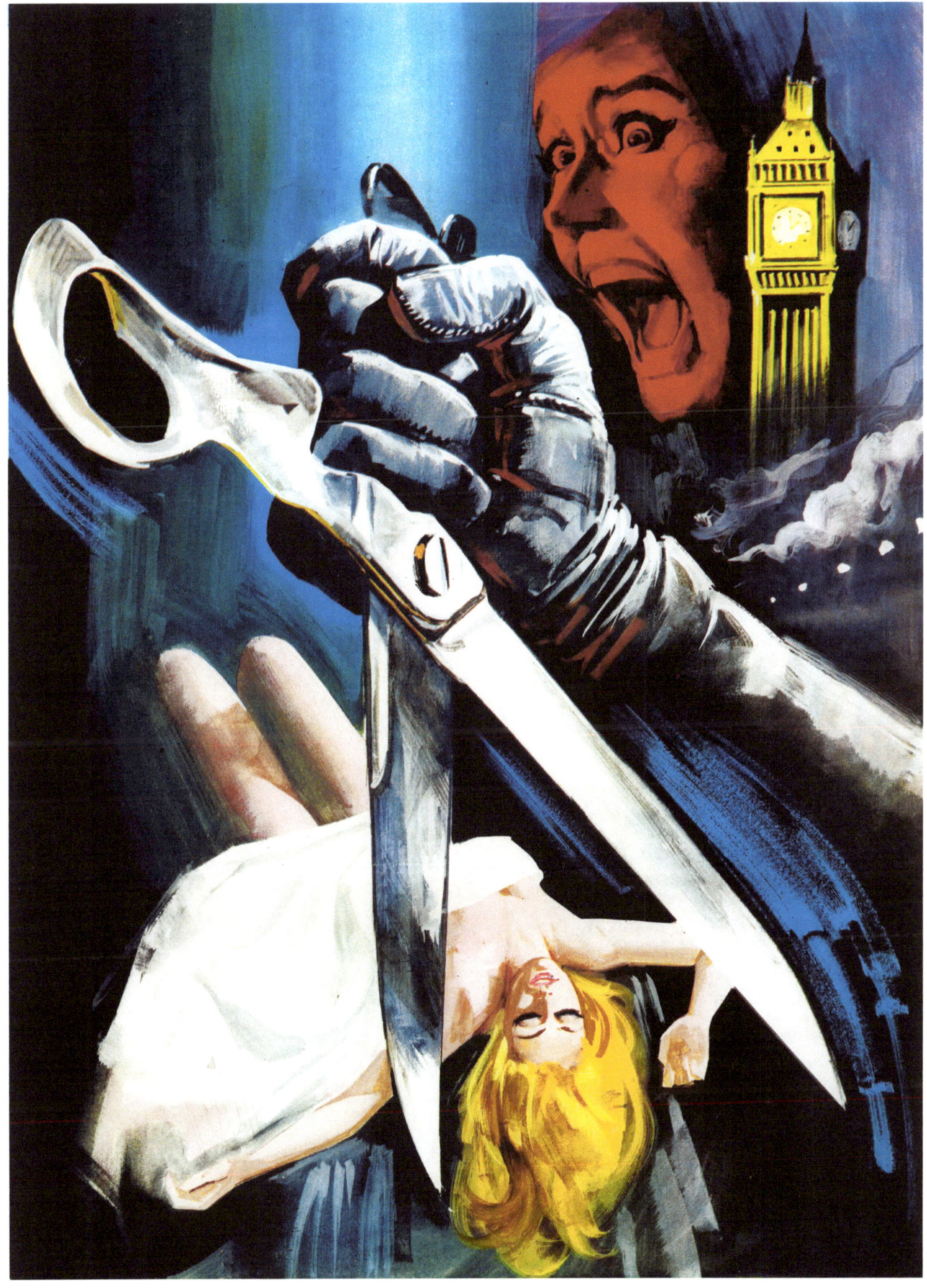

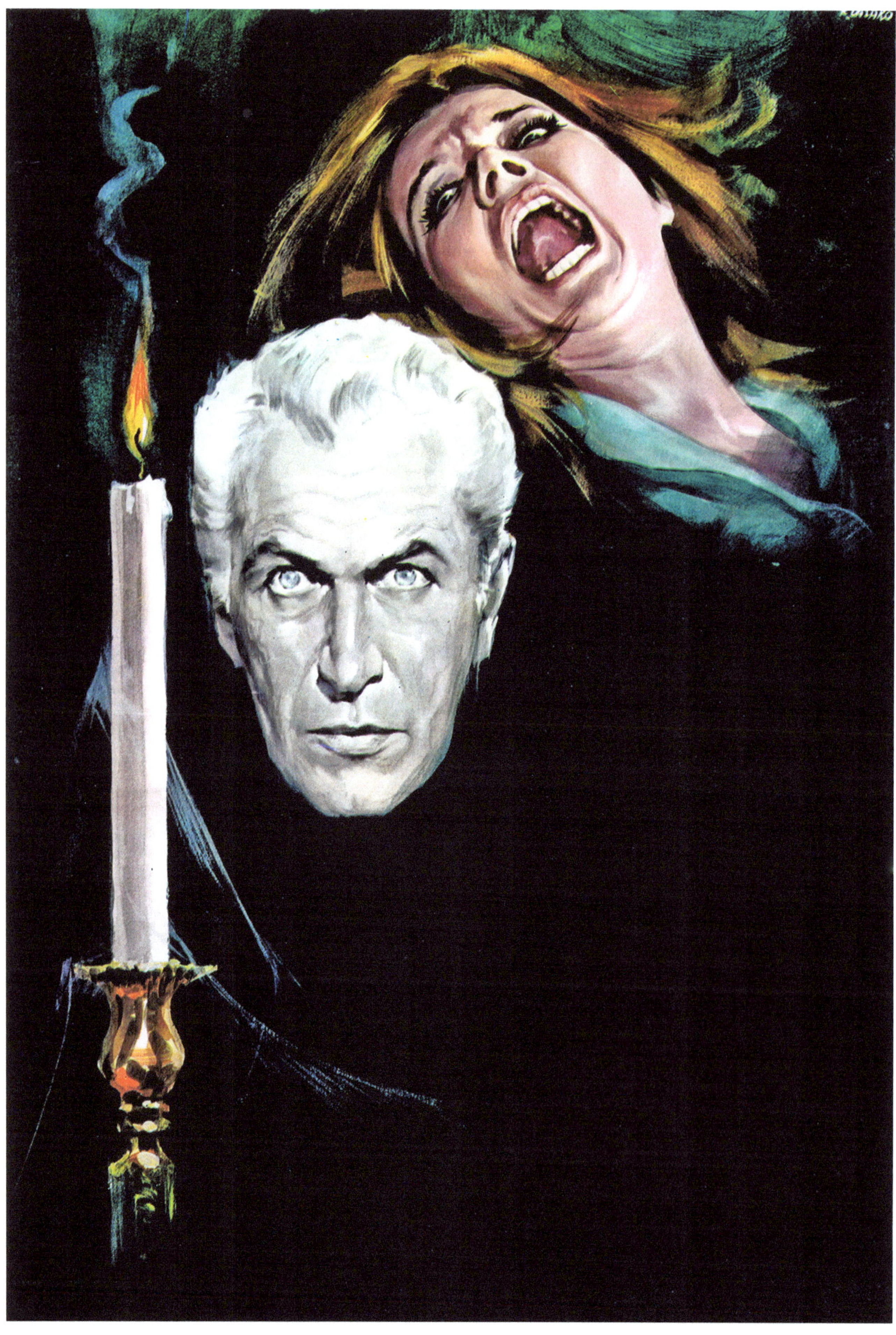

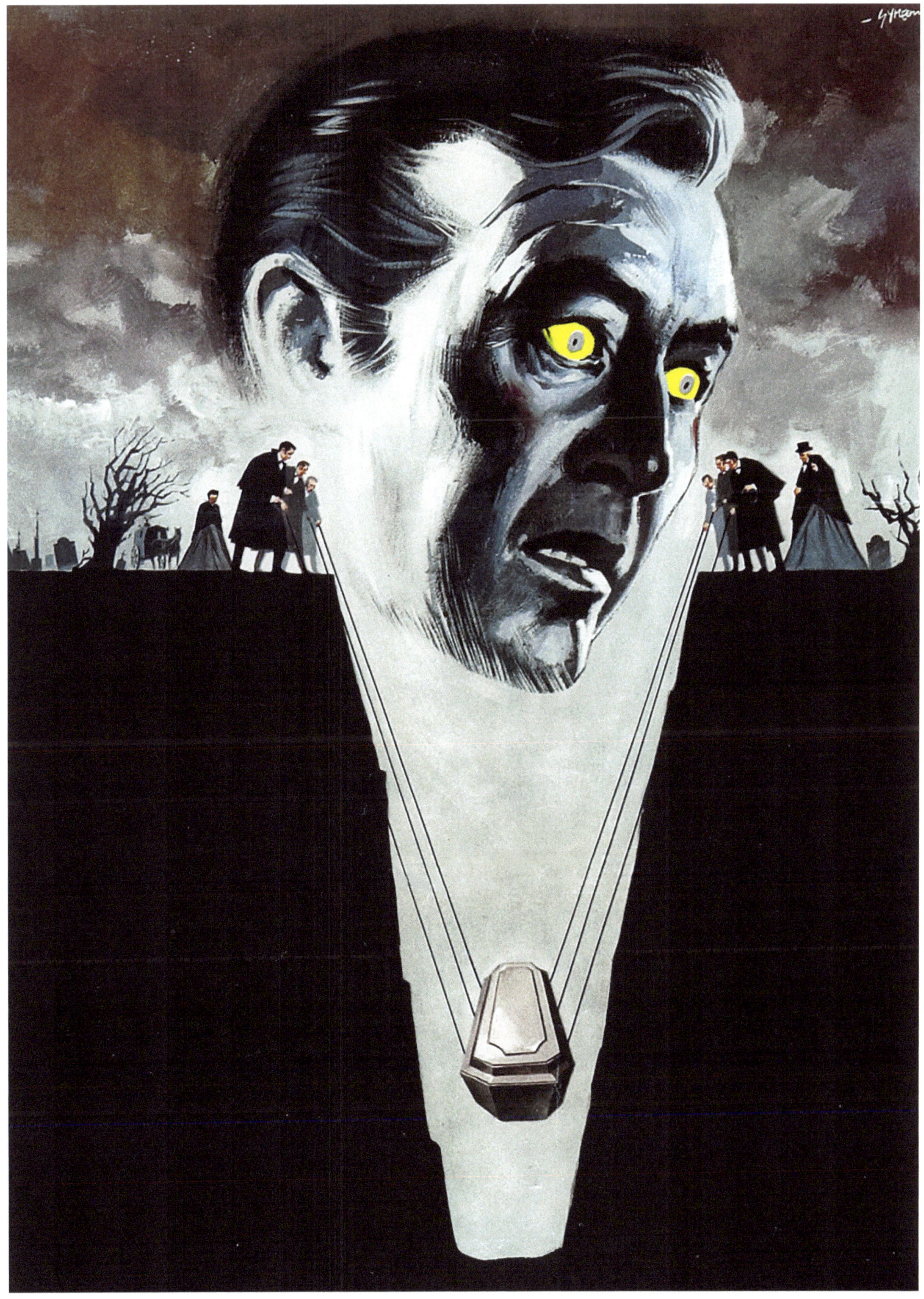

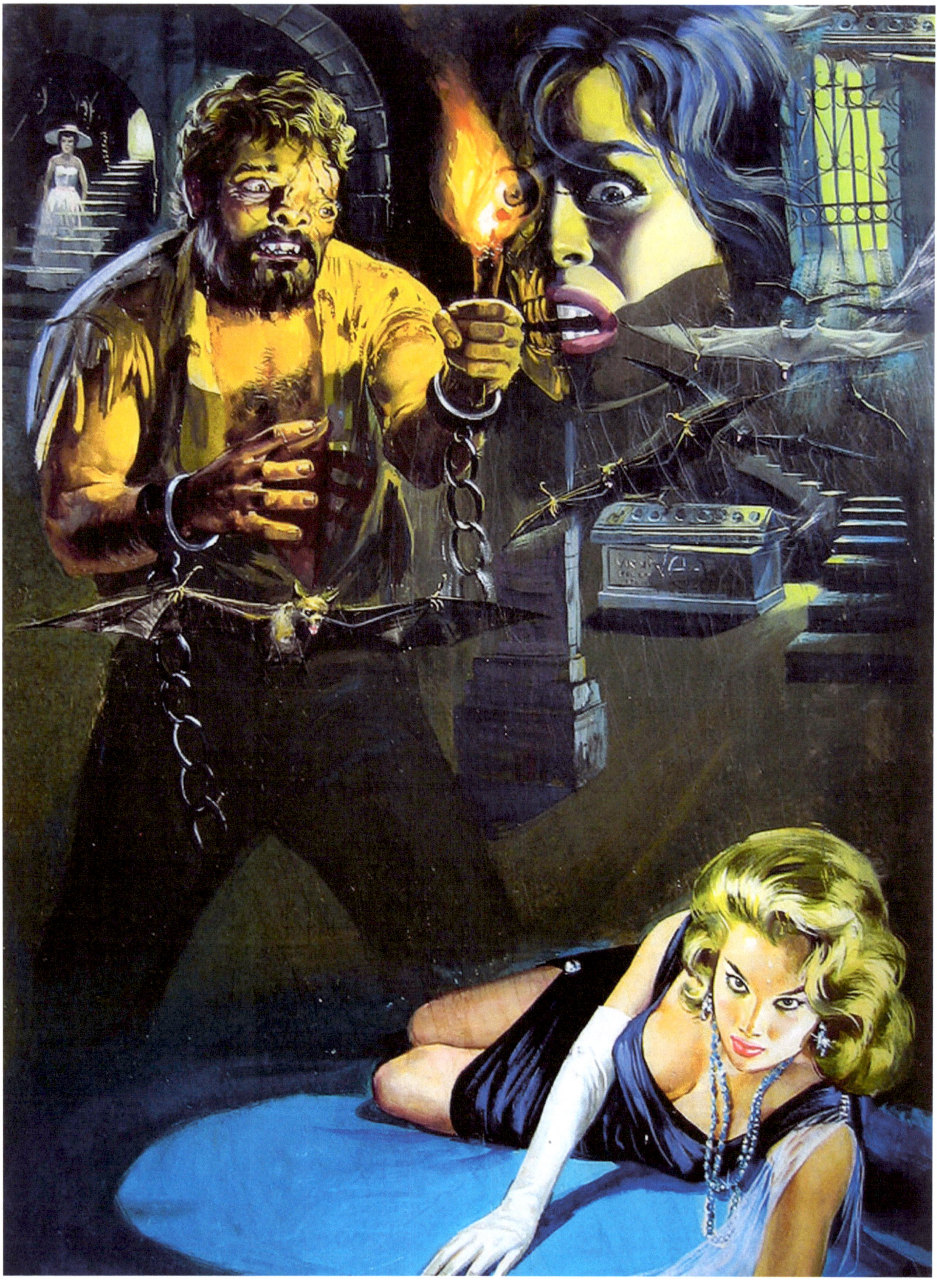

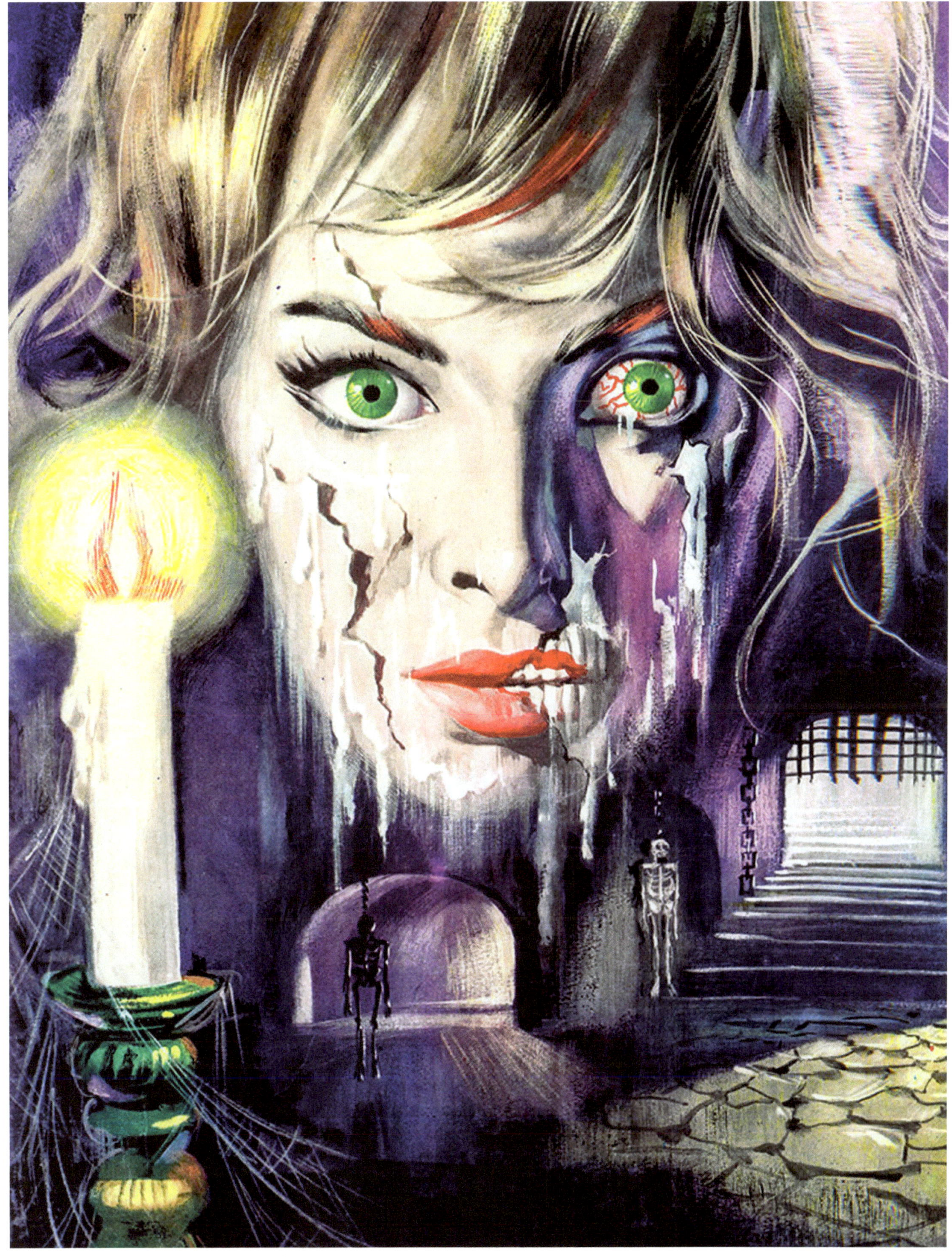

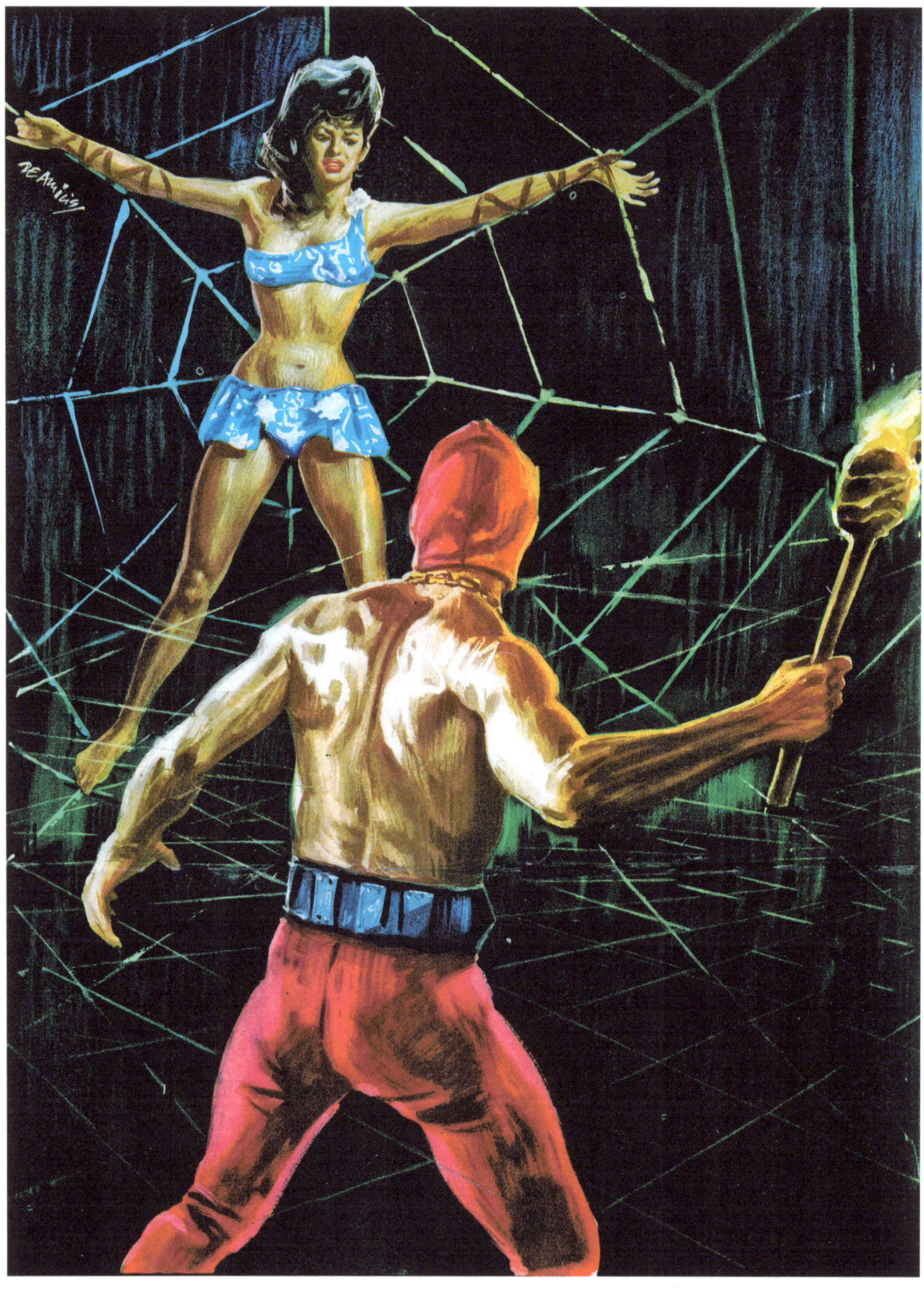

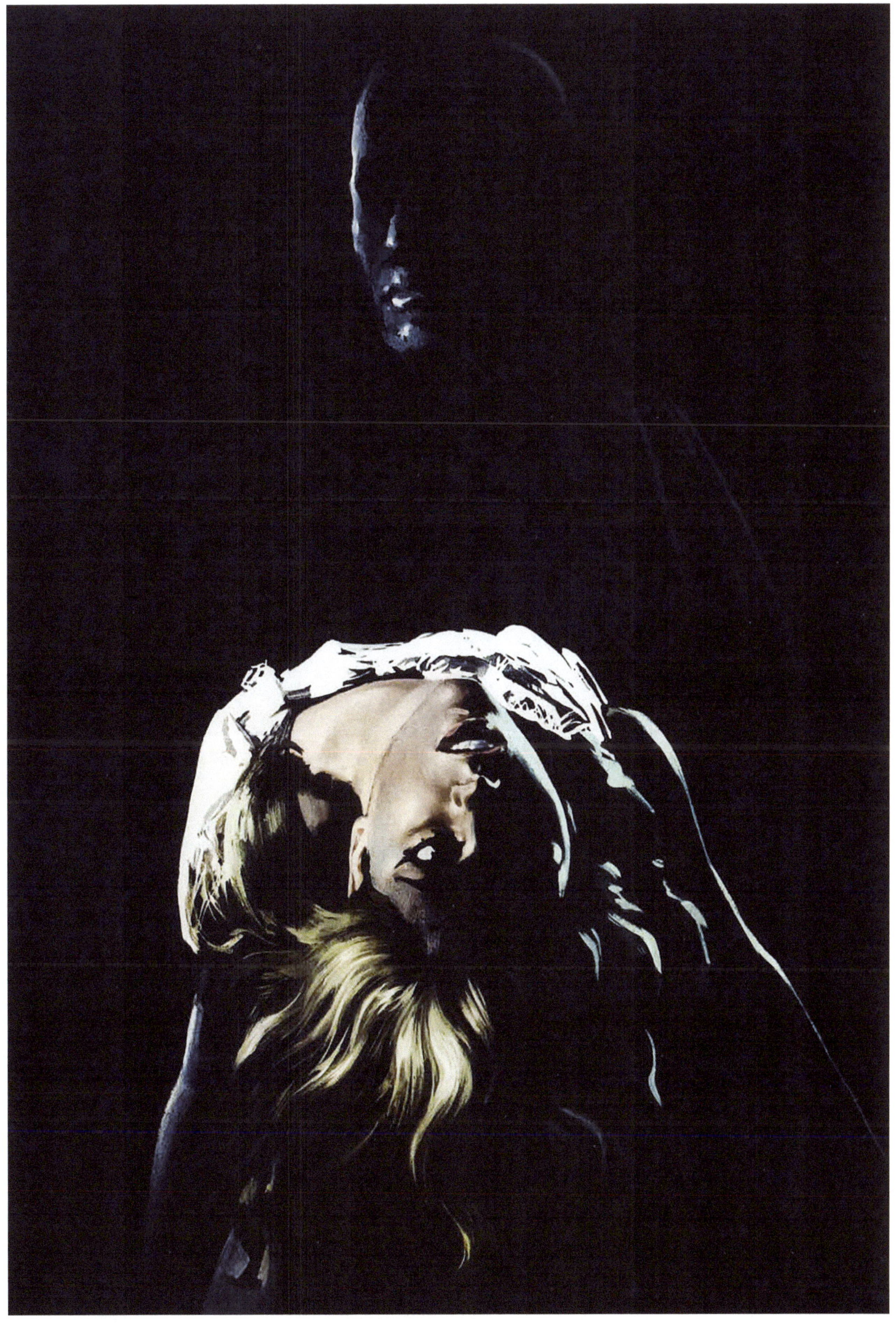

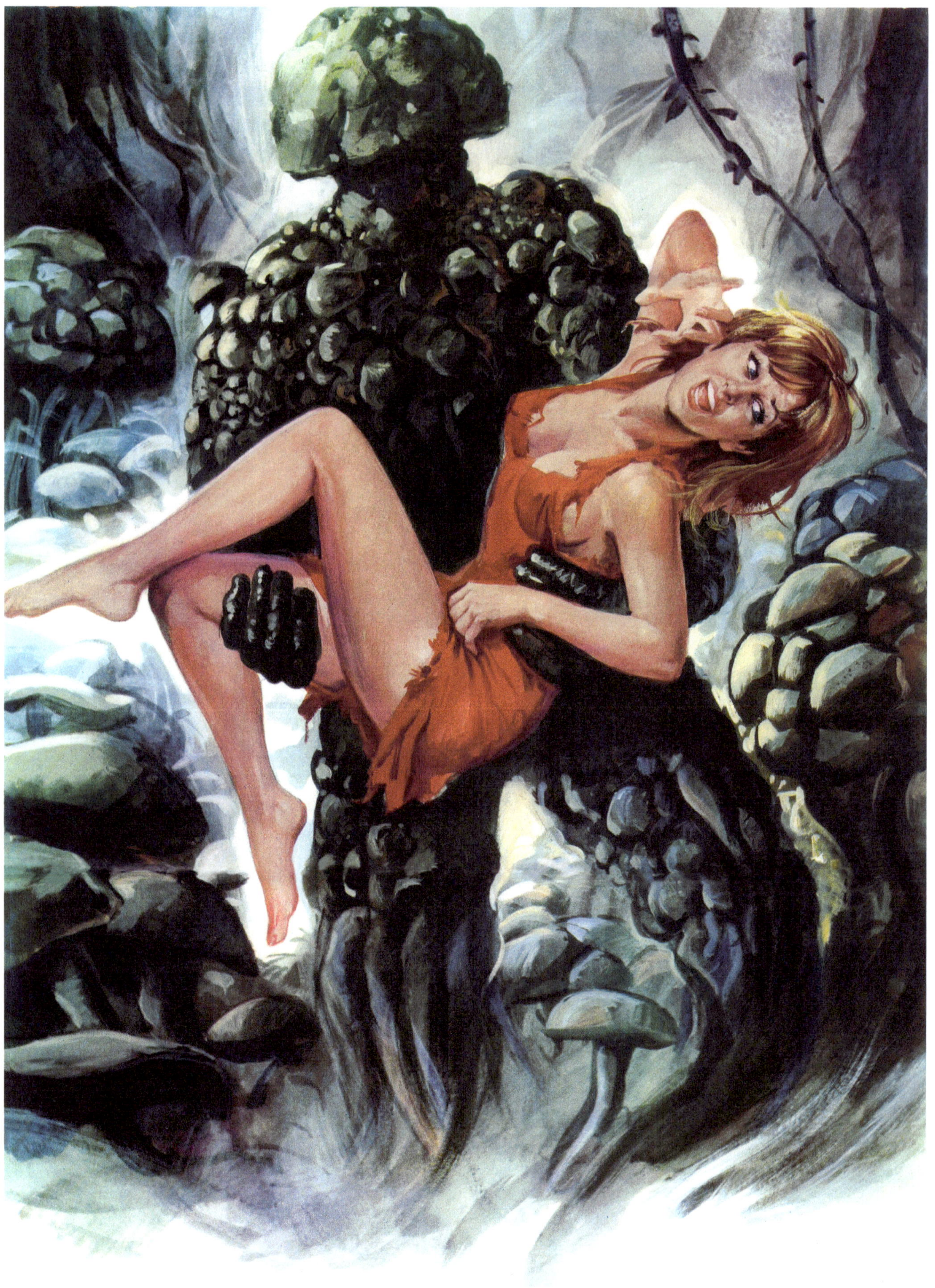

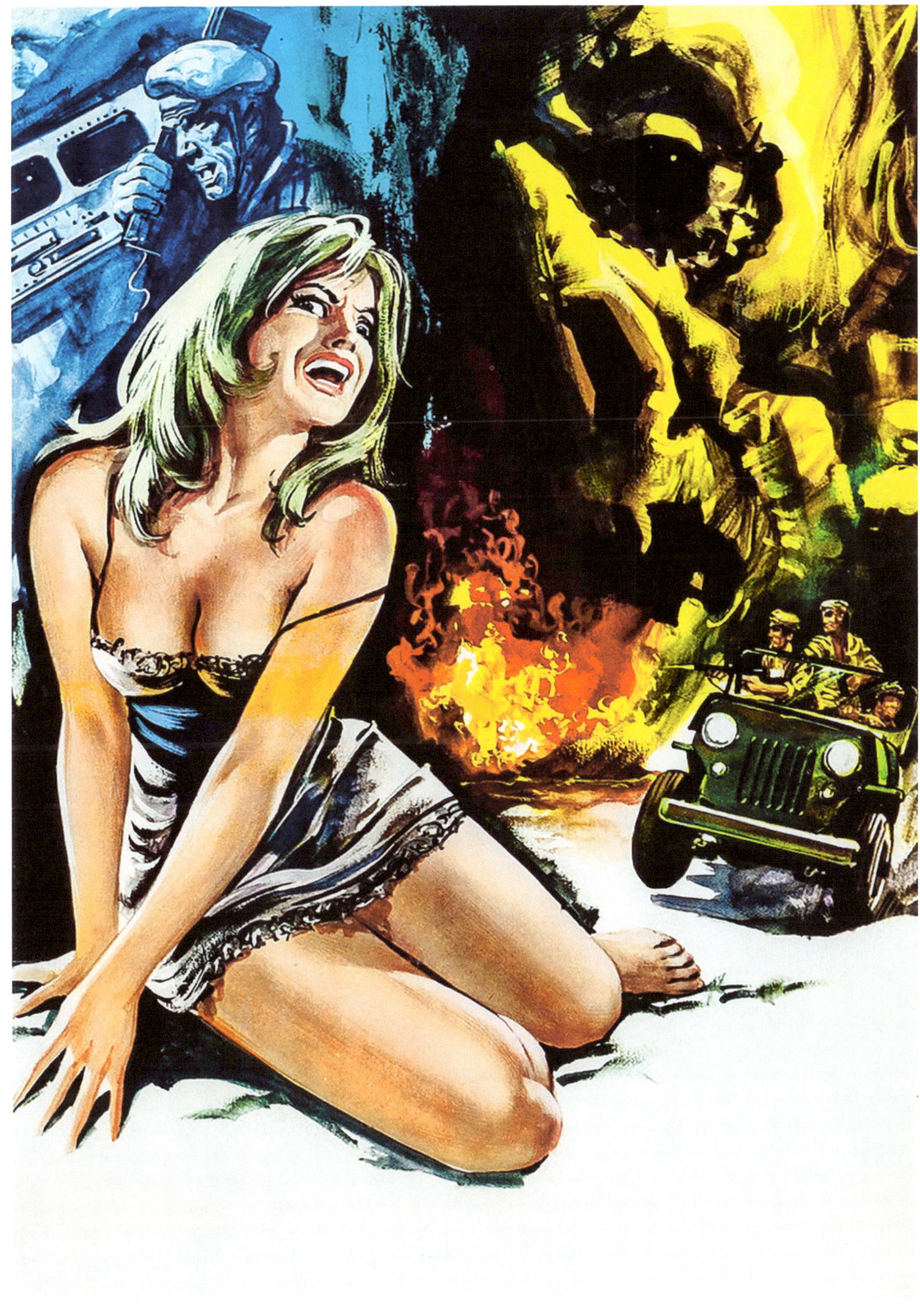

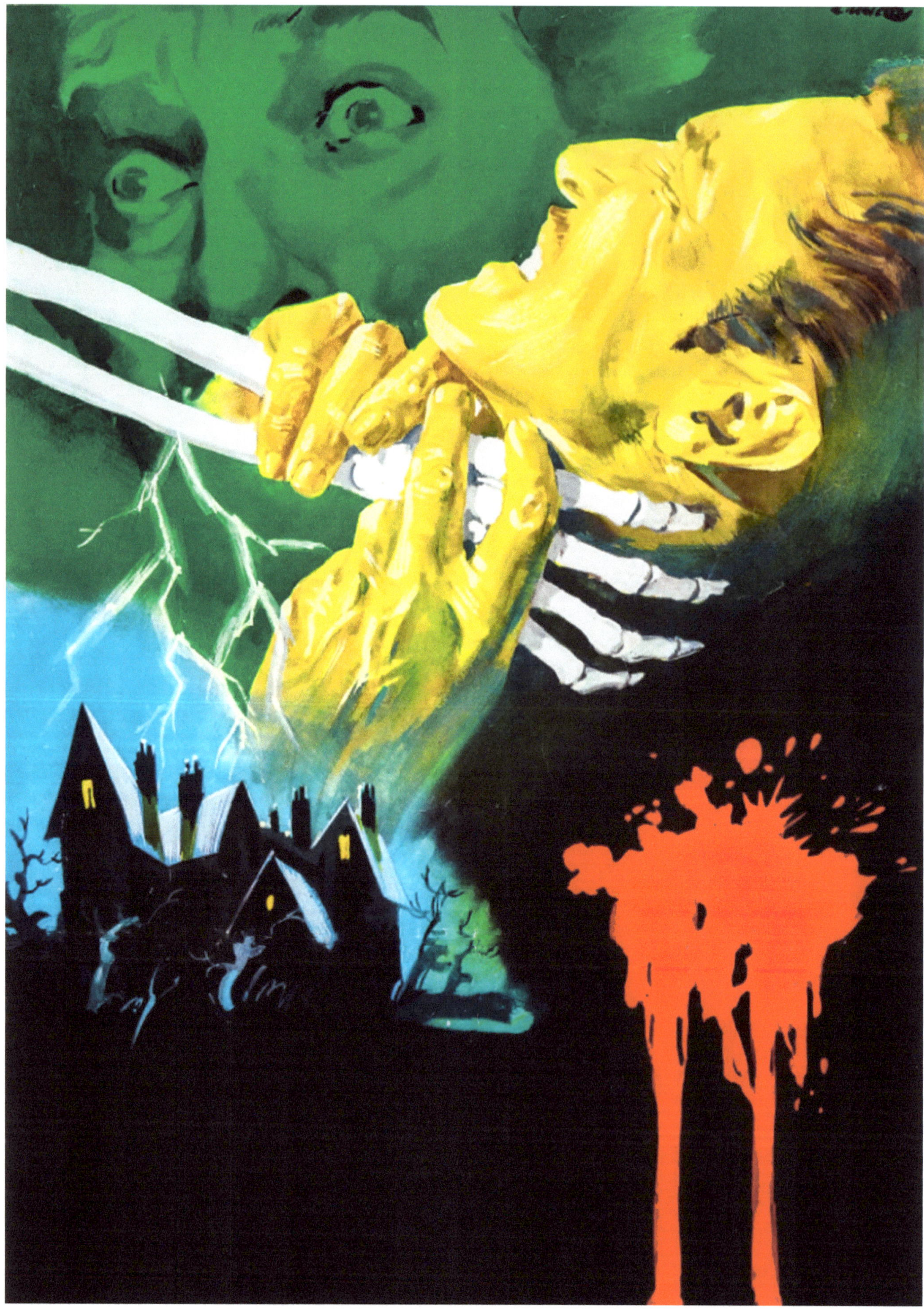

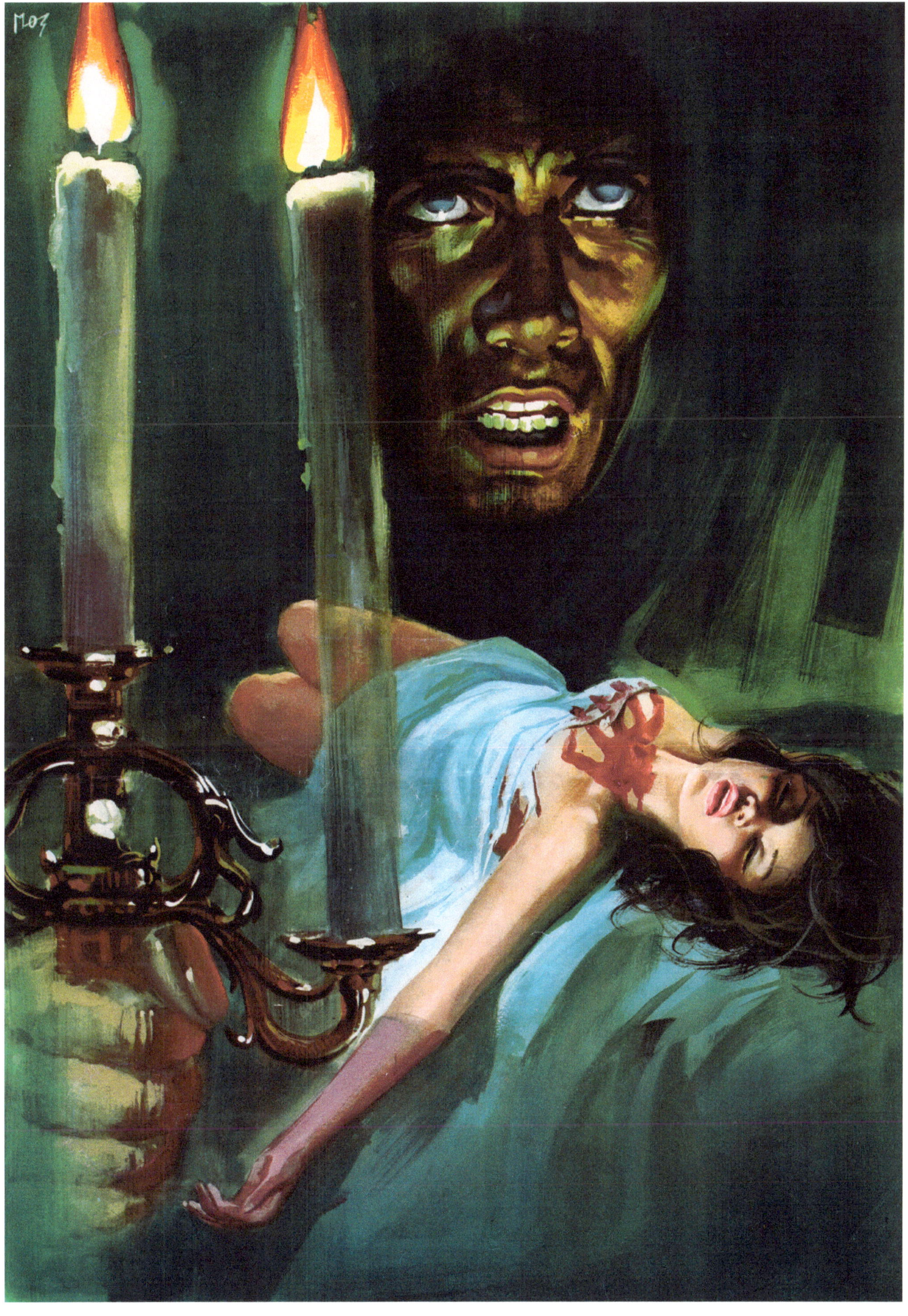

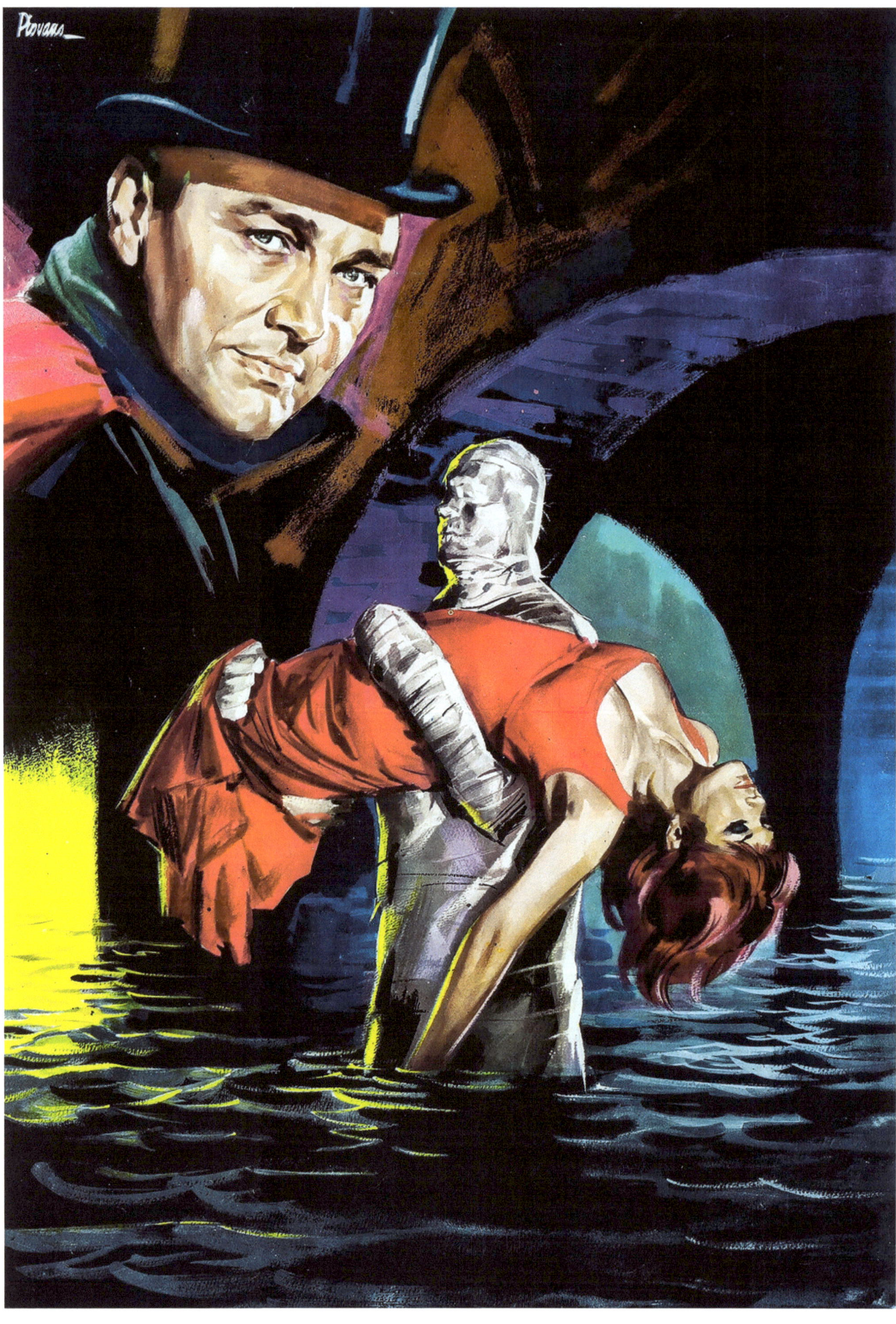

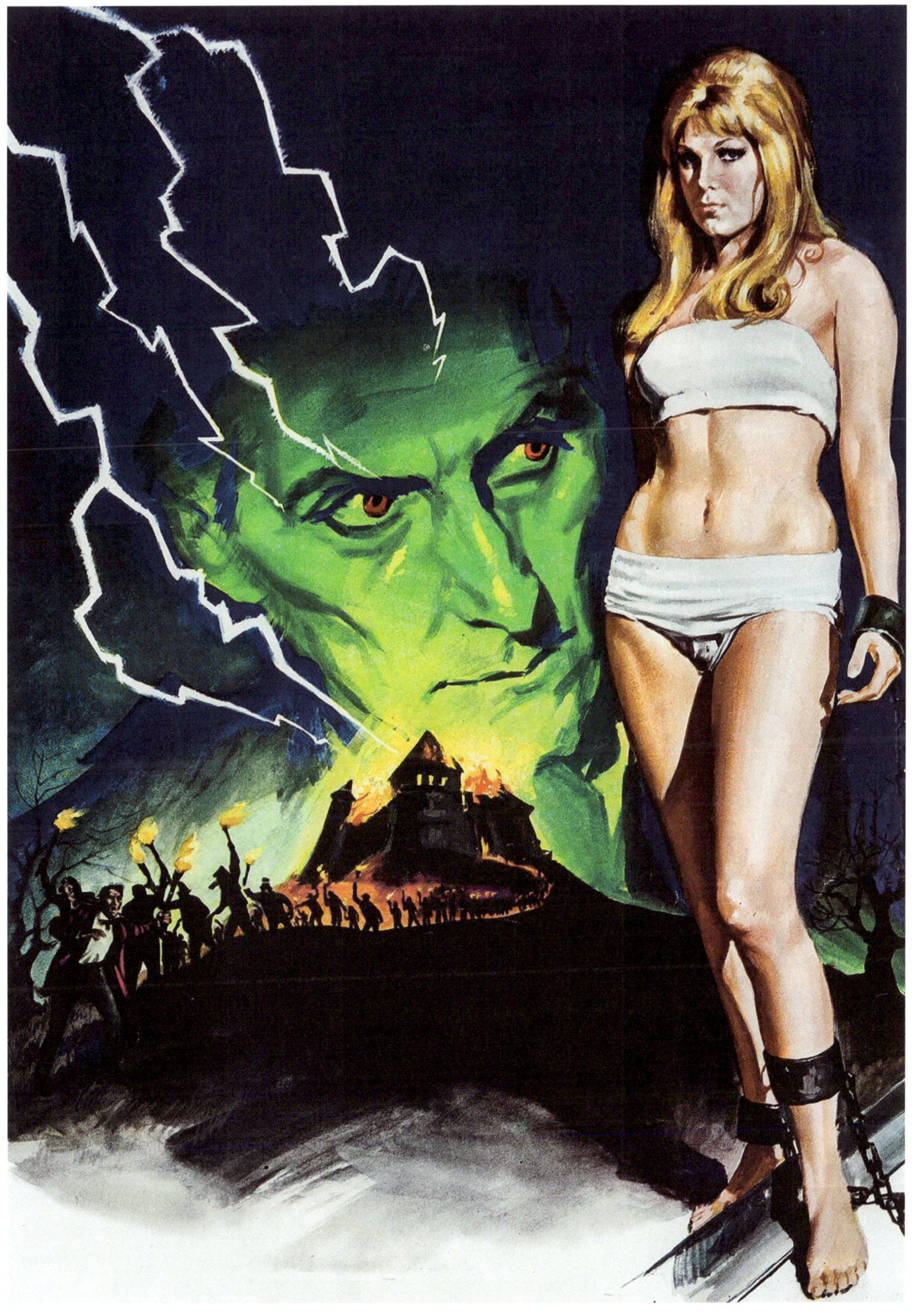

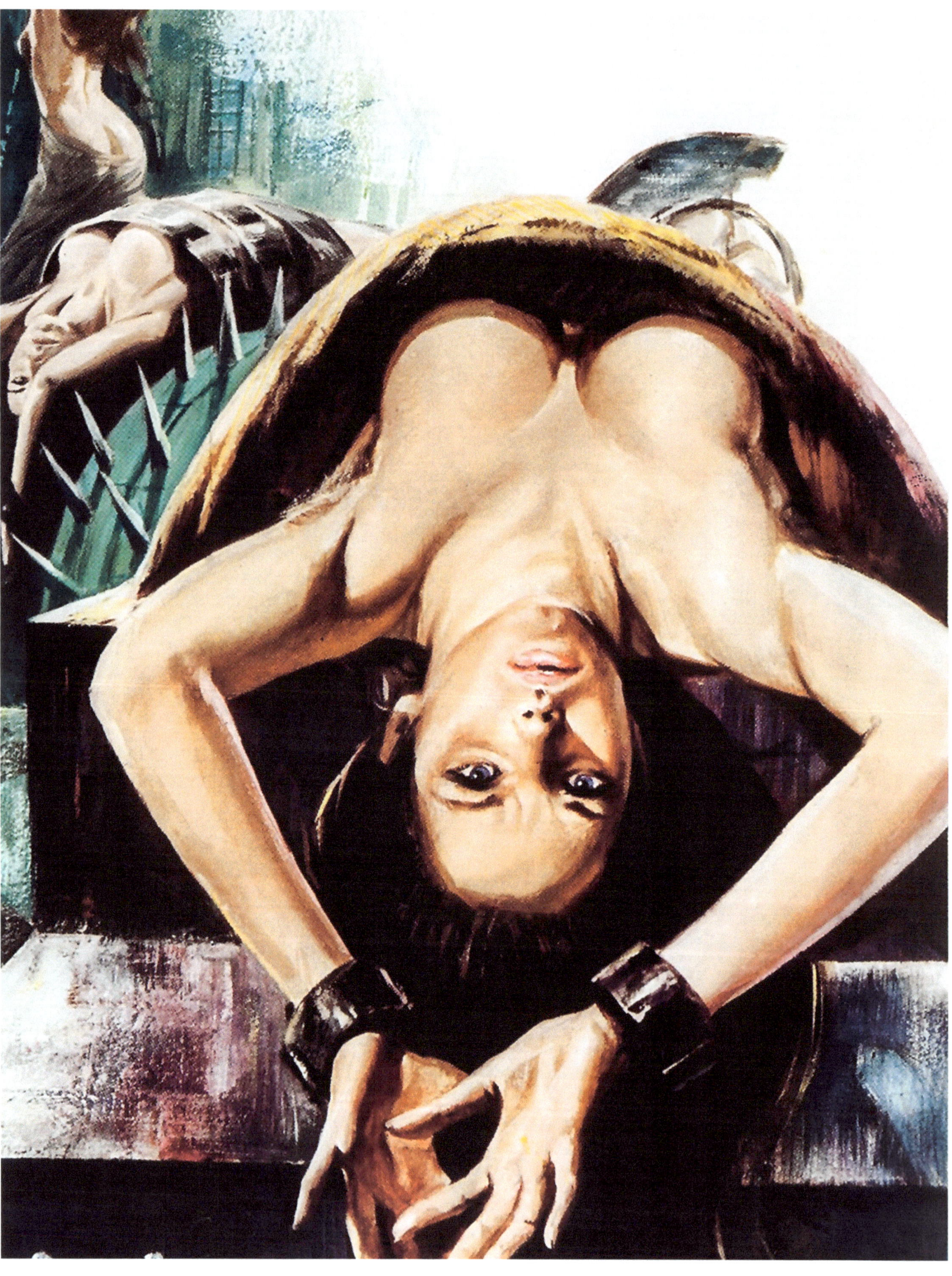

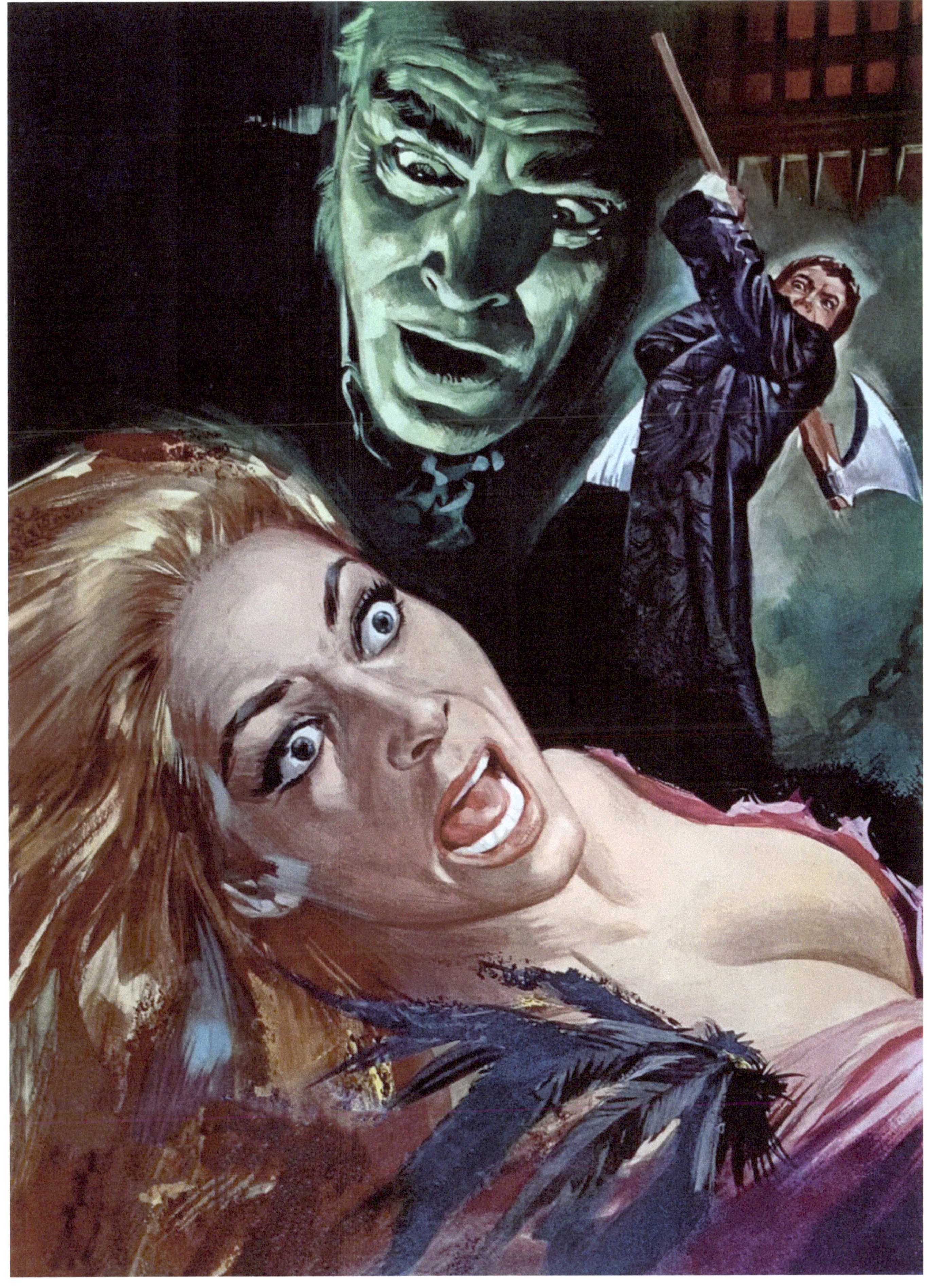

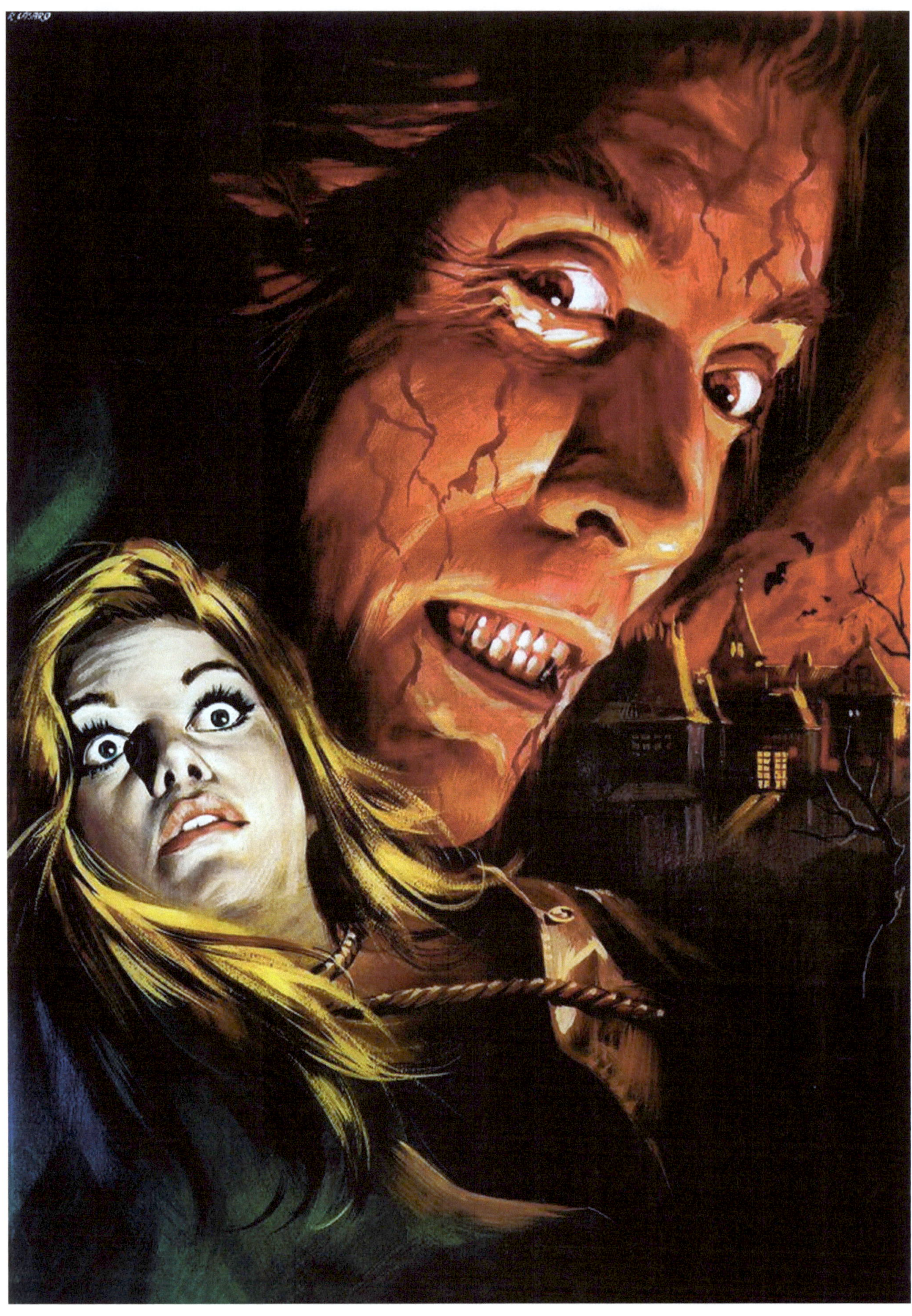

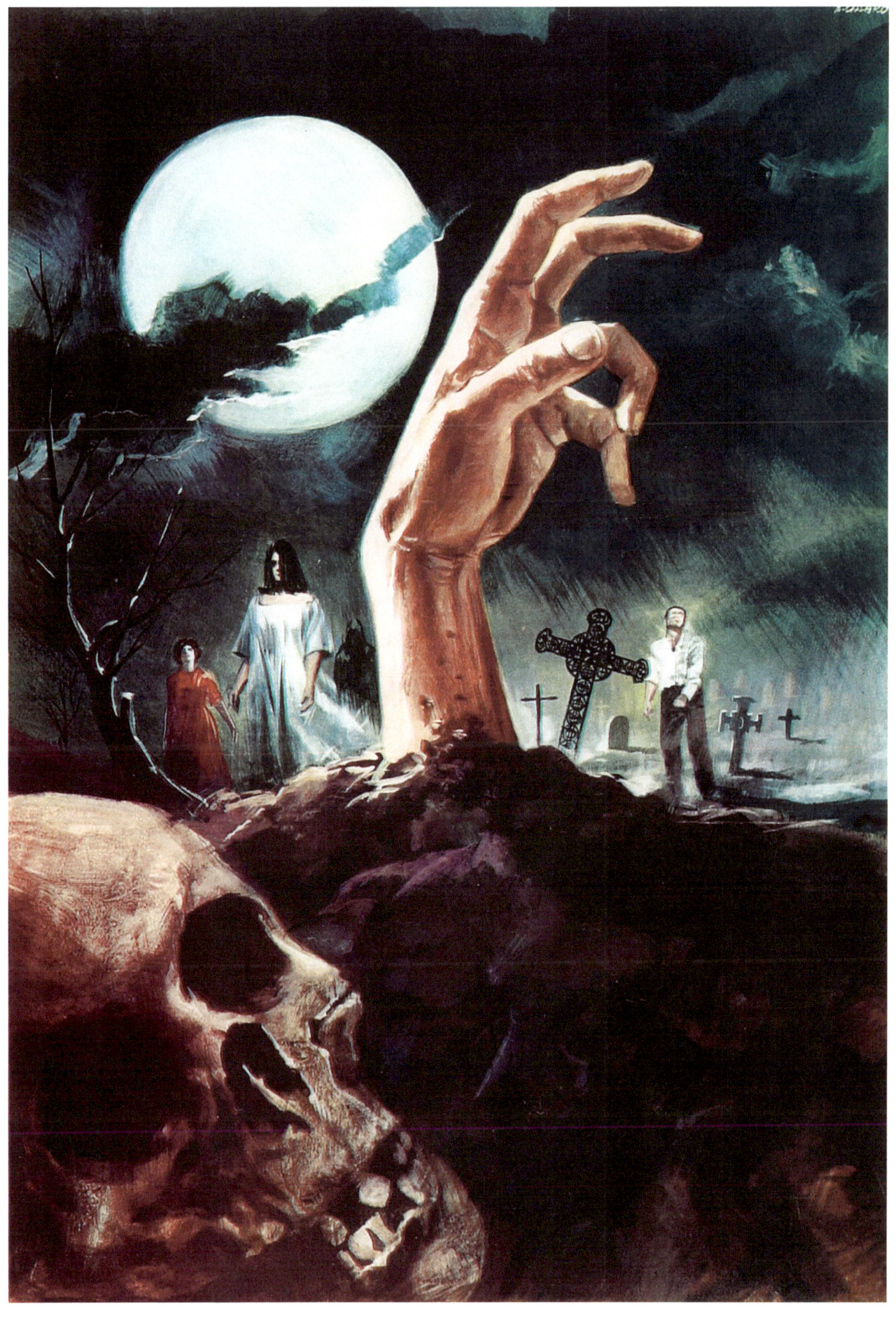

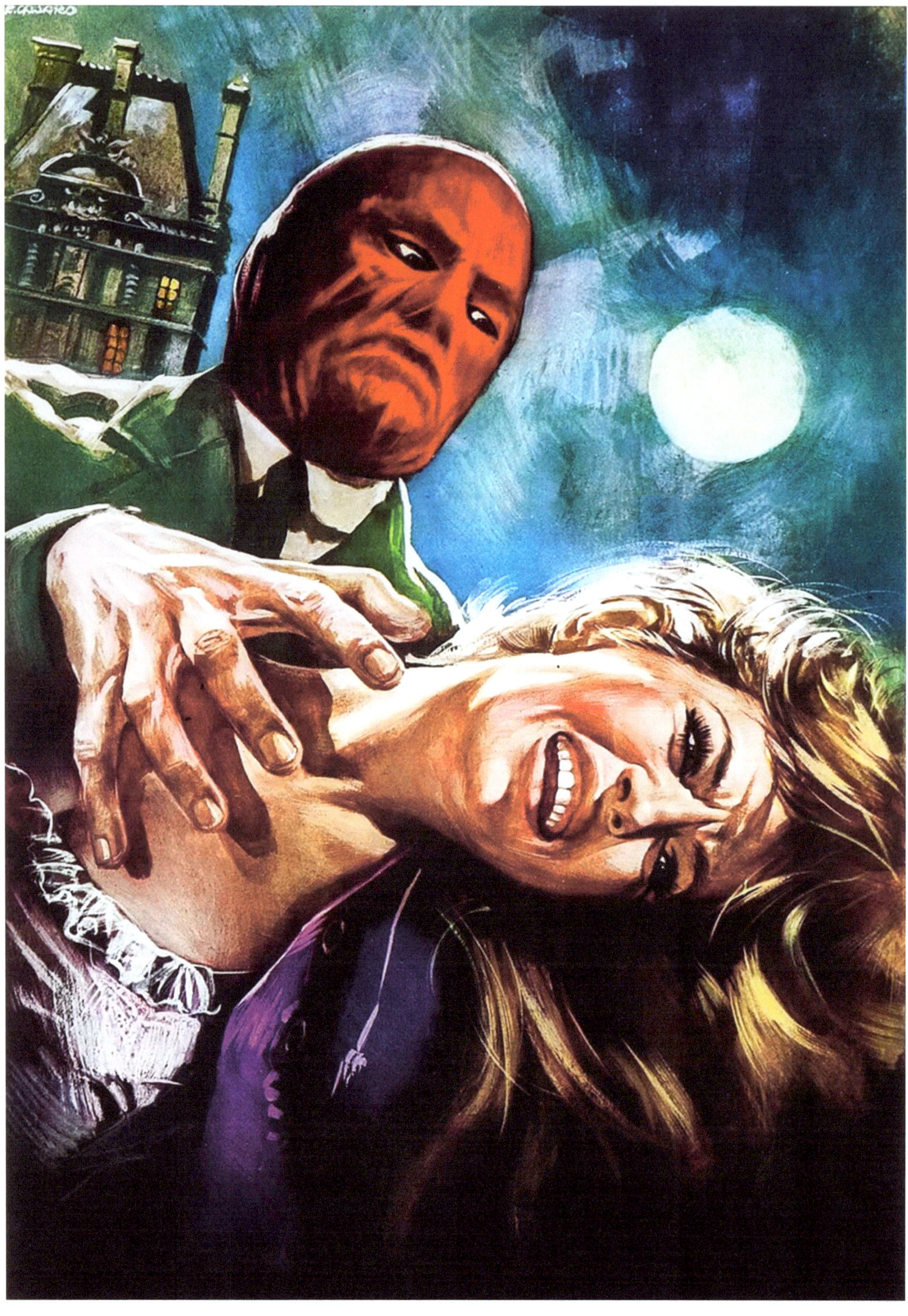

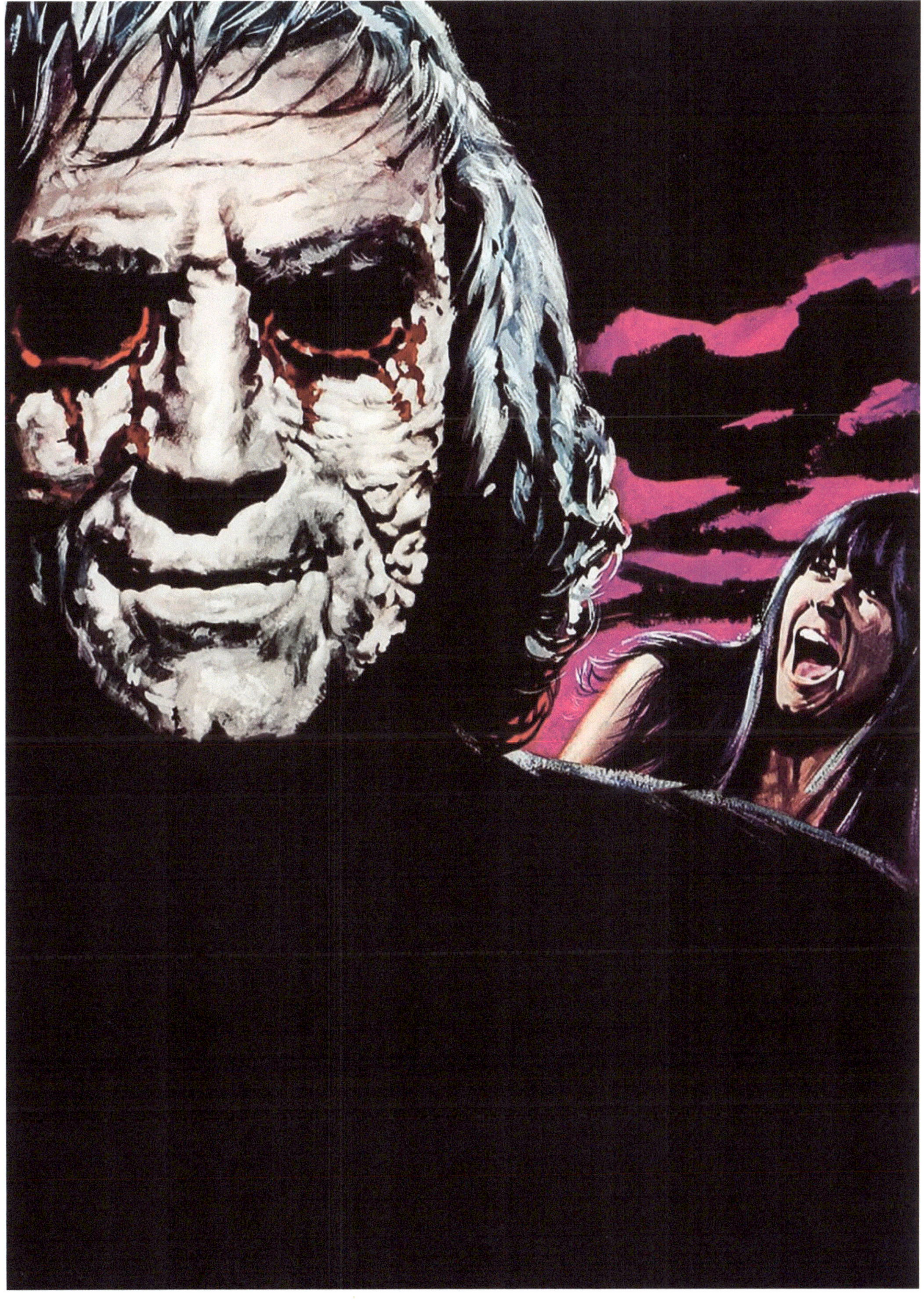

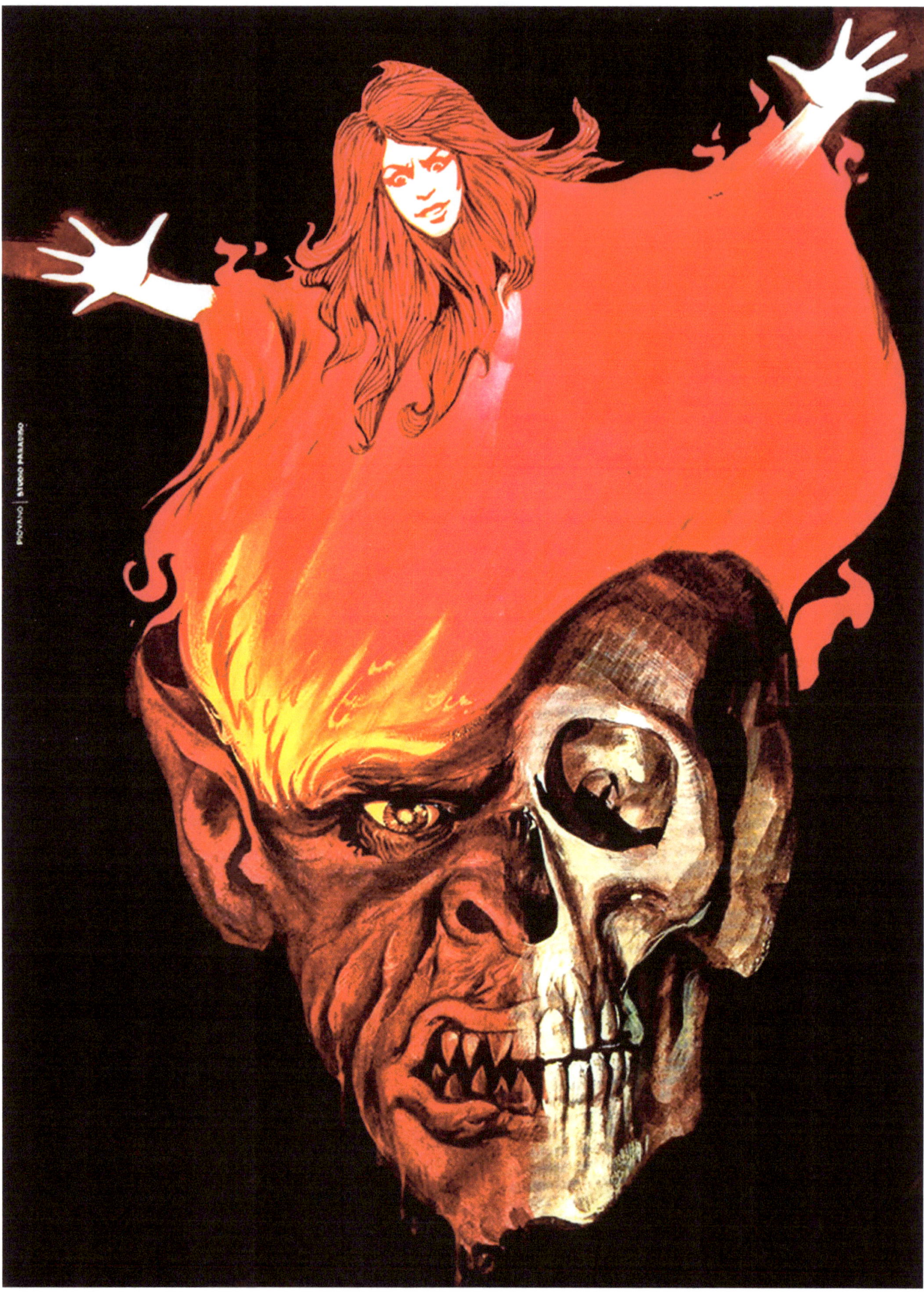
PIOVANO | STUDIO PARADISO

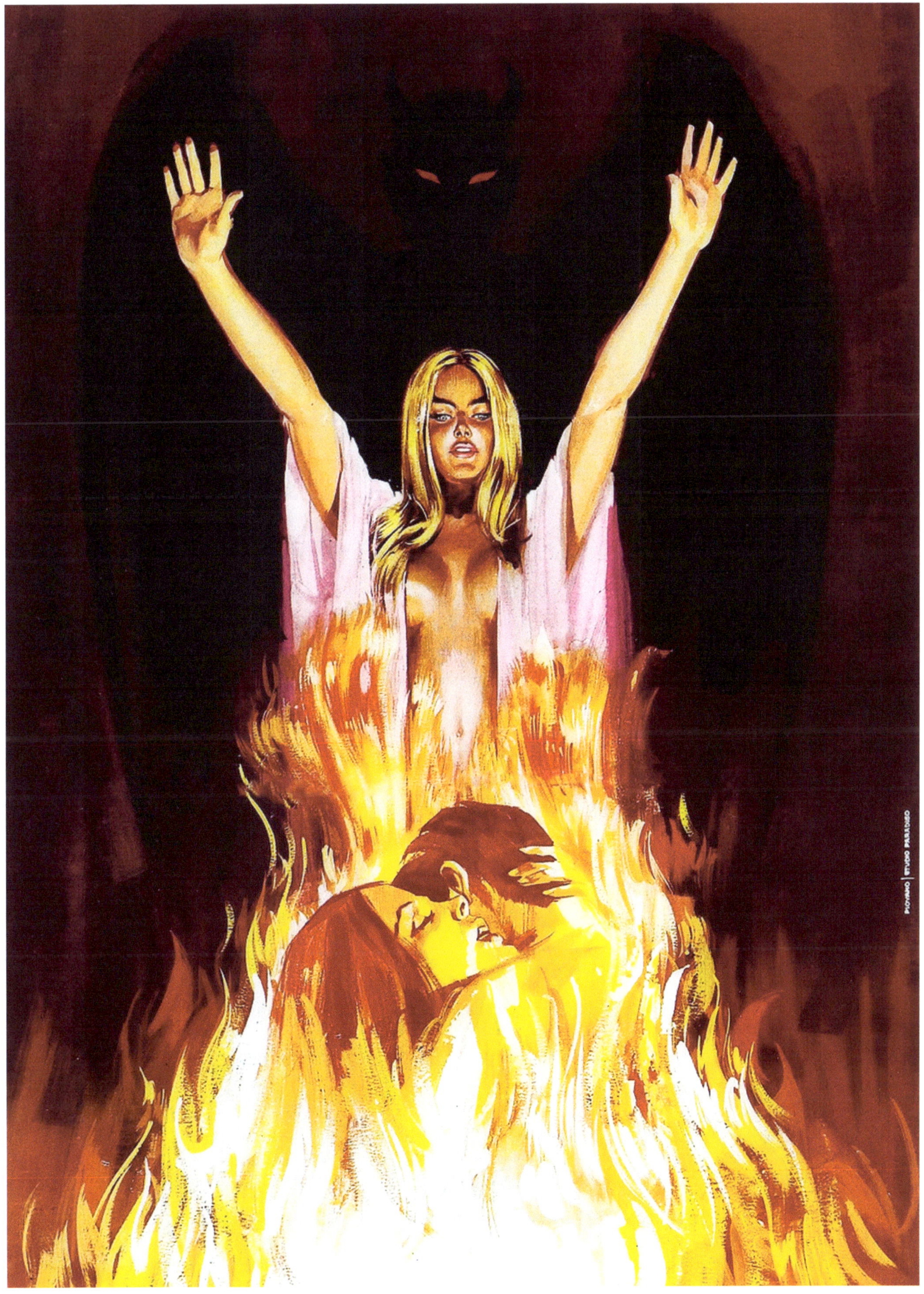
PIOVANO | STUDIO PARADISO

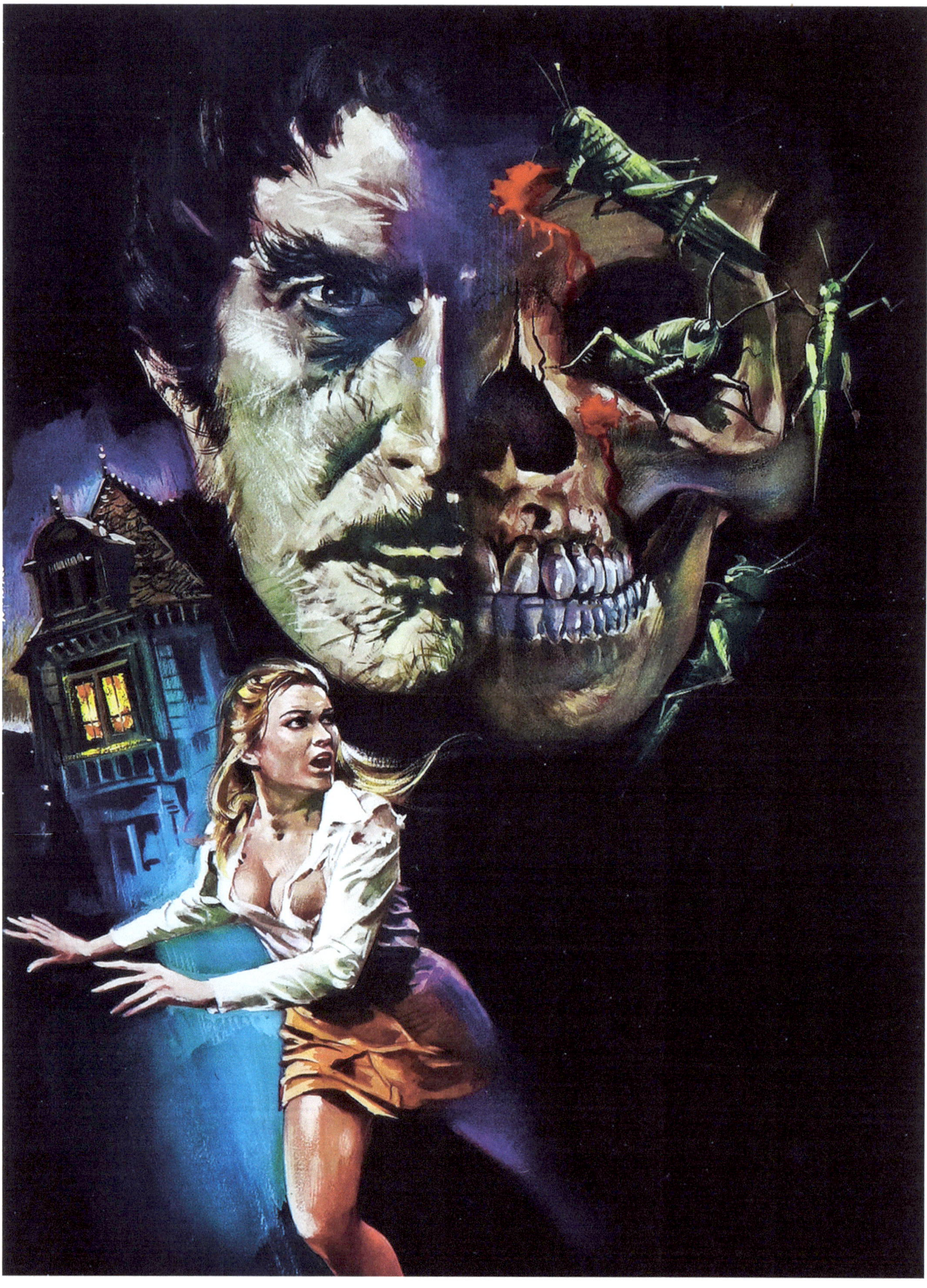

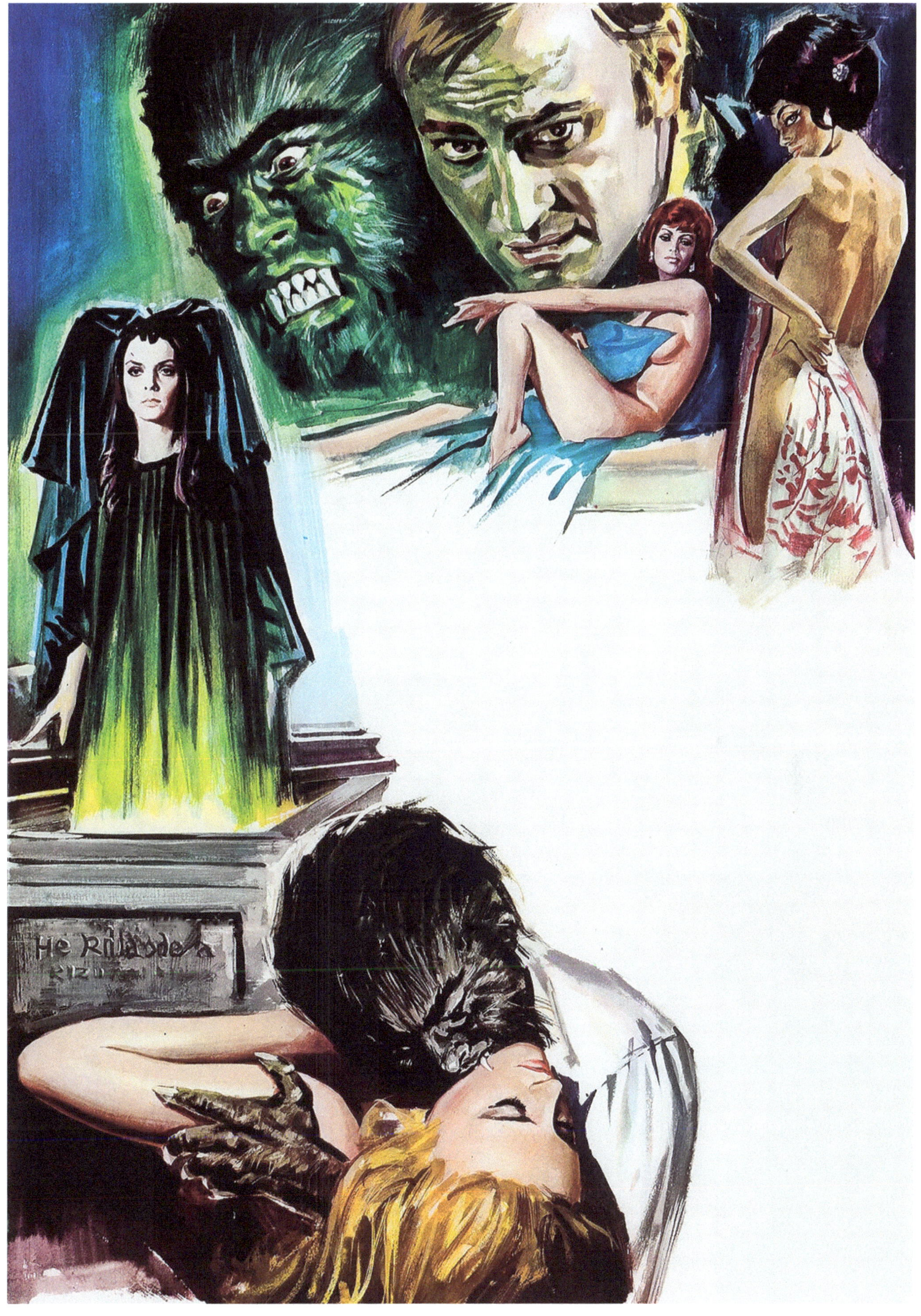

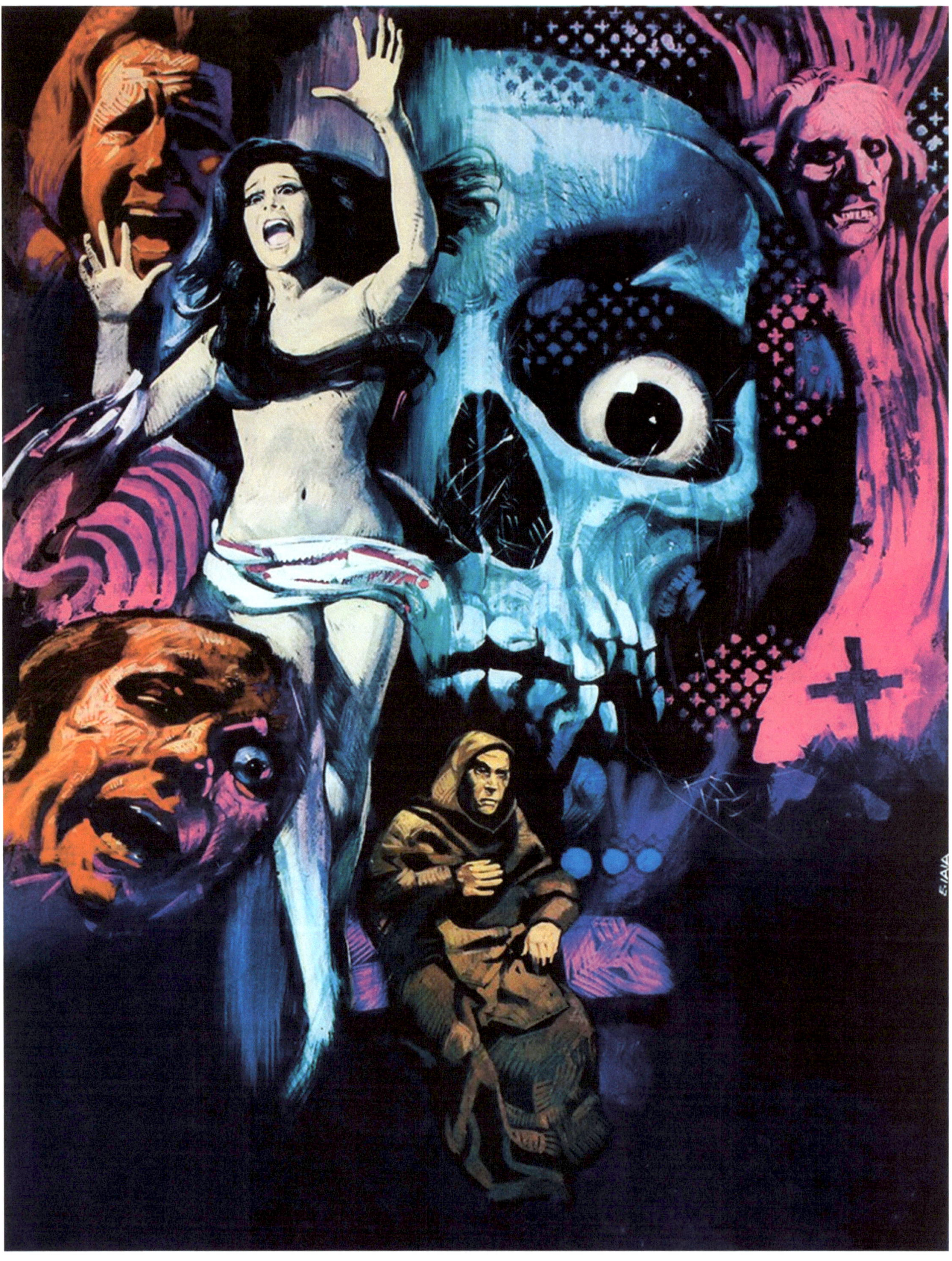

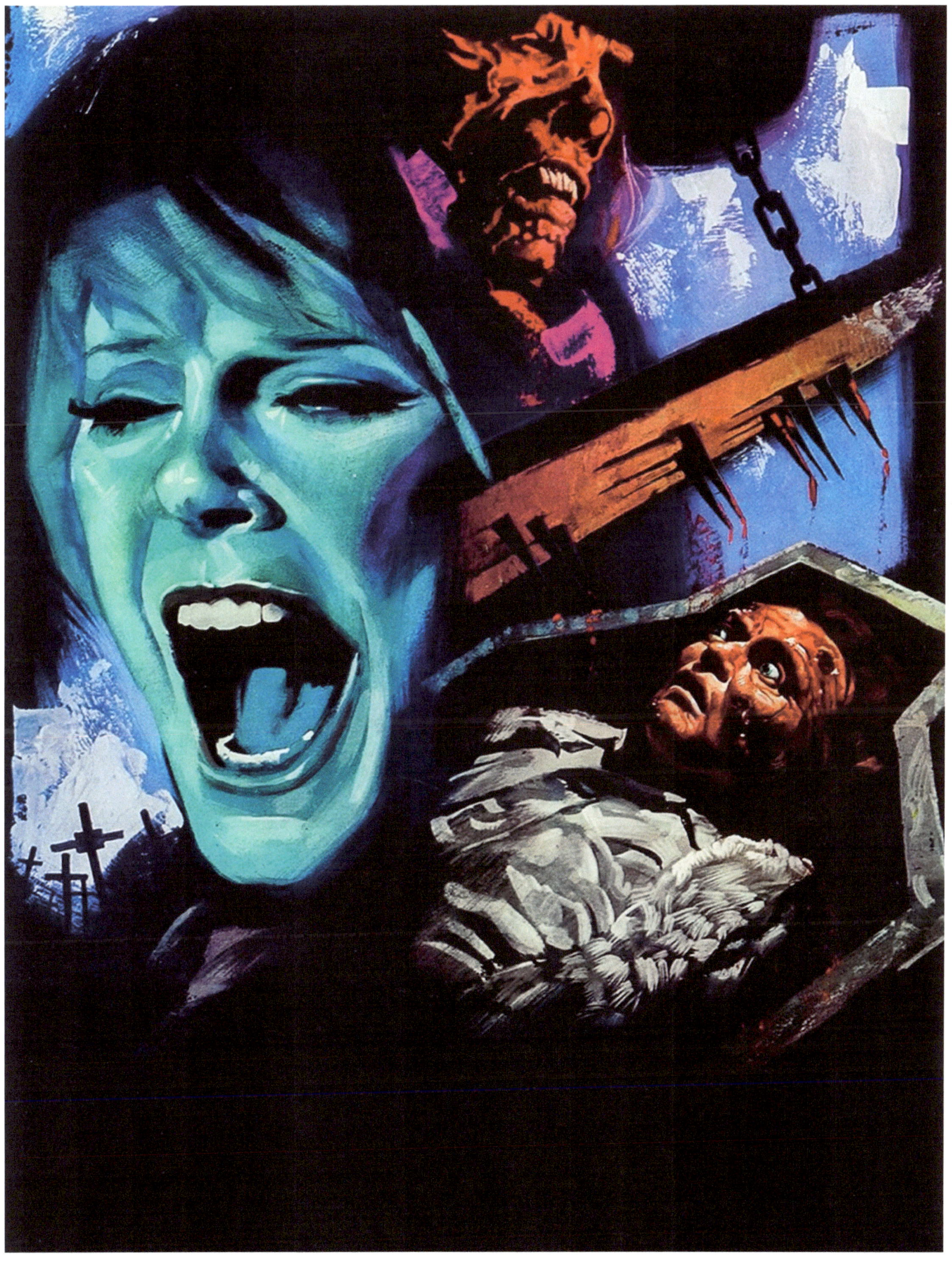

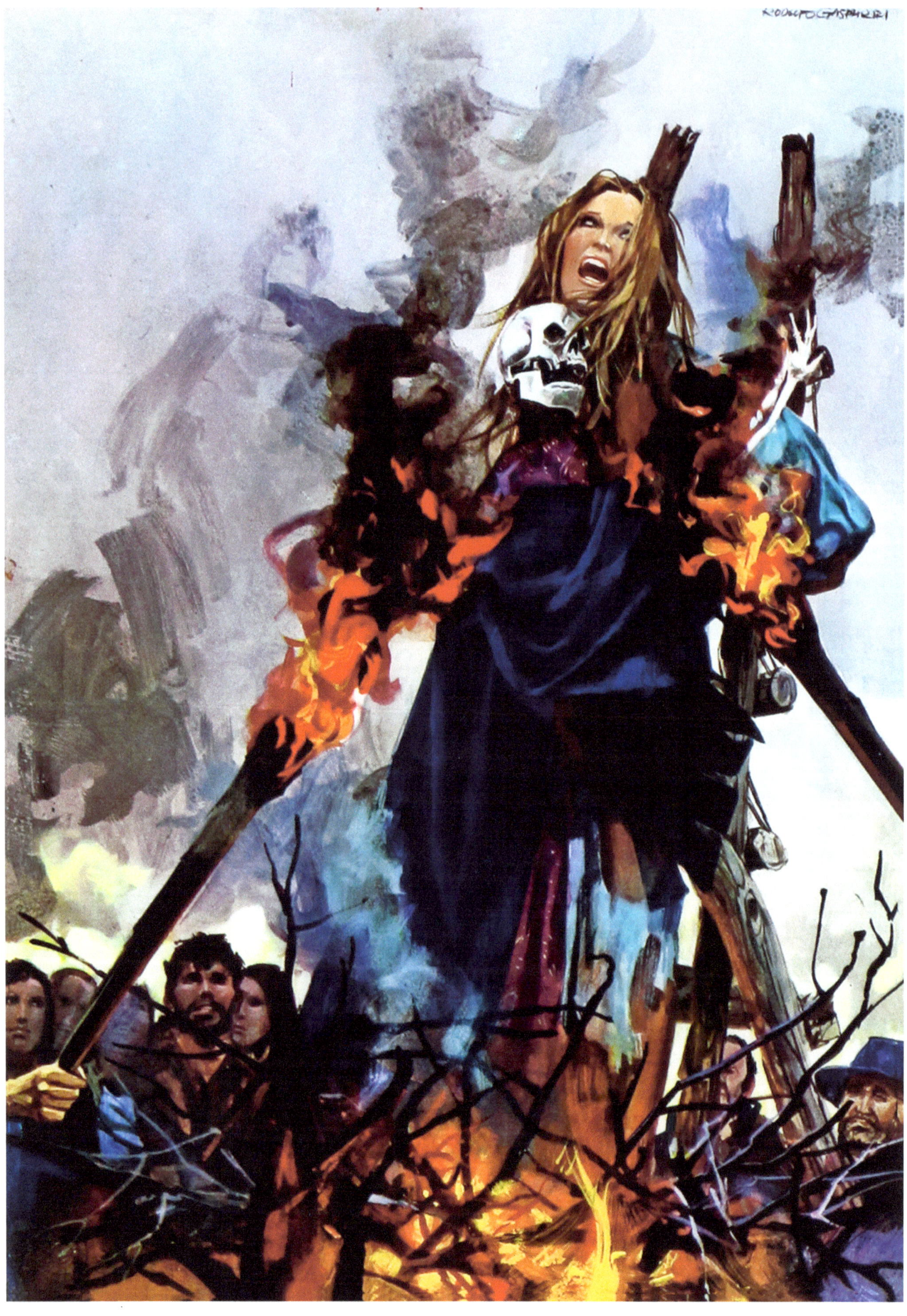

RODOLFO GASPARRI

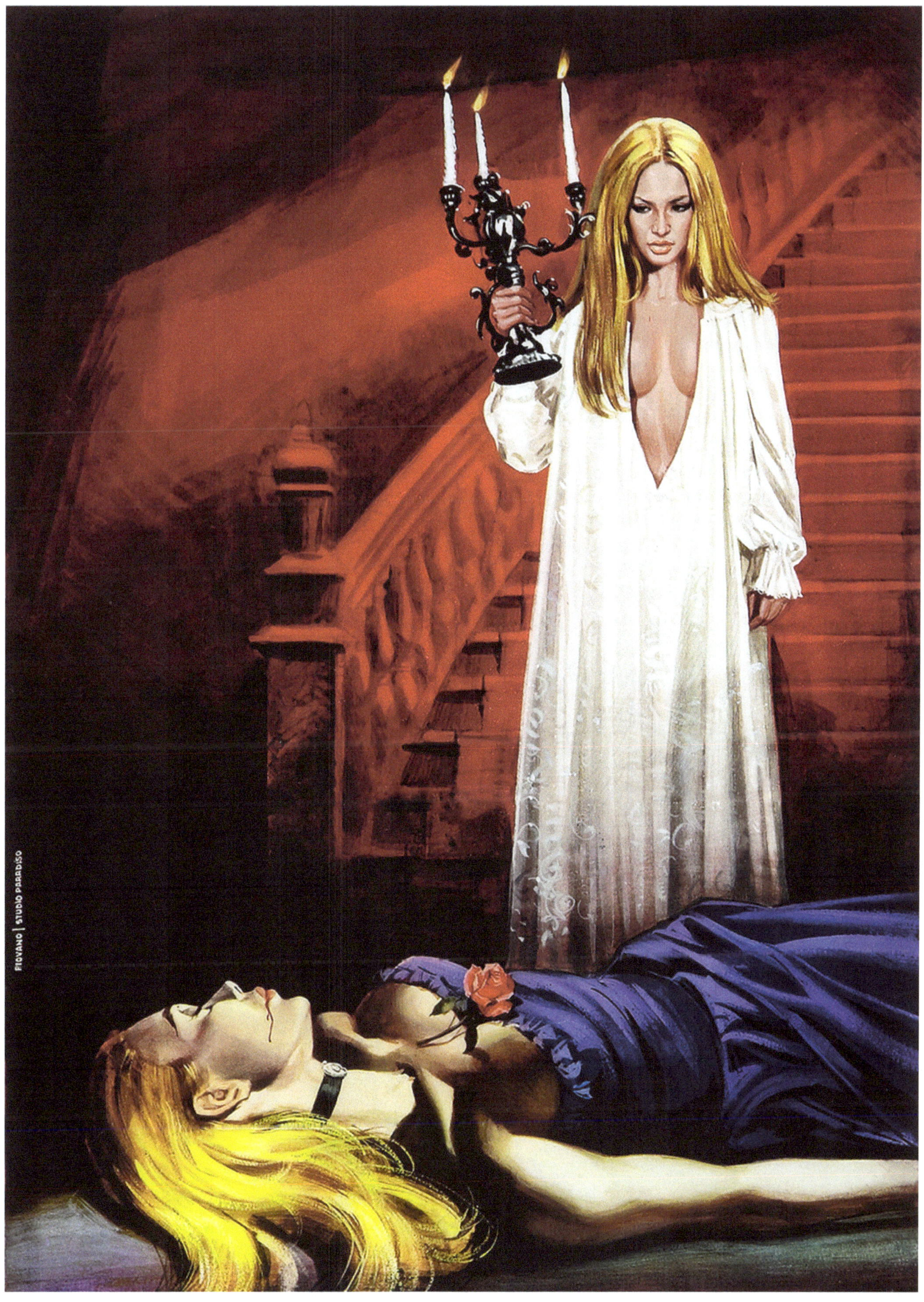
FIOVANO | STUDIO PARADISO

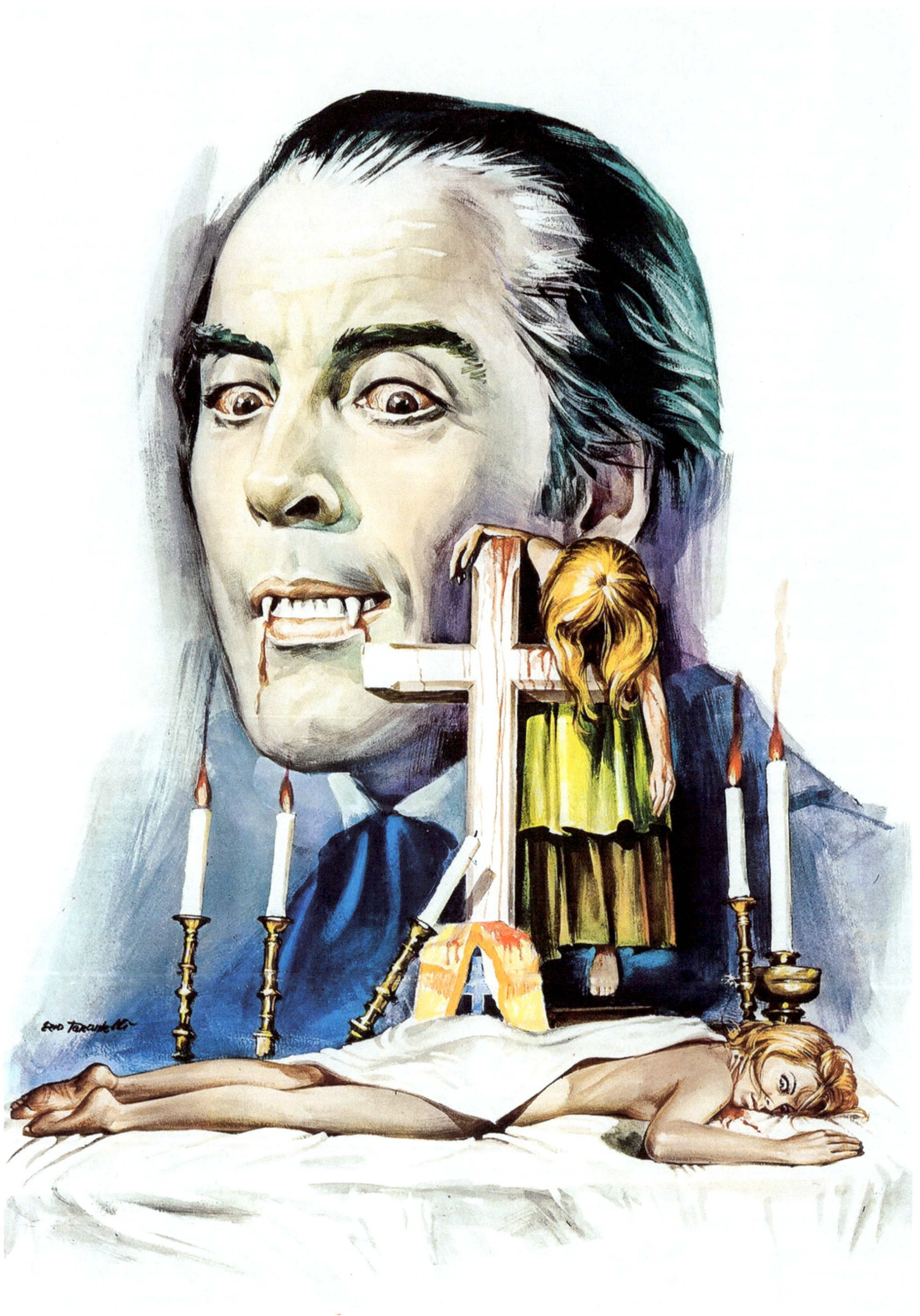

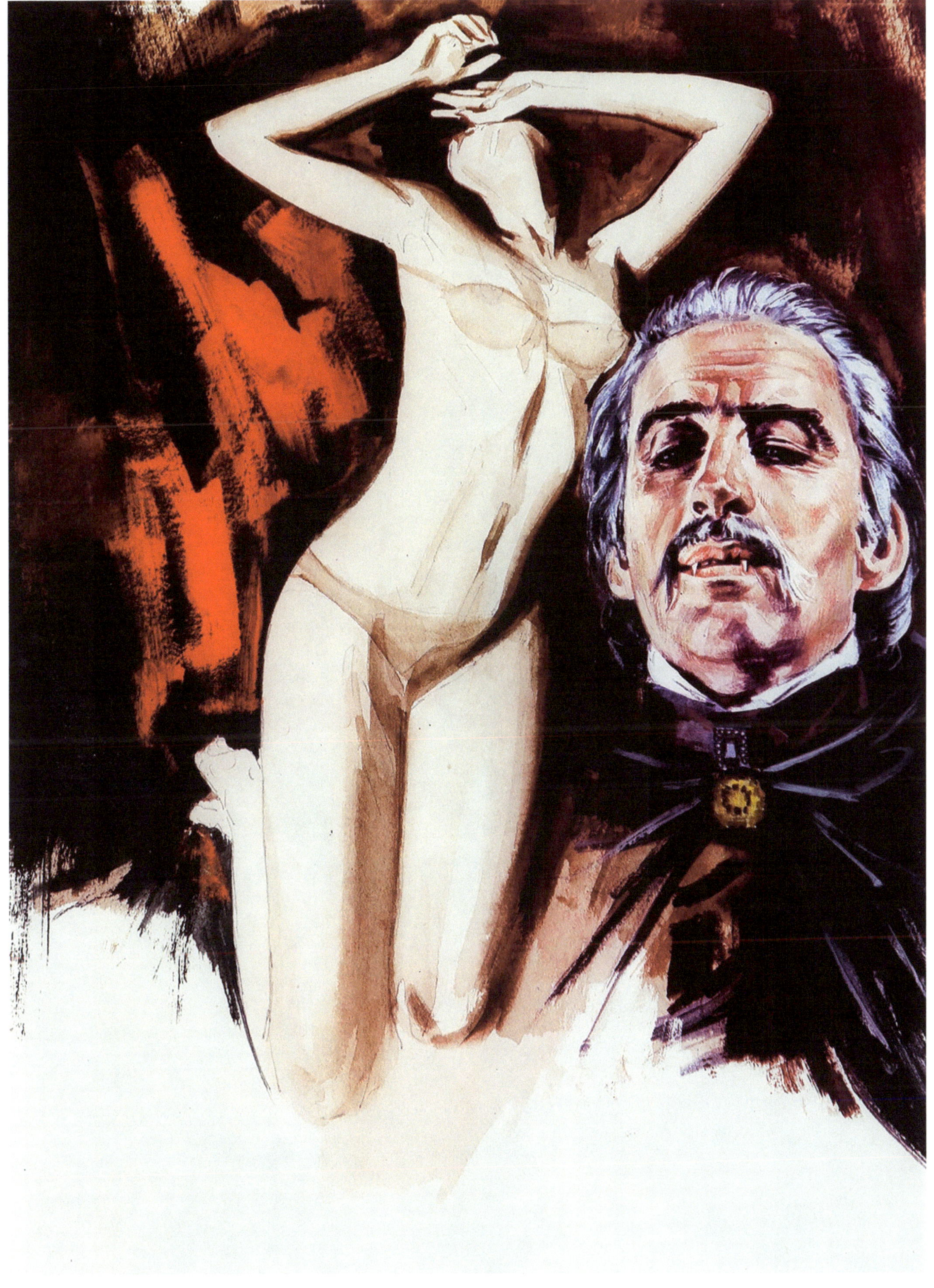

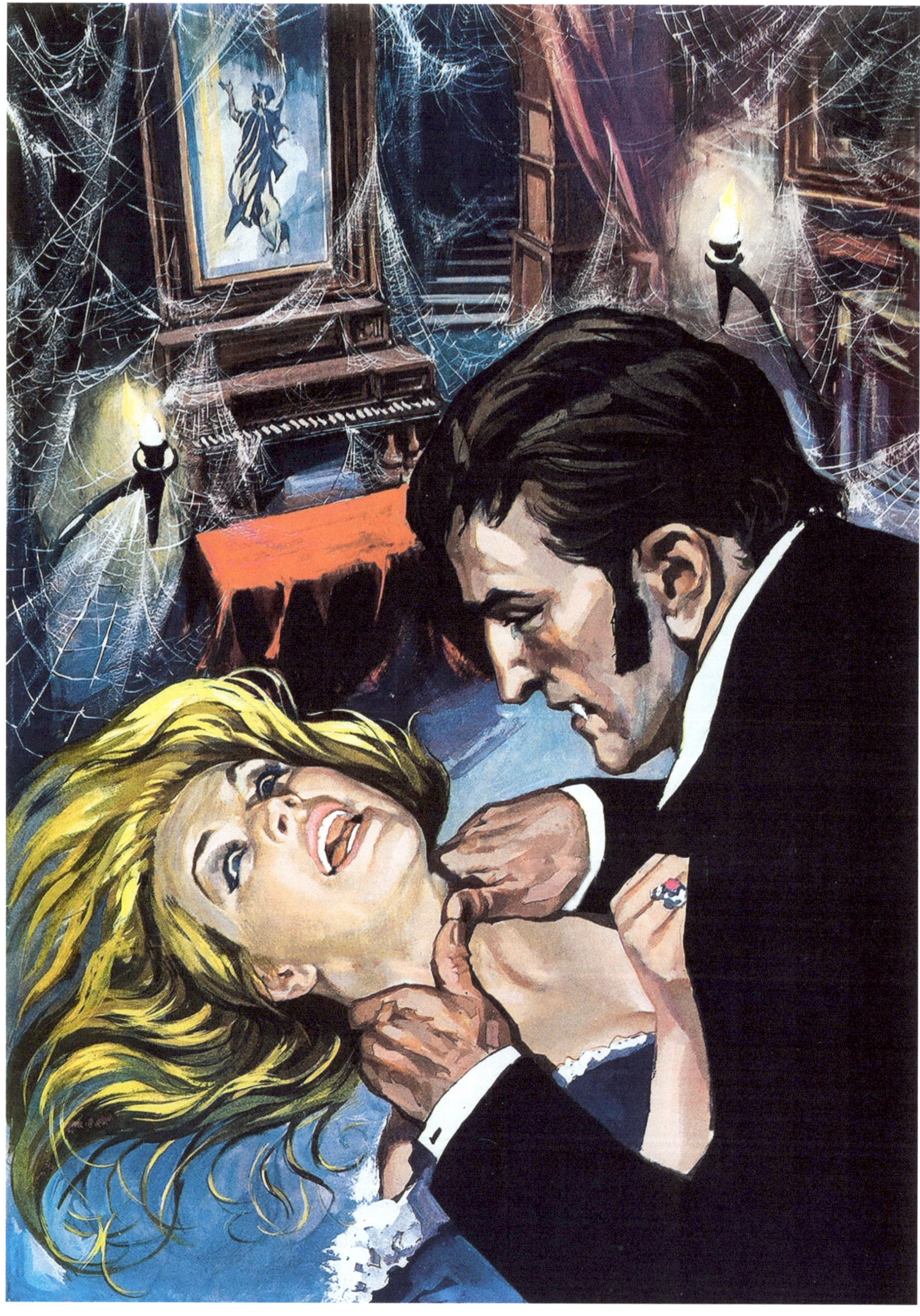

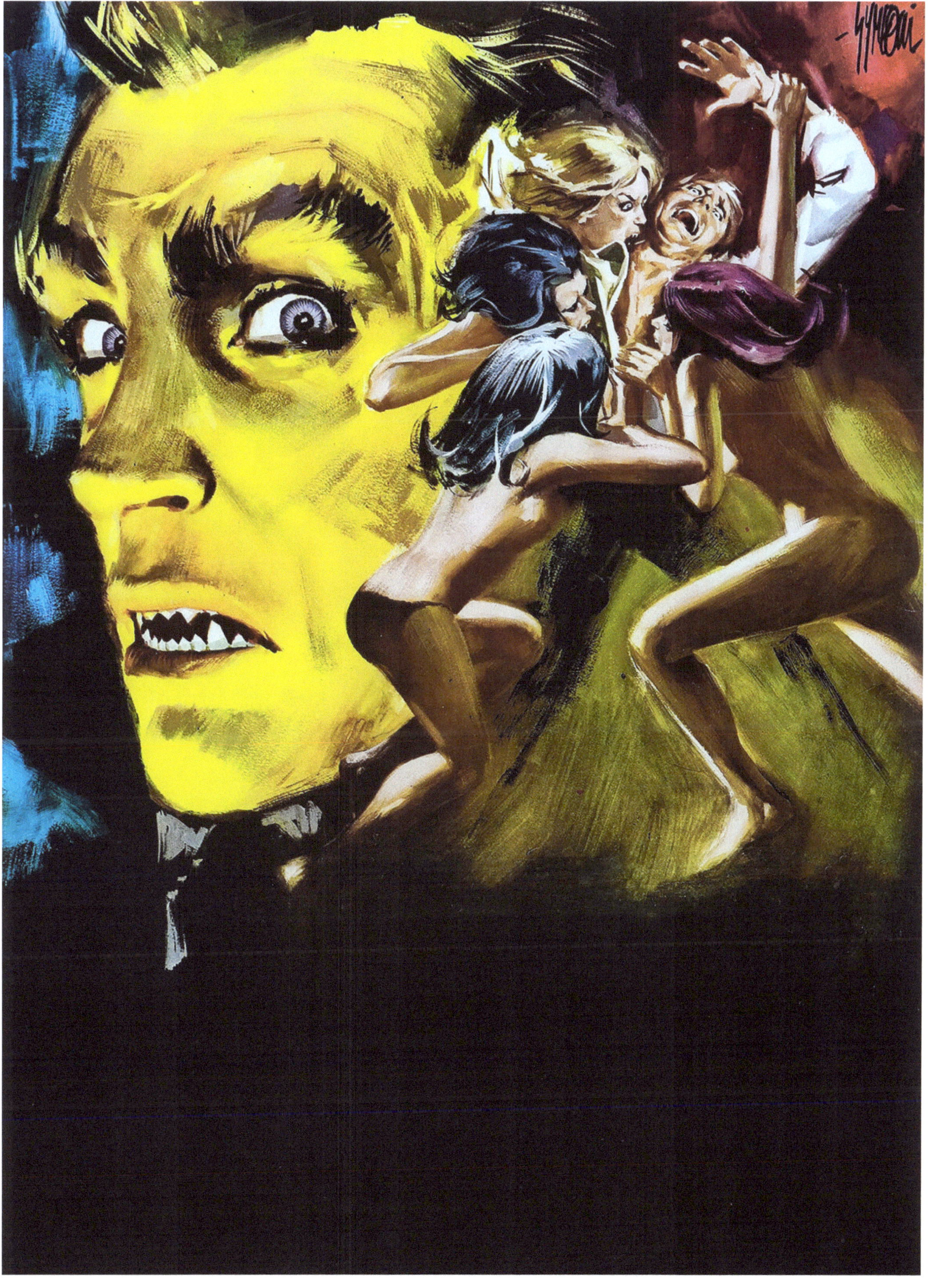

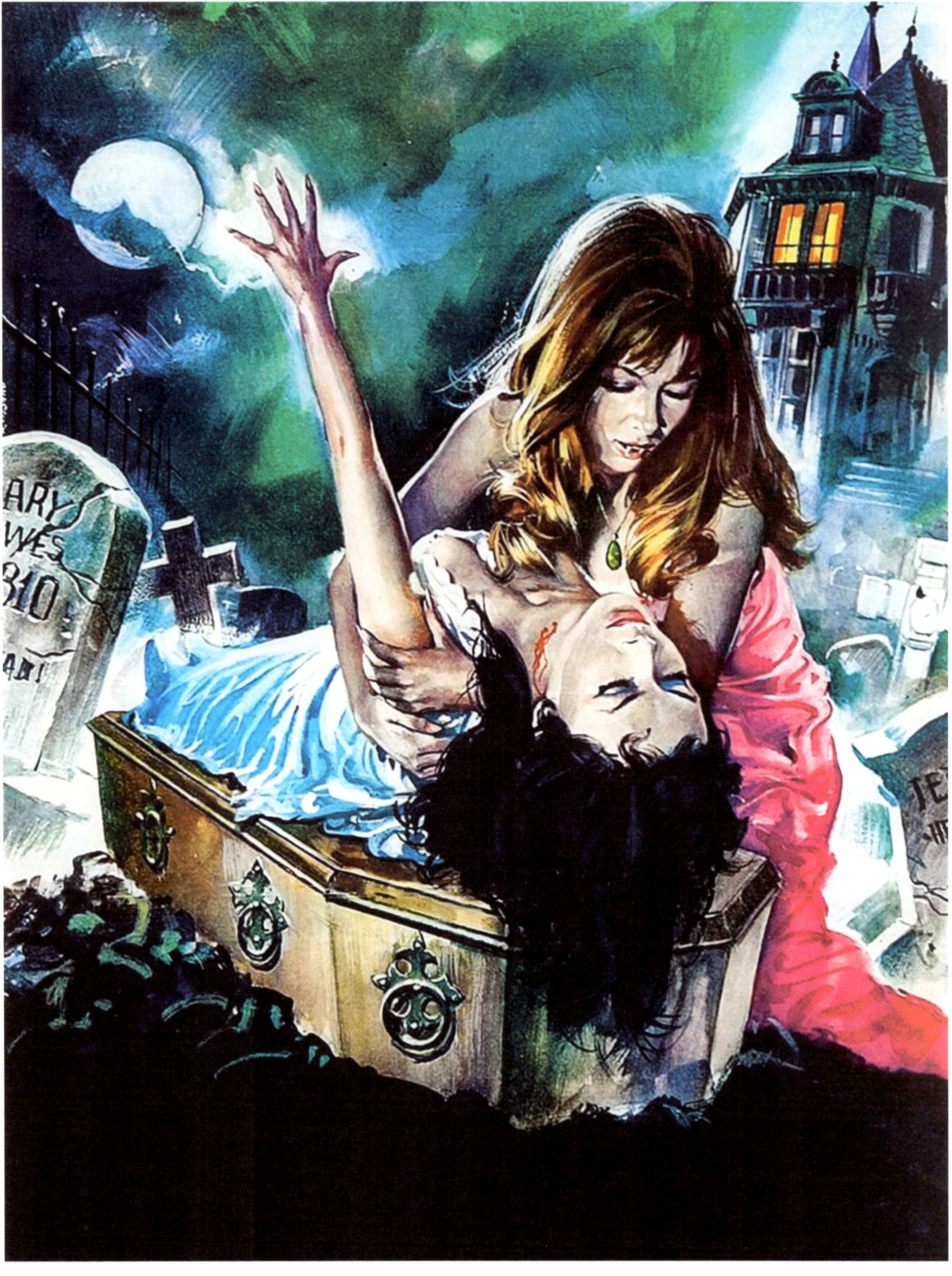

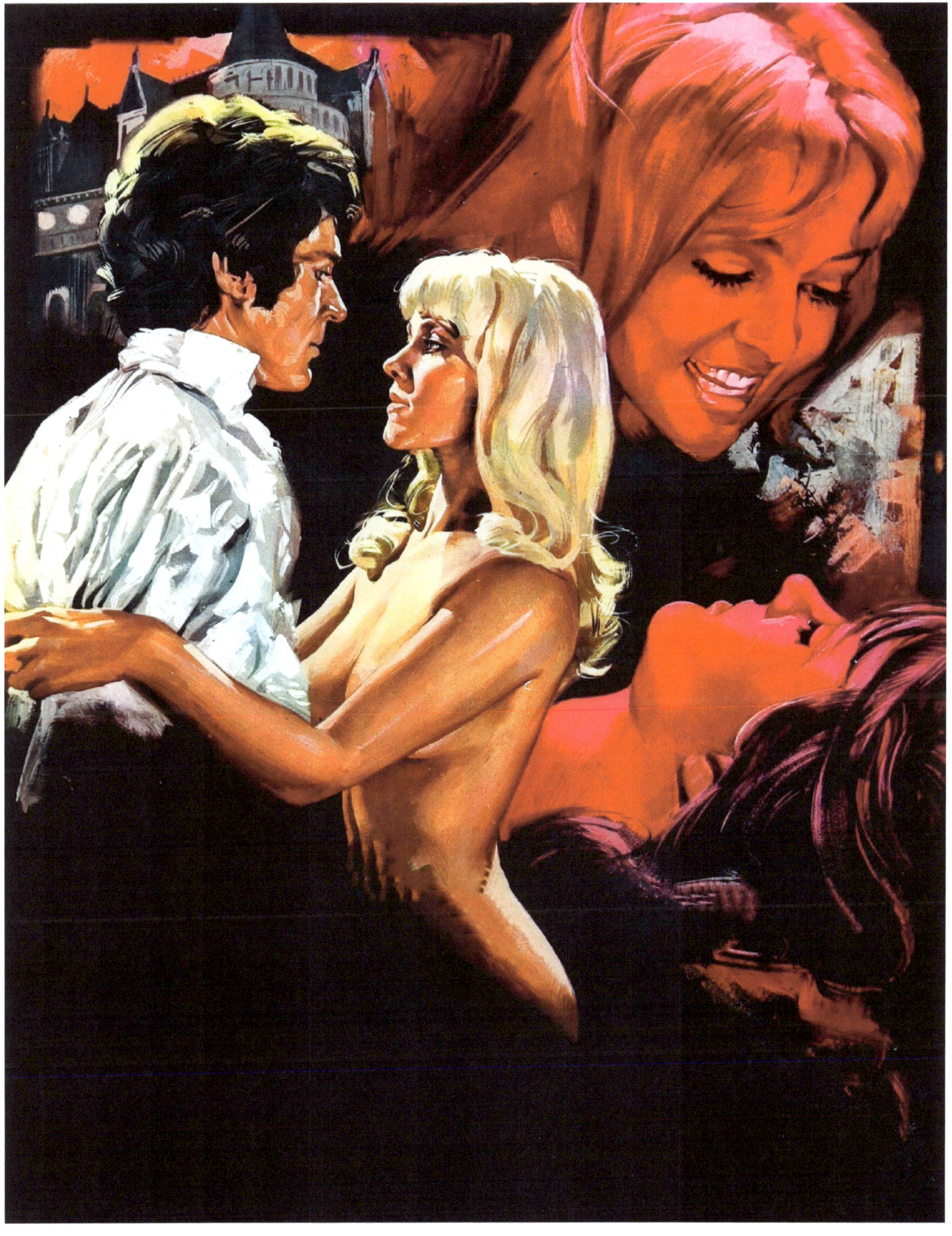

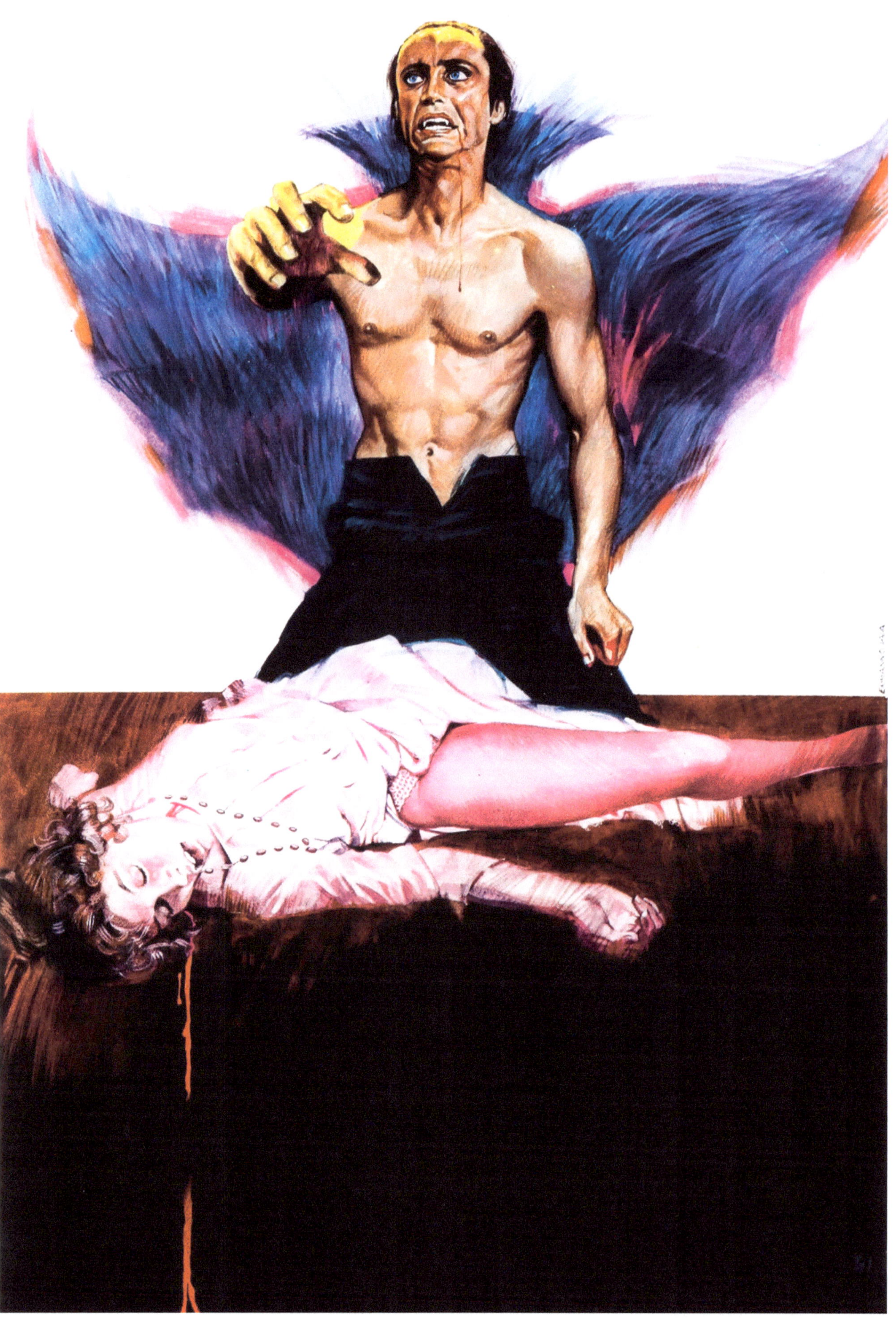

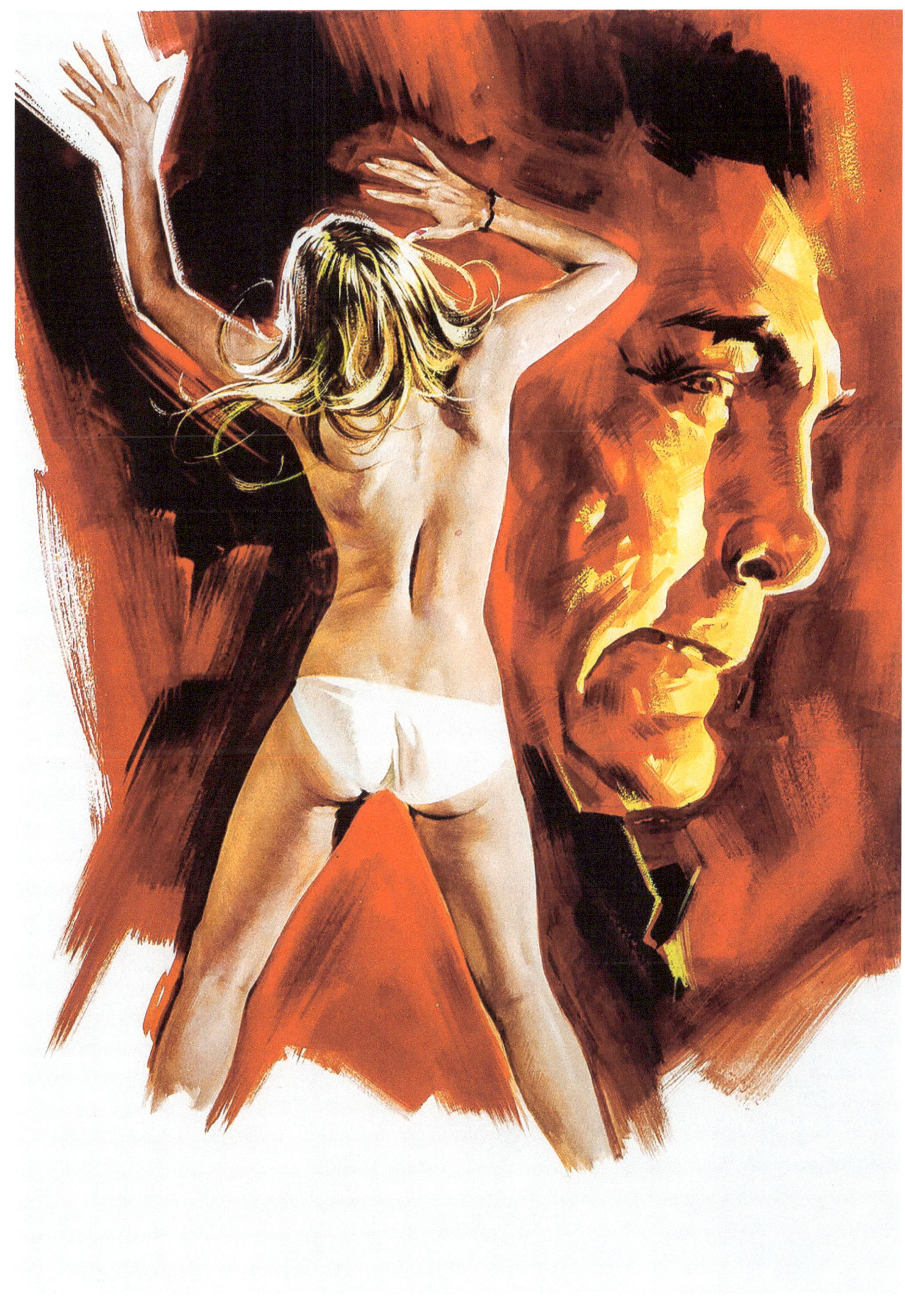

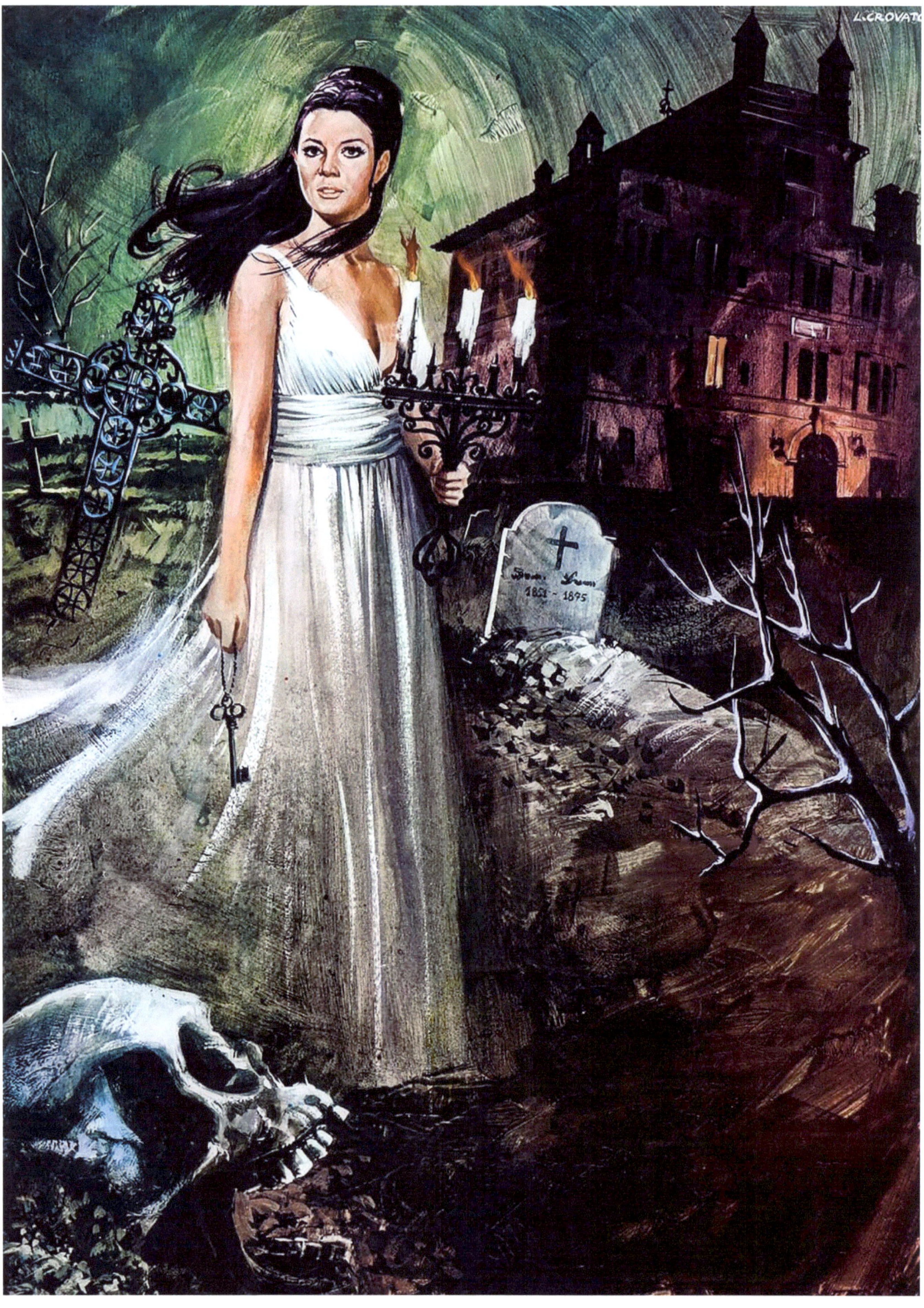

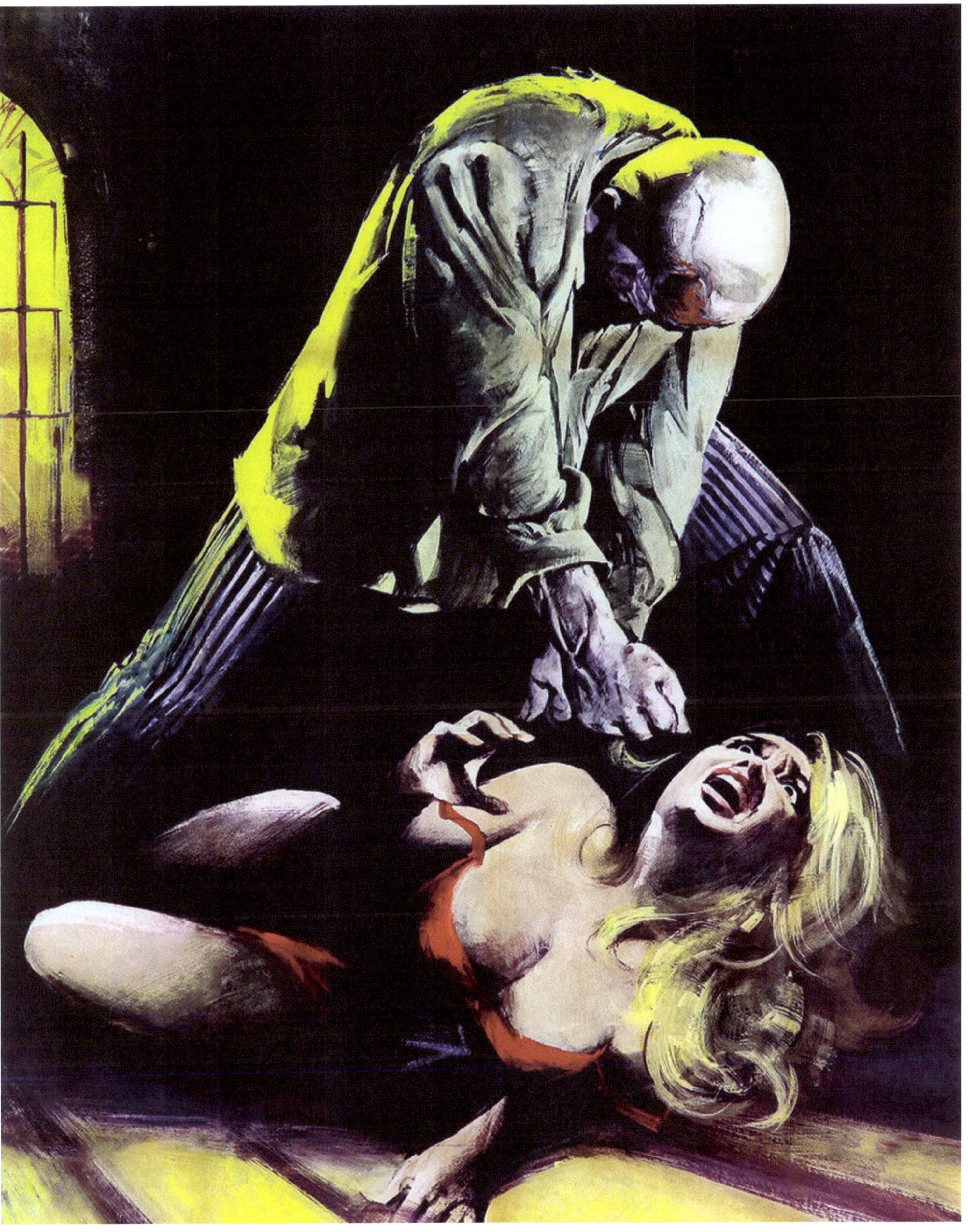

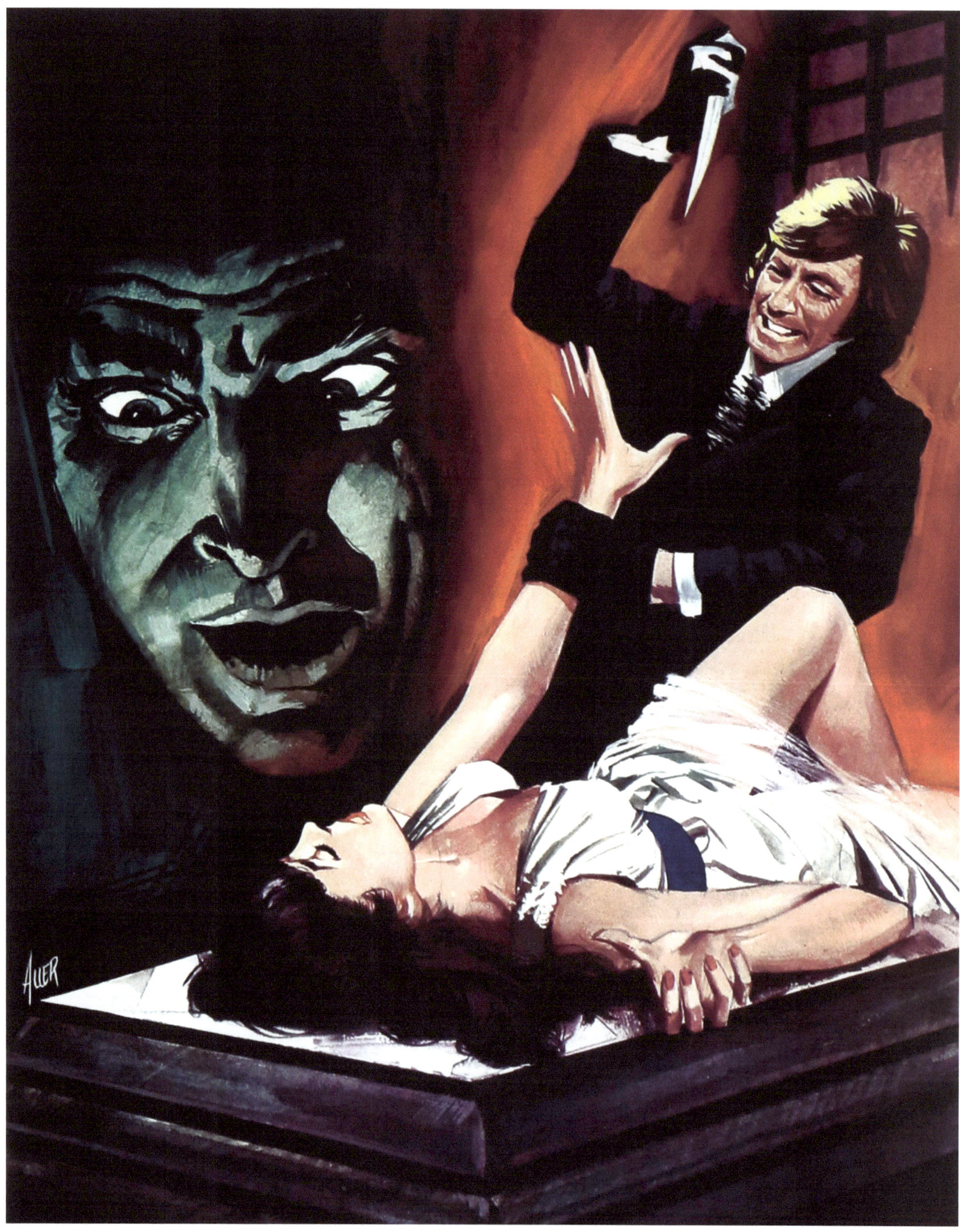

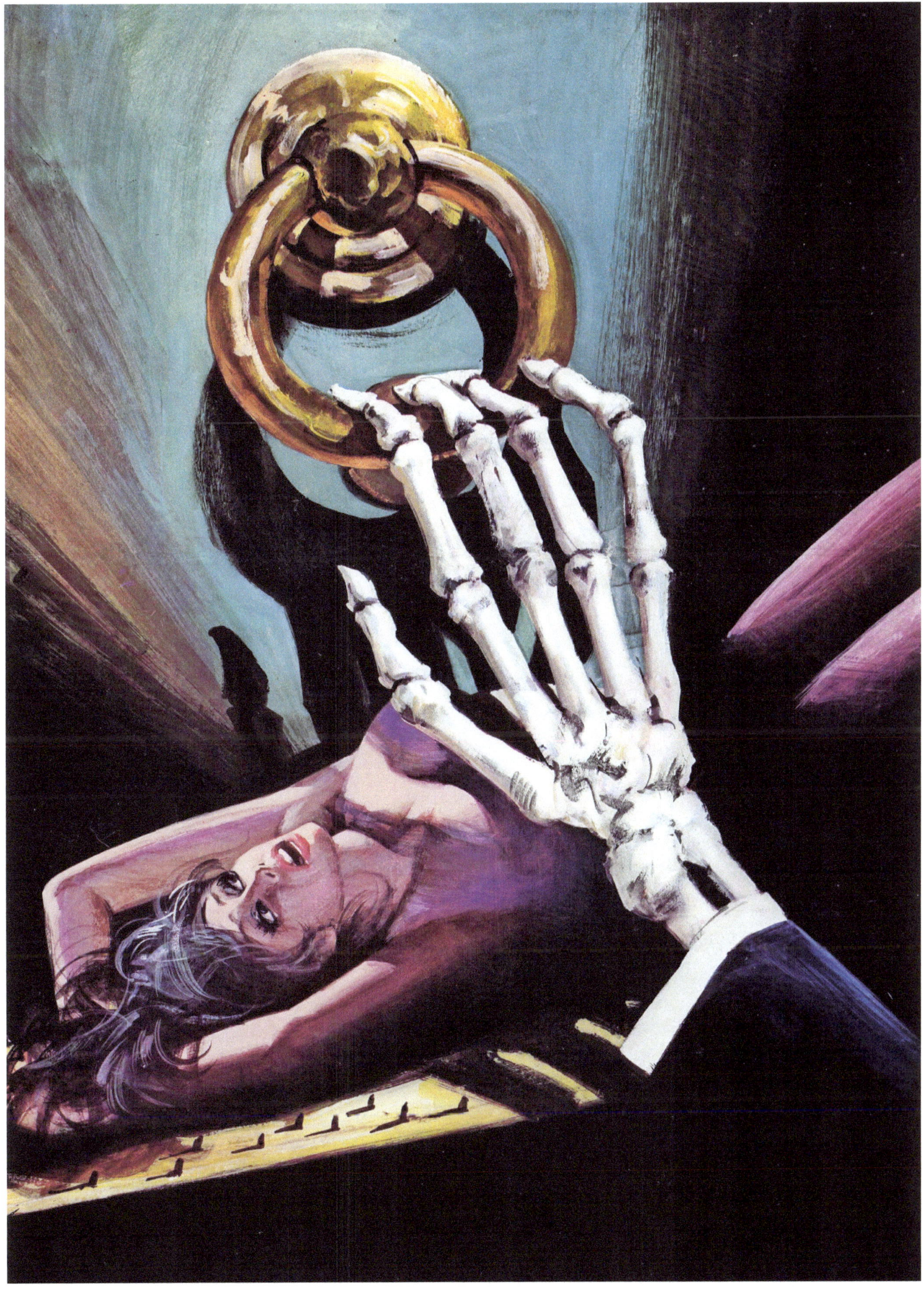

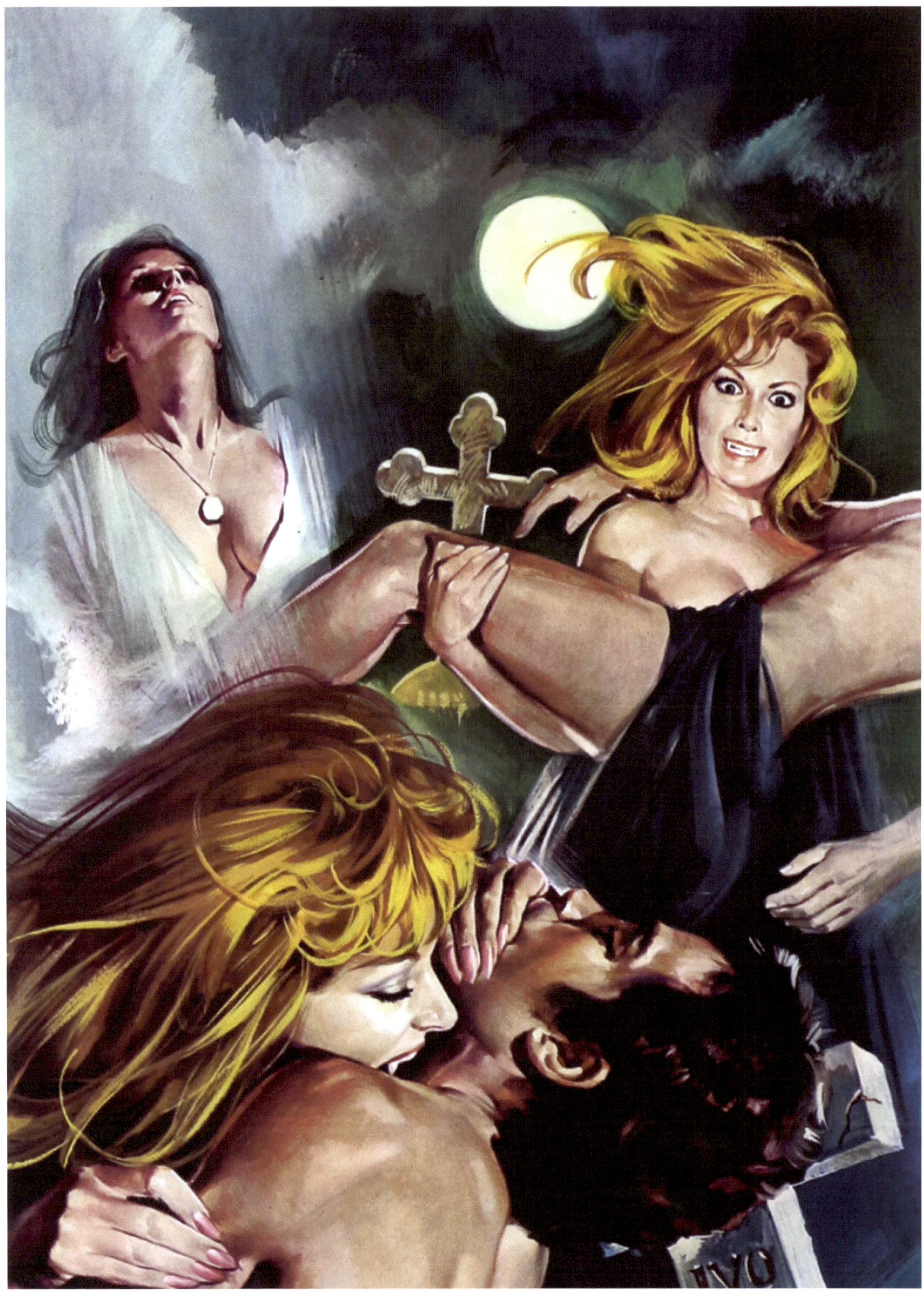

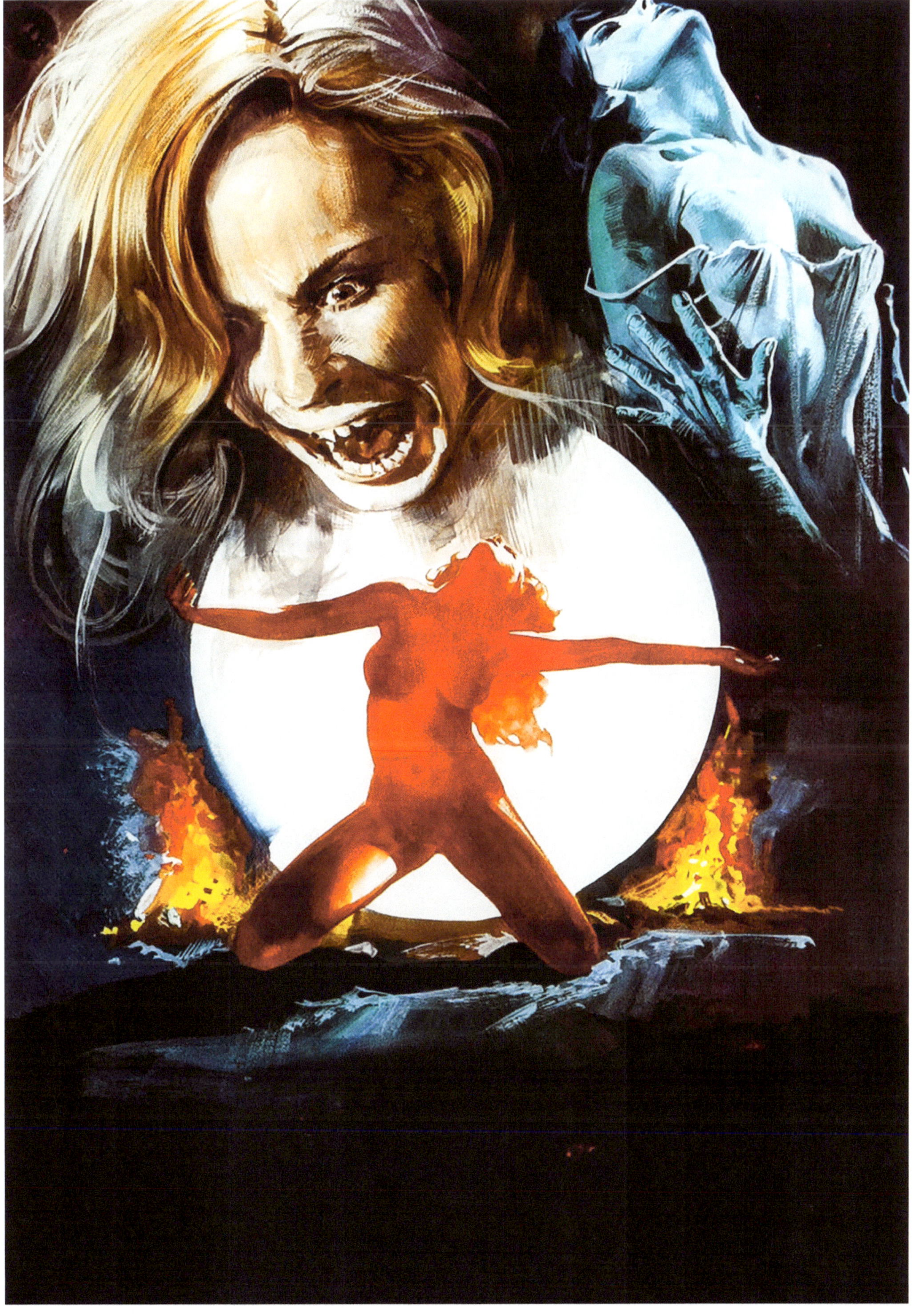

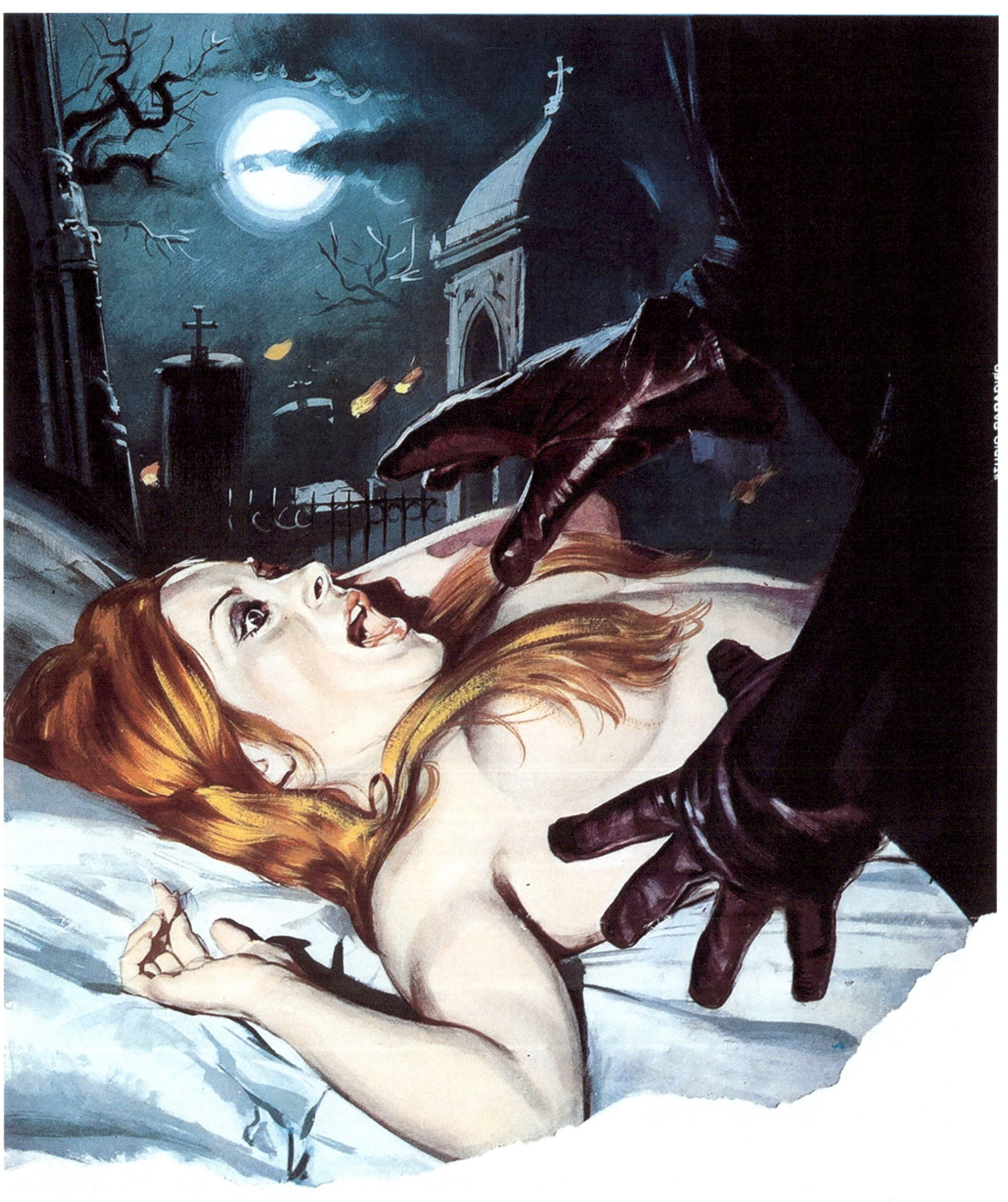

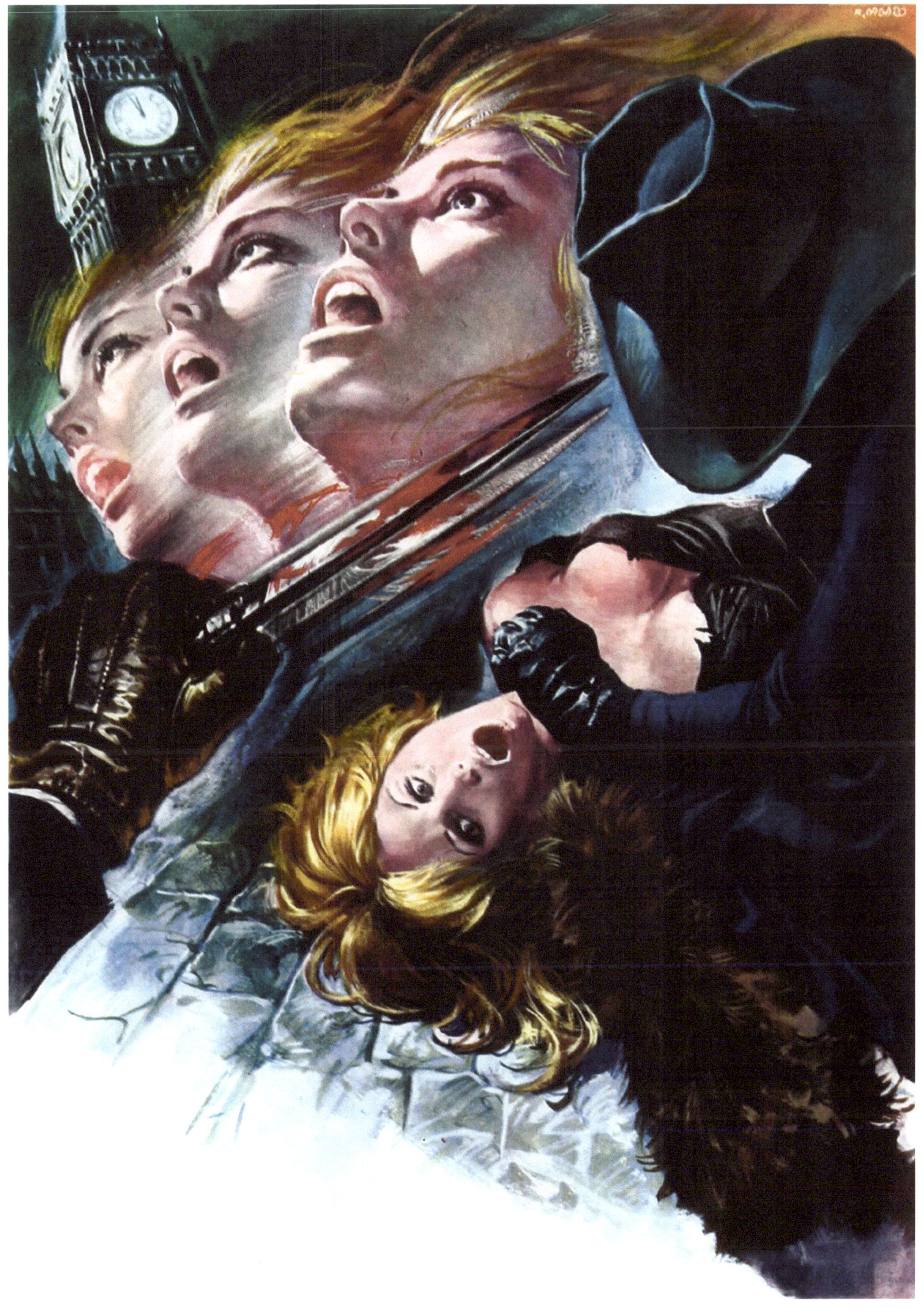

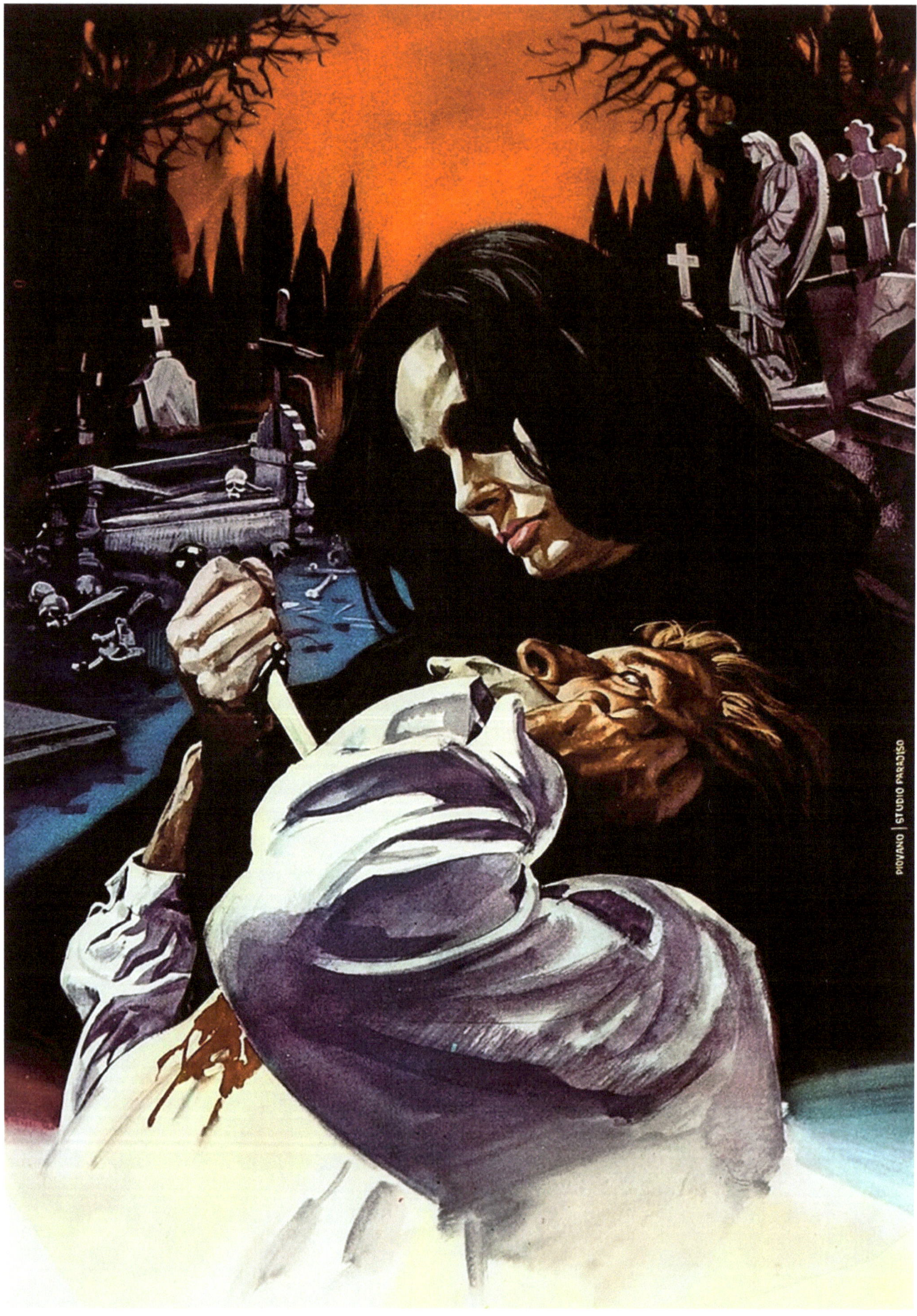
PIOVANO | STUDIO PARADISO

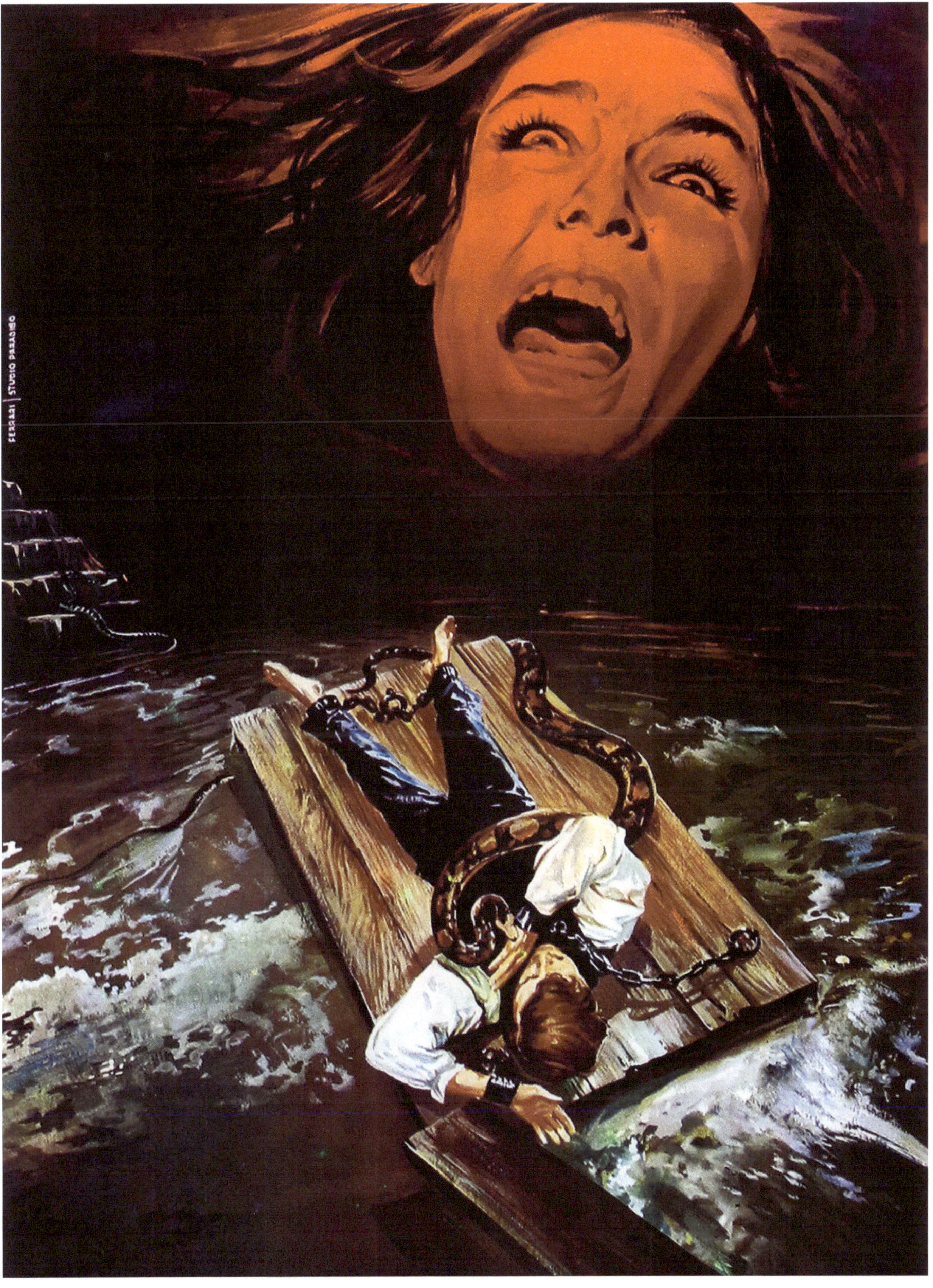
FERRARI | STUDIO PARADISO

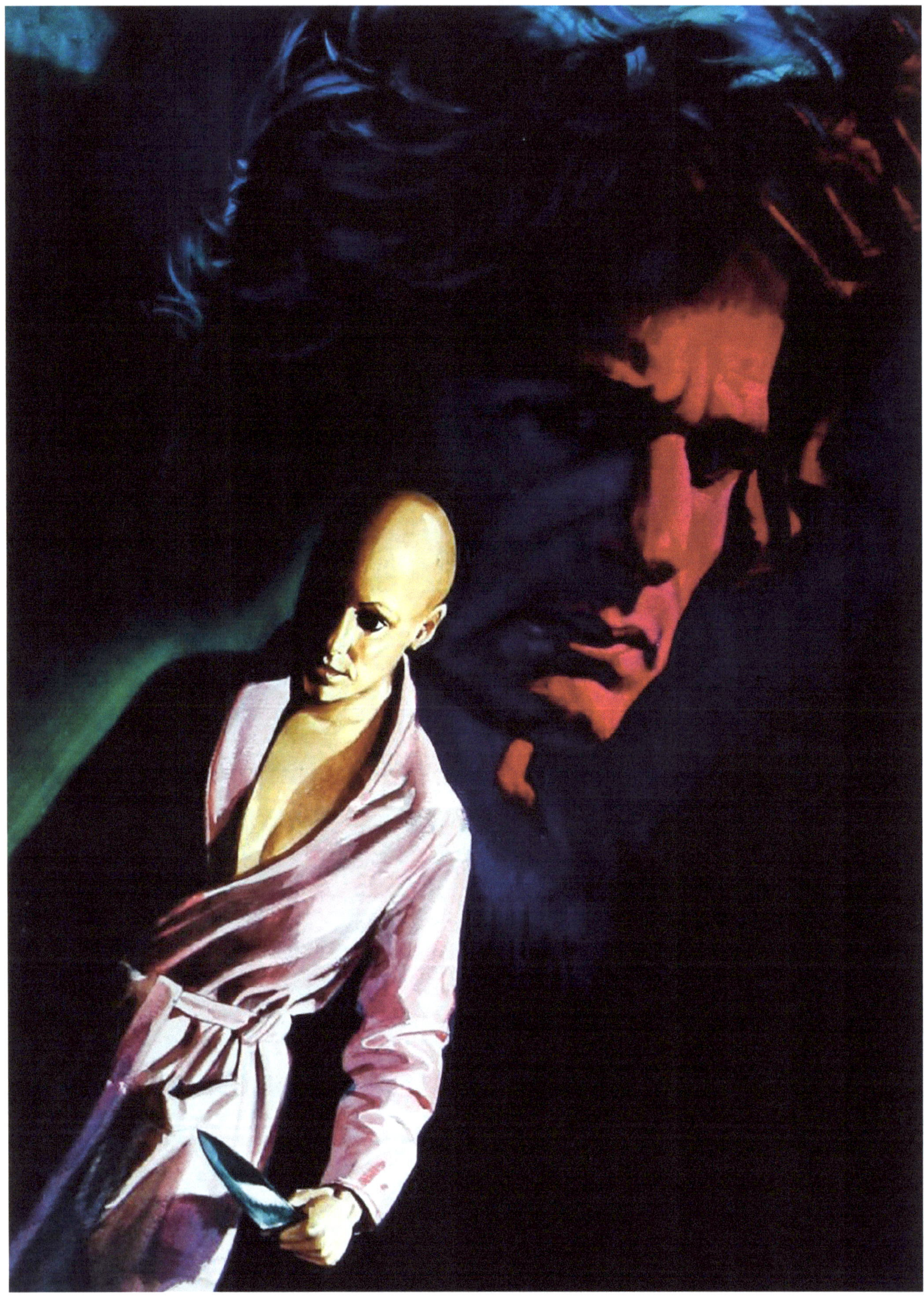

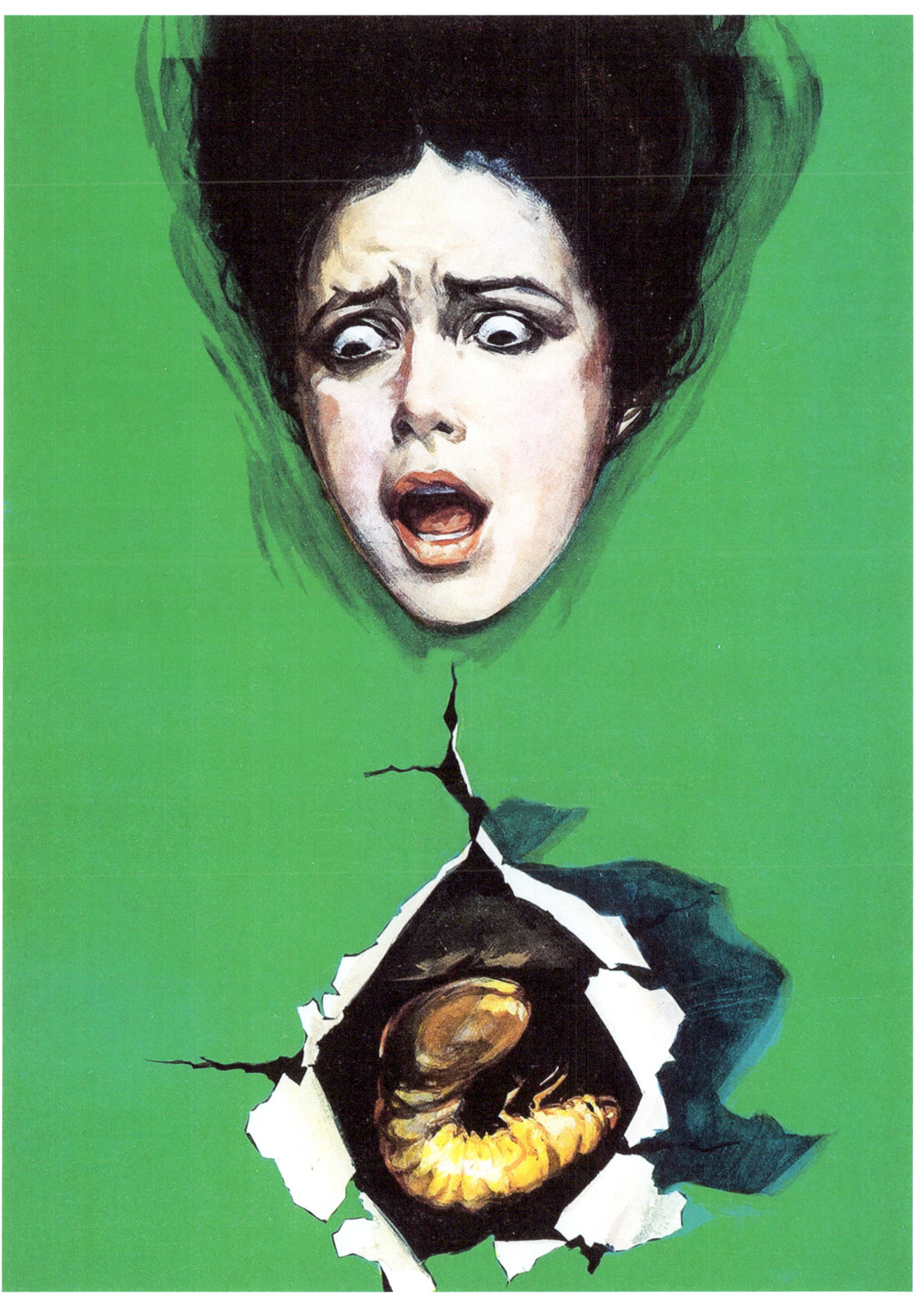

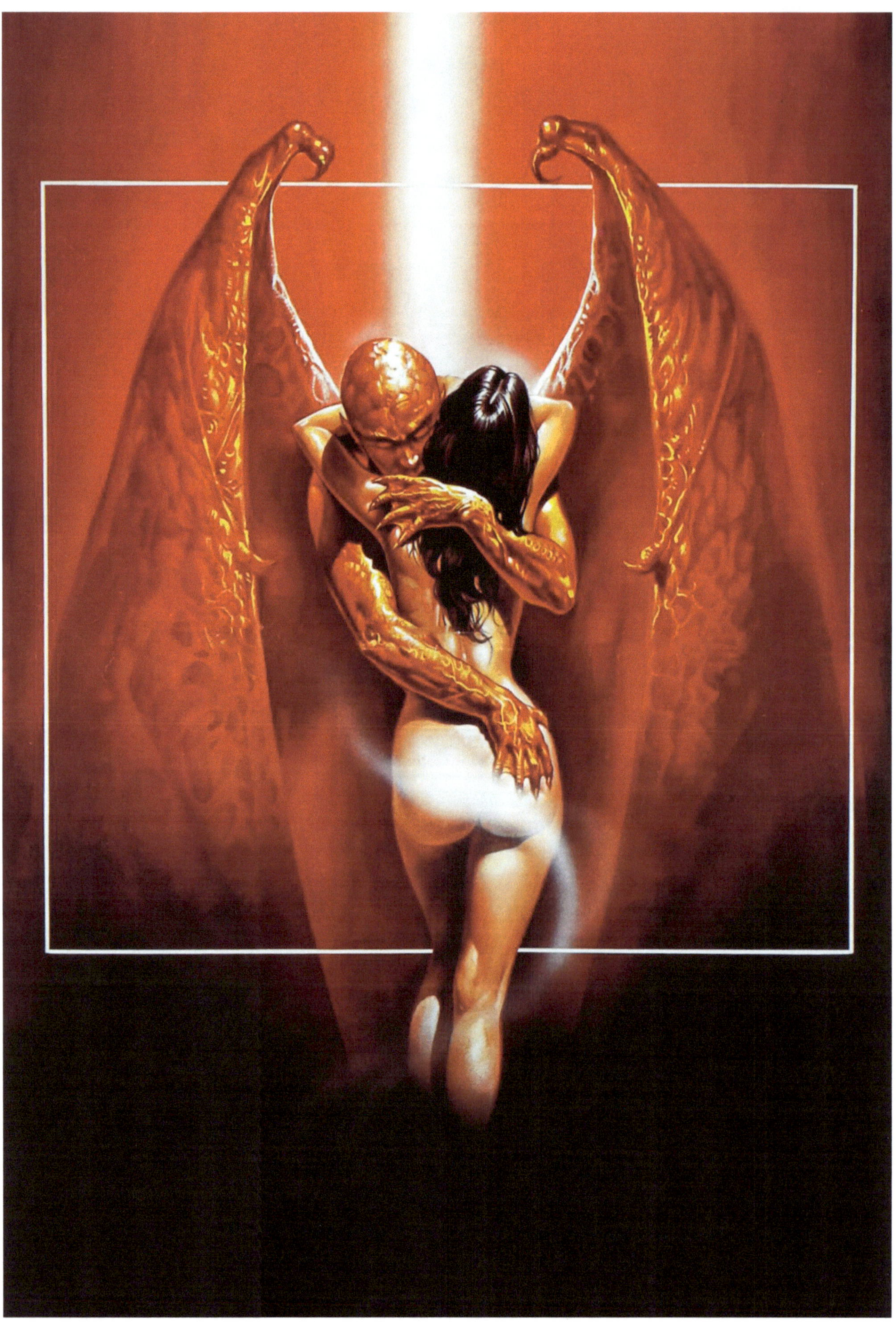

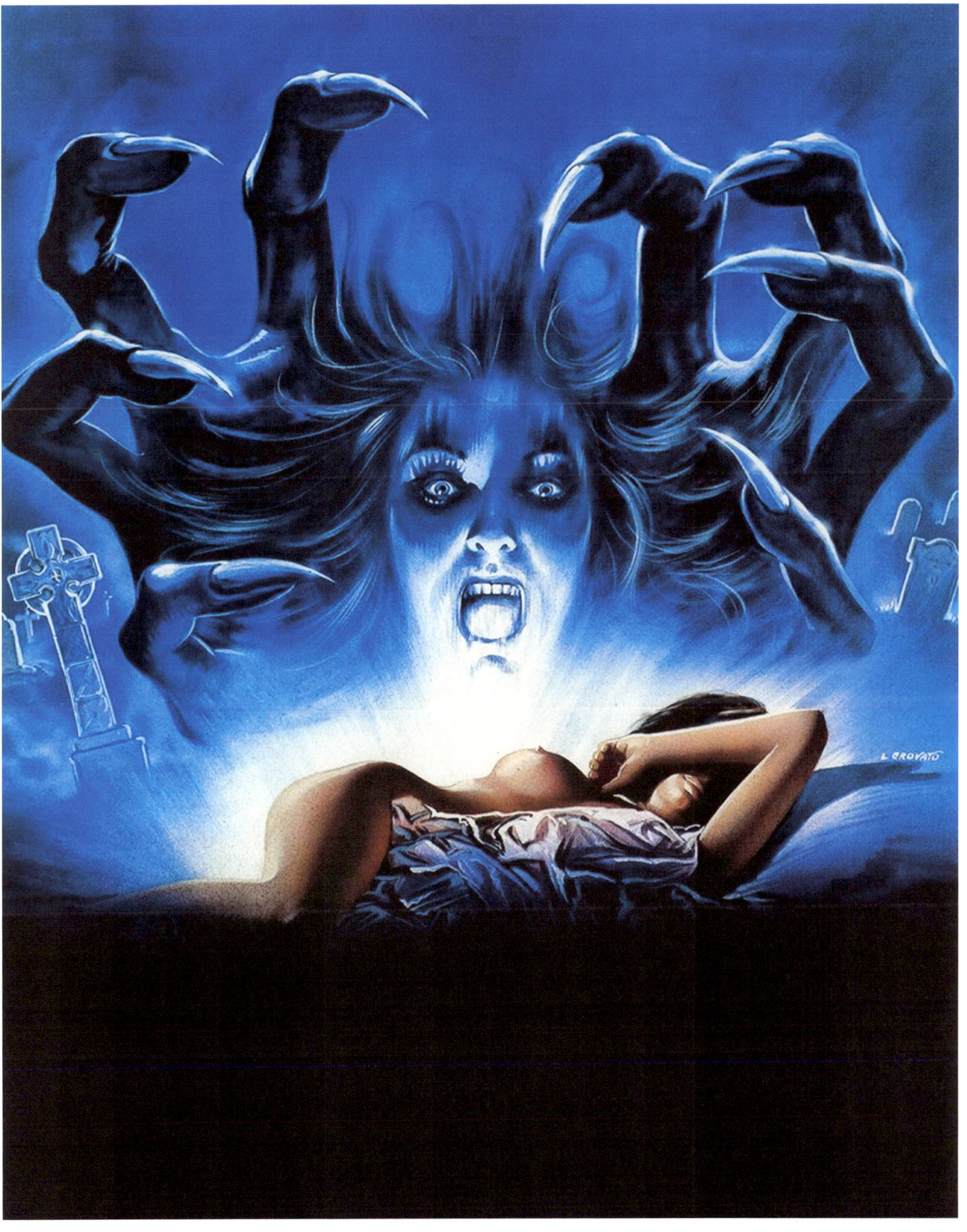
L. BROVATO

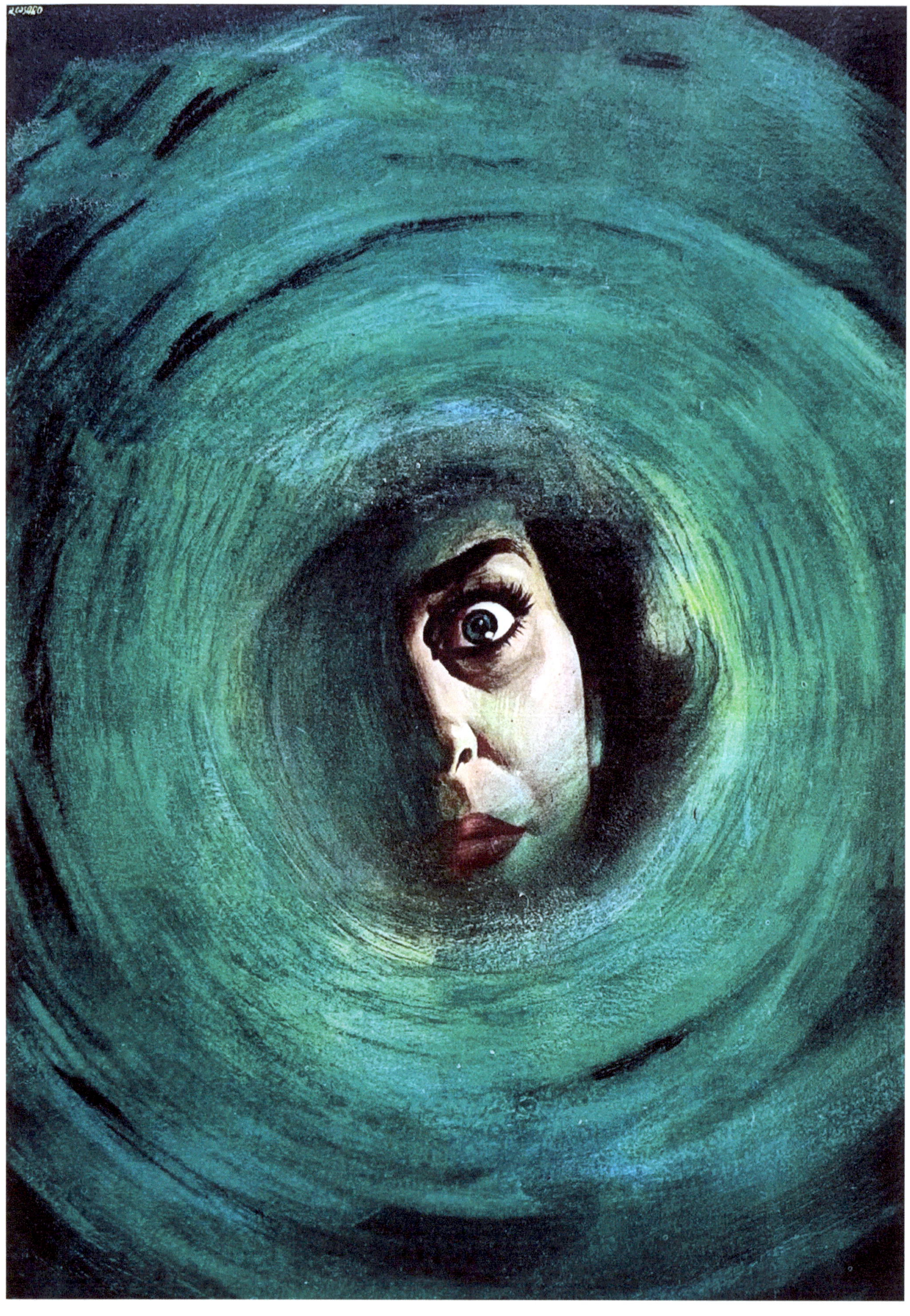

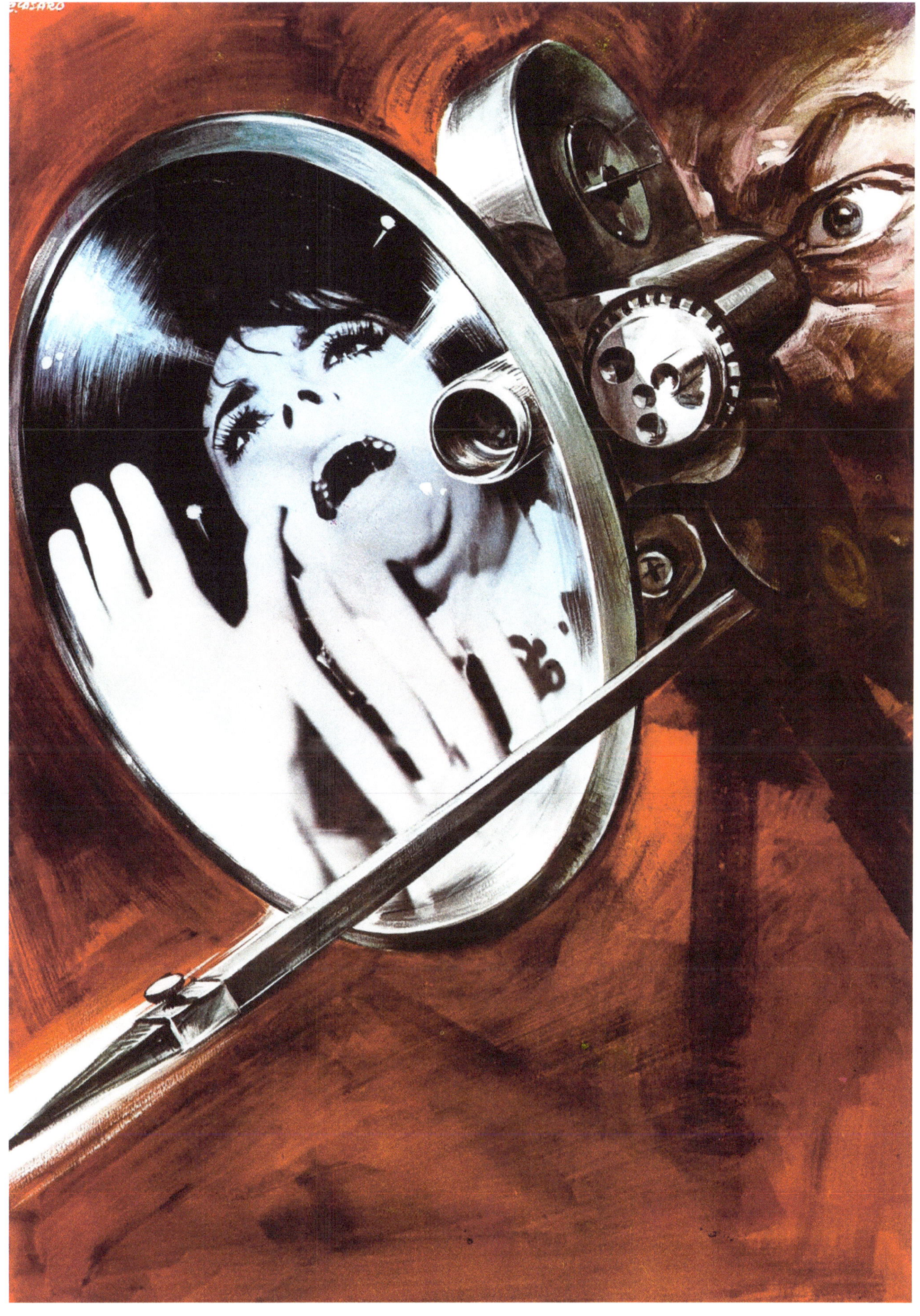

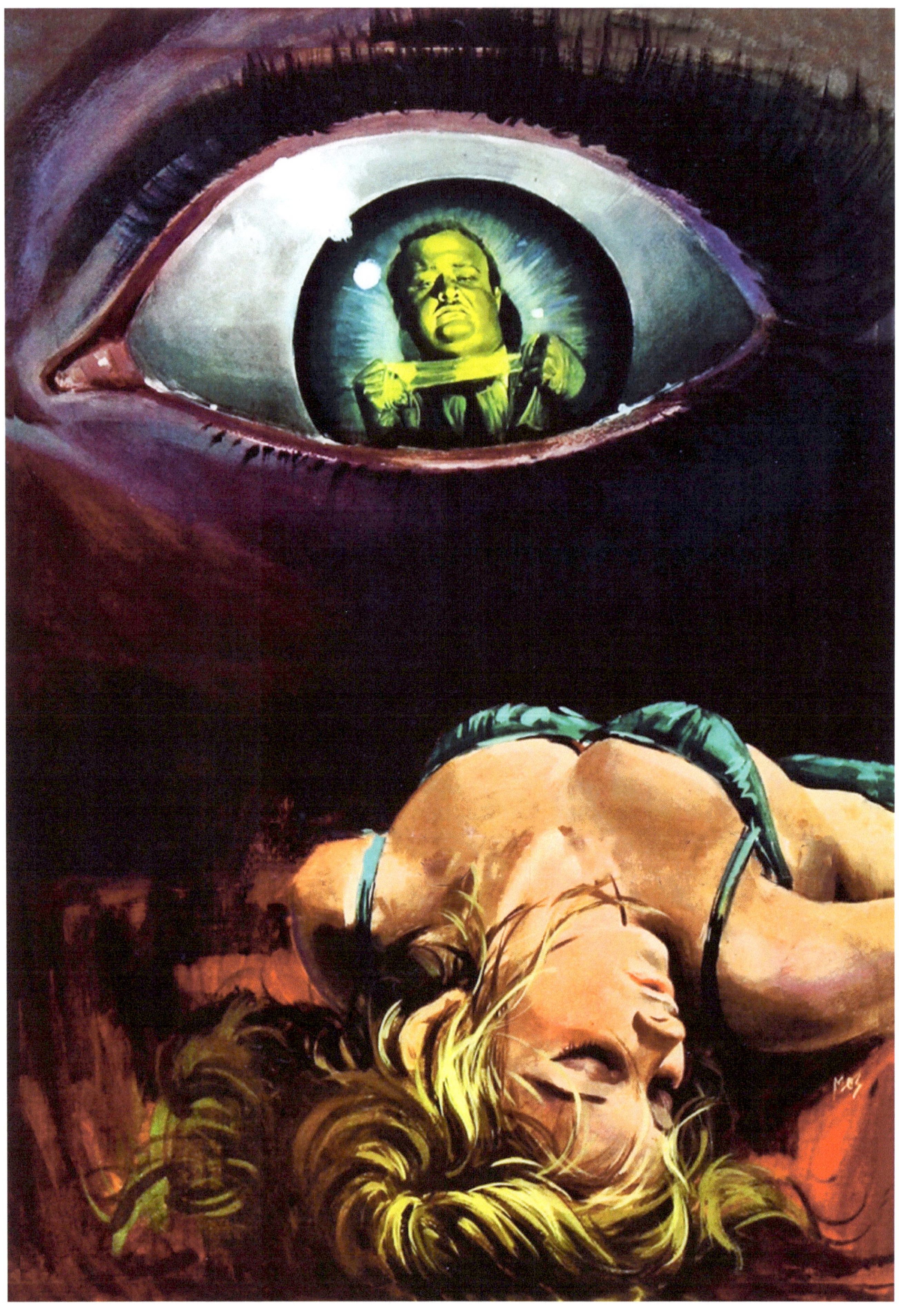

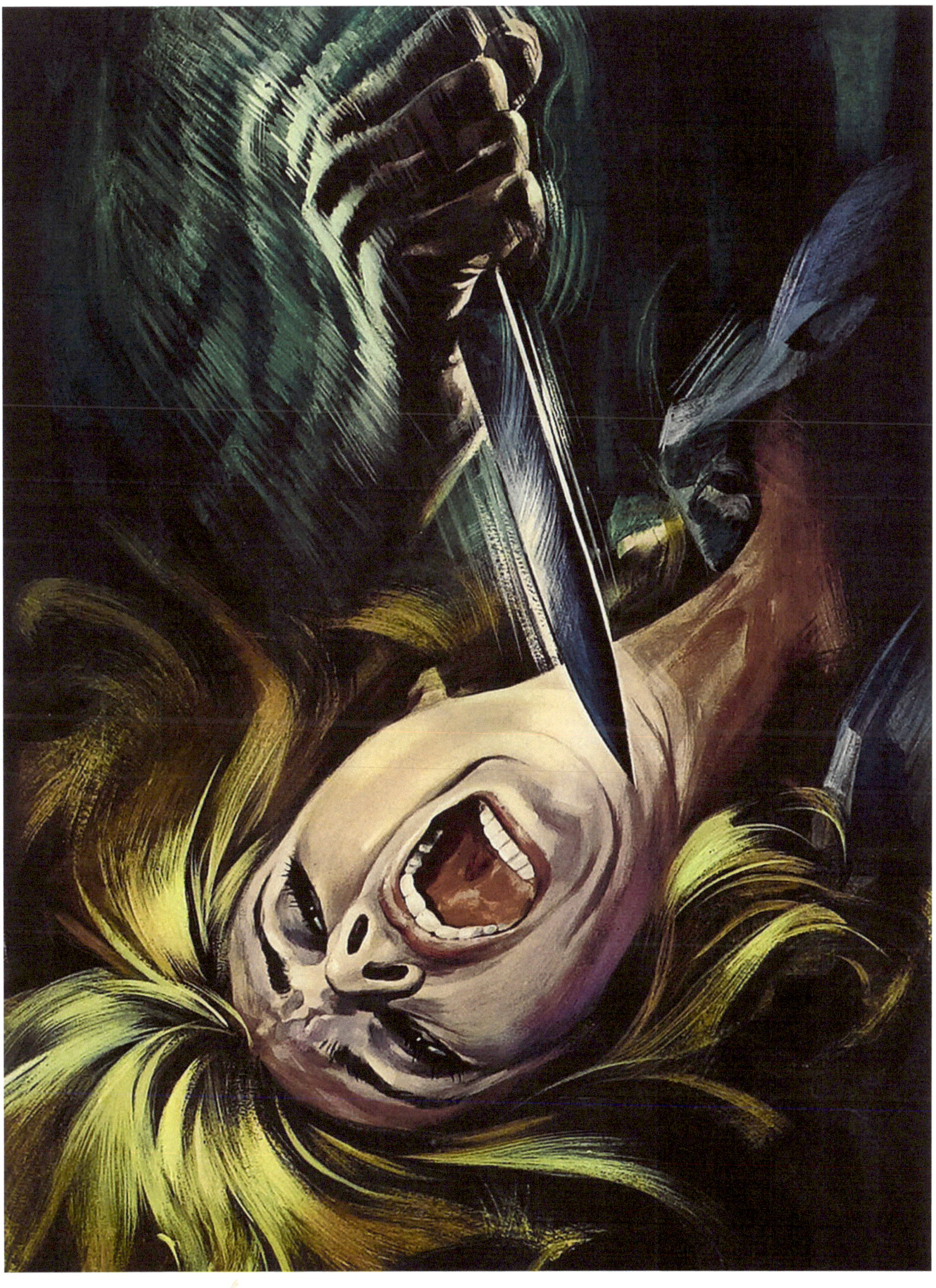

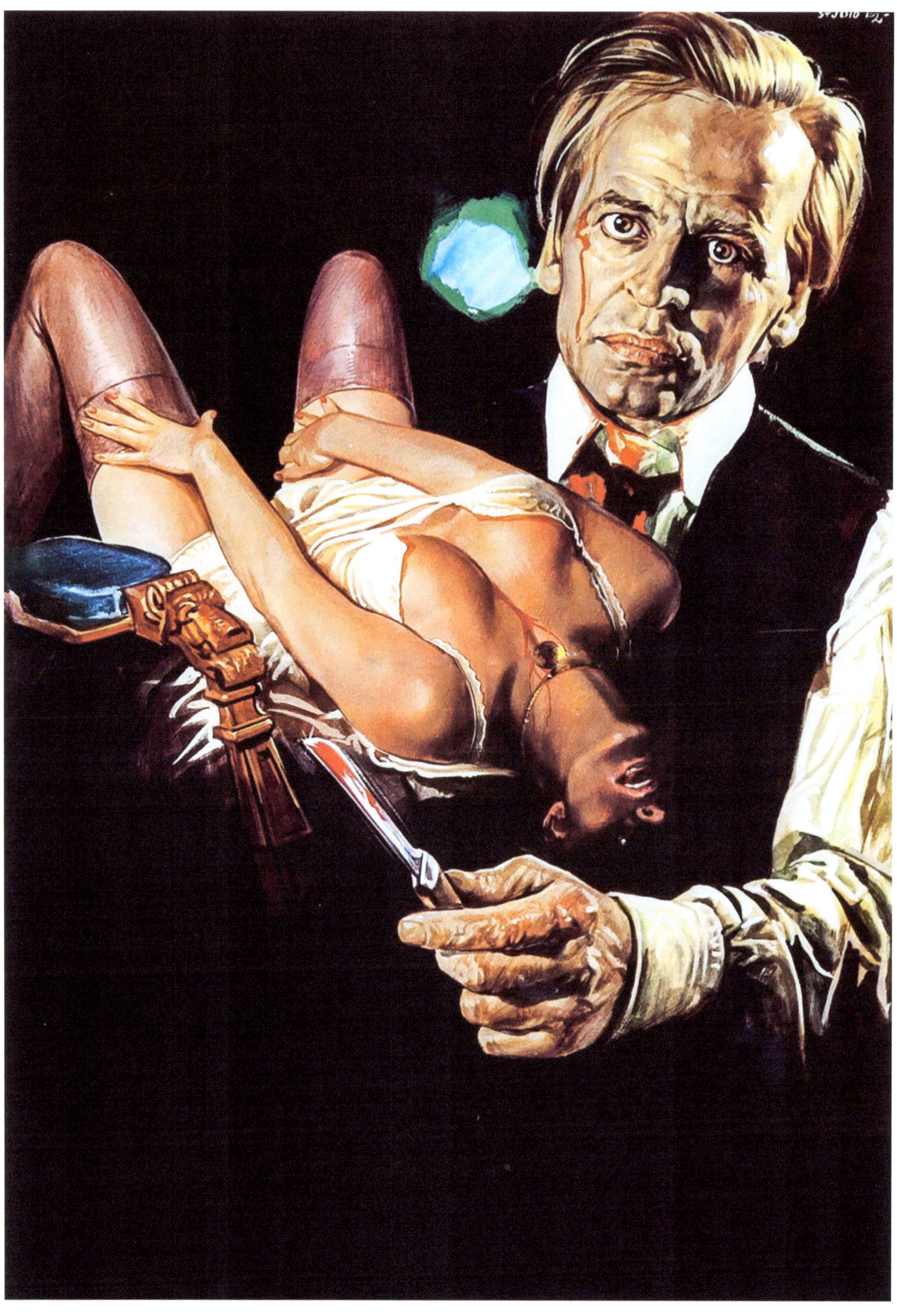

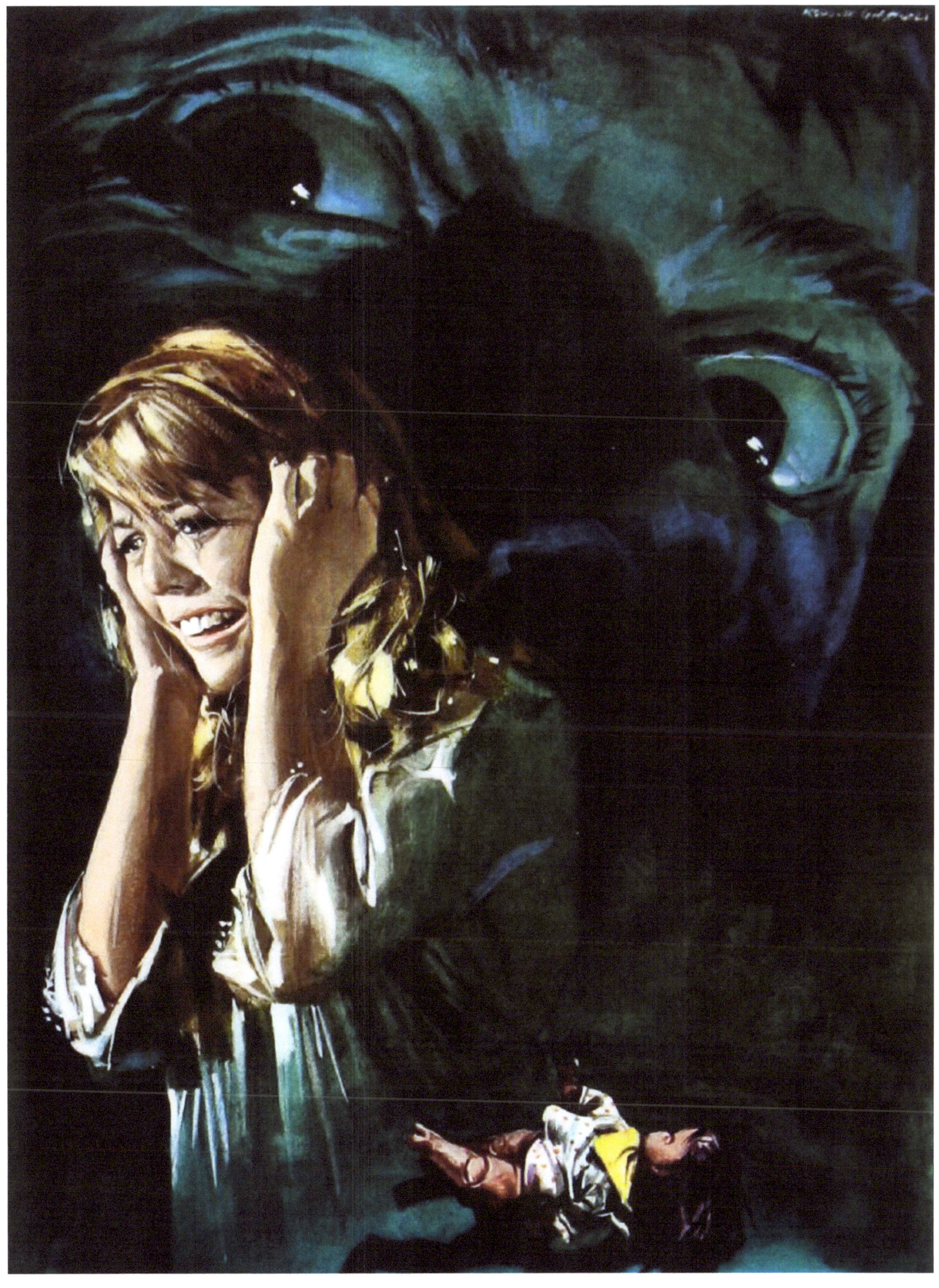

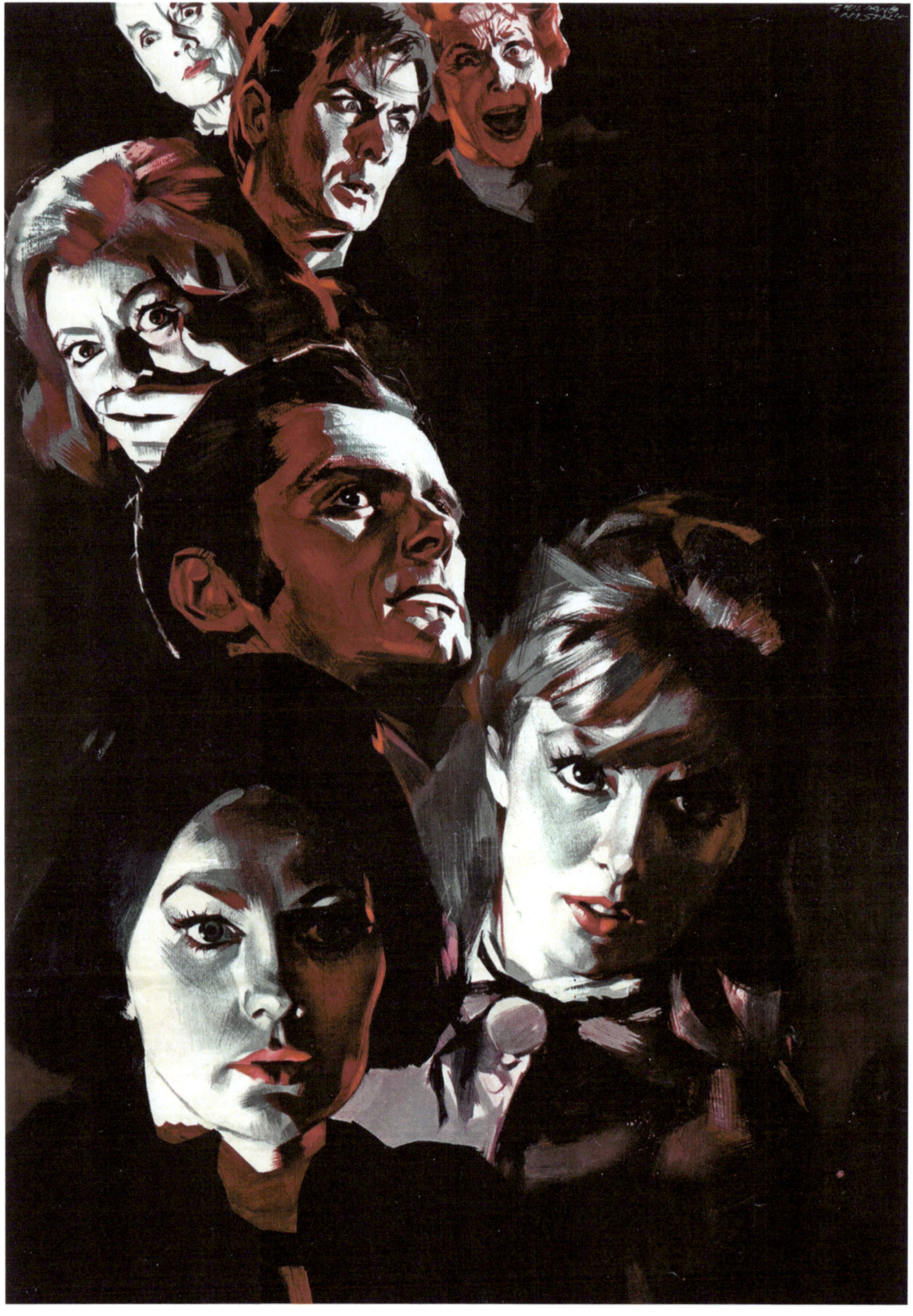

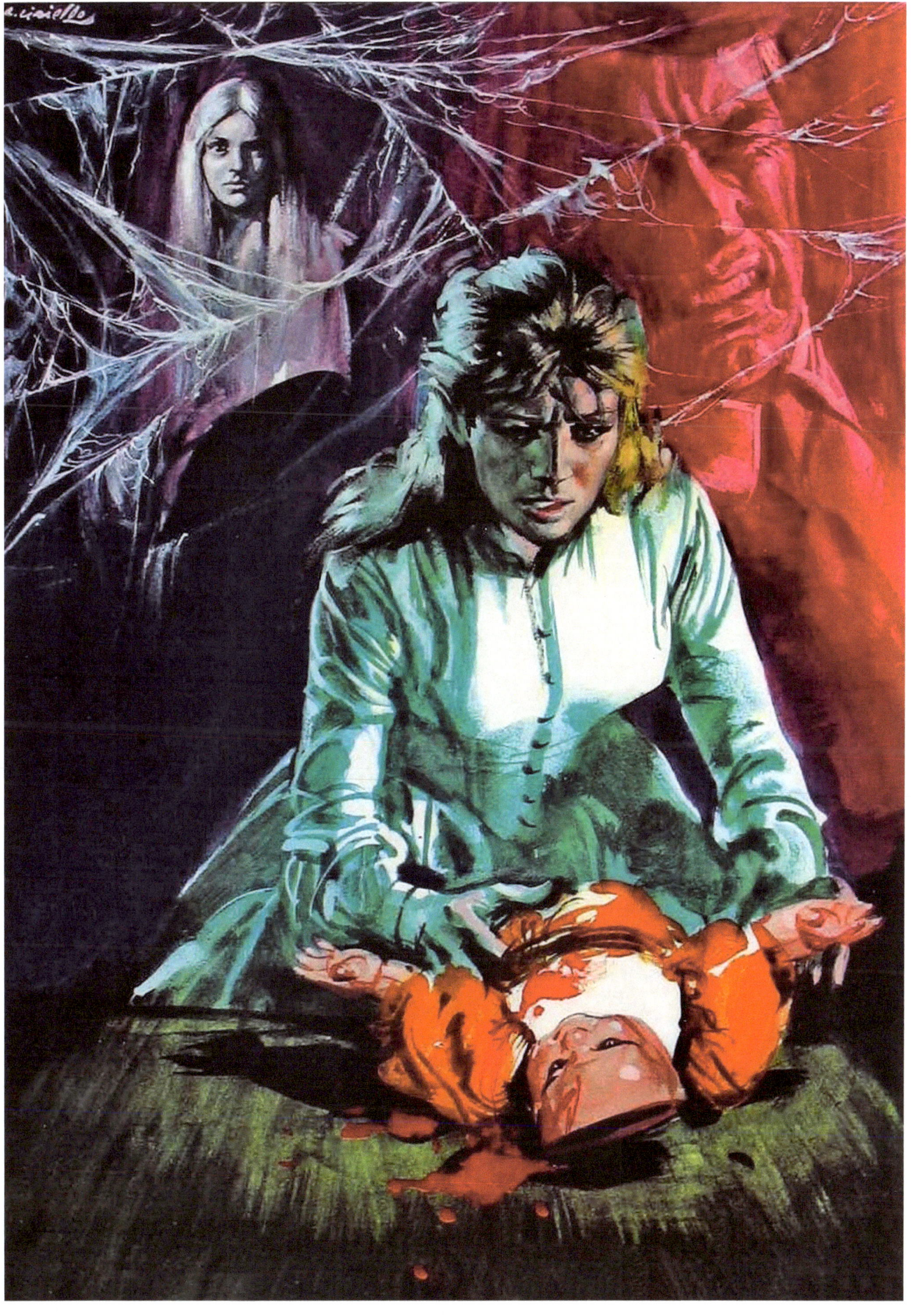

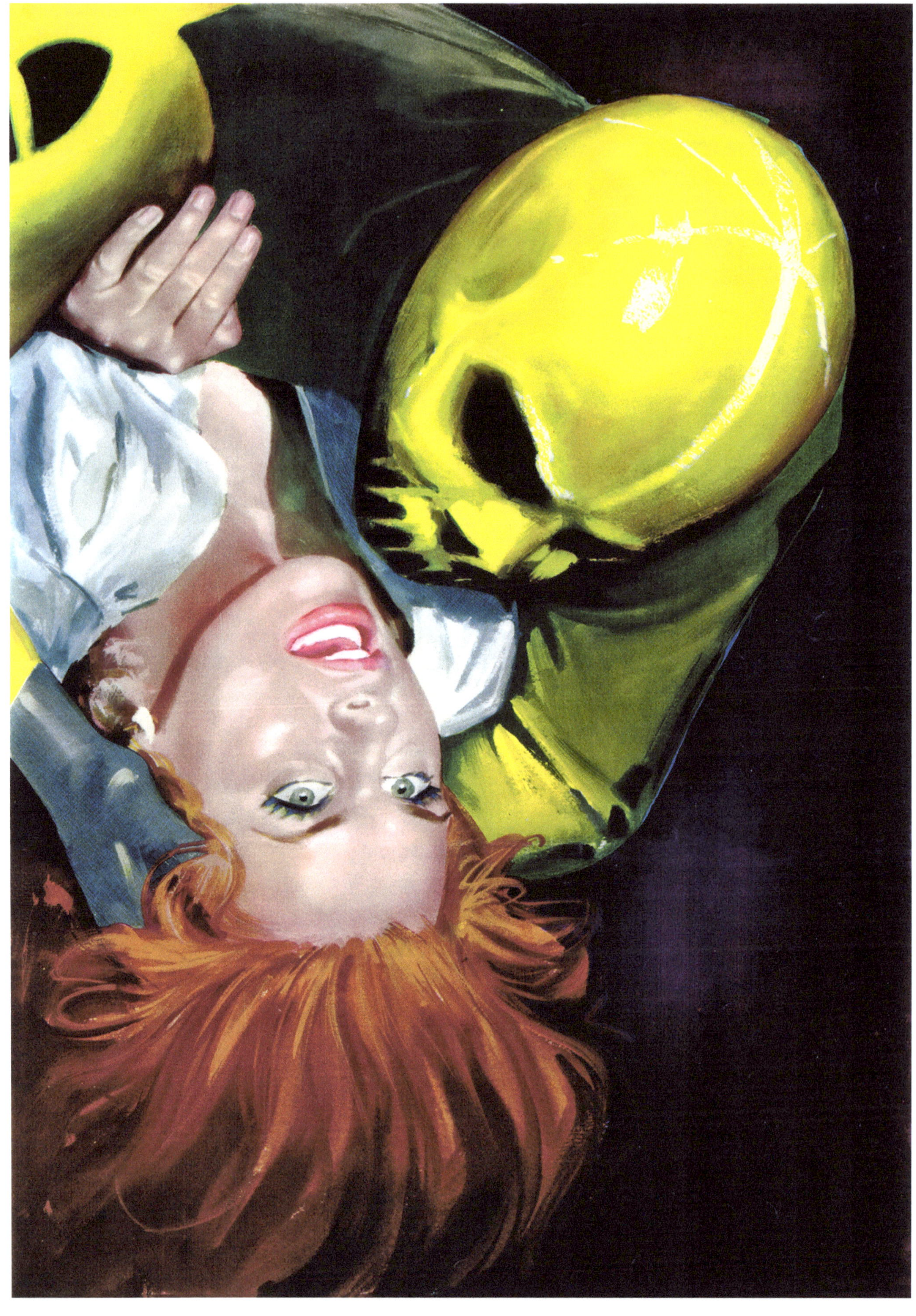

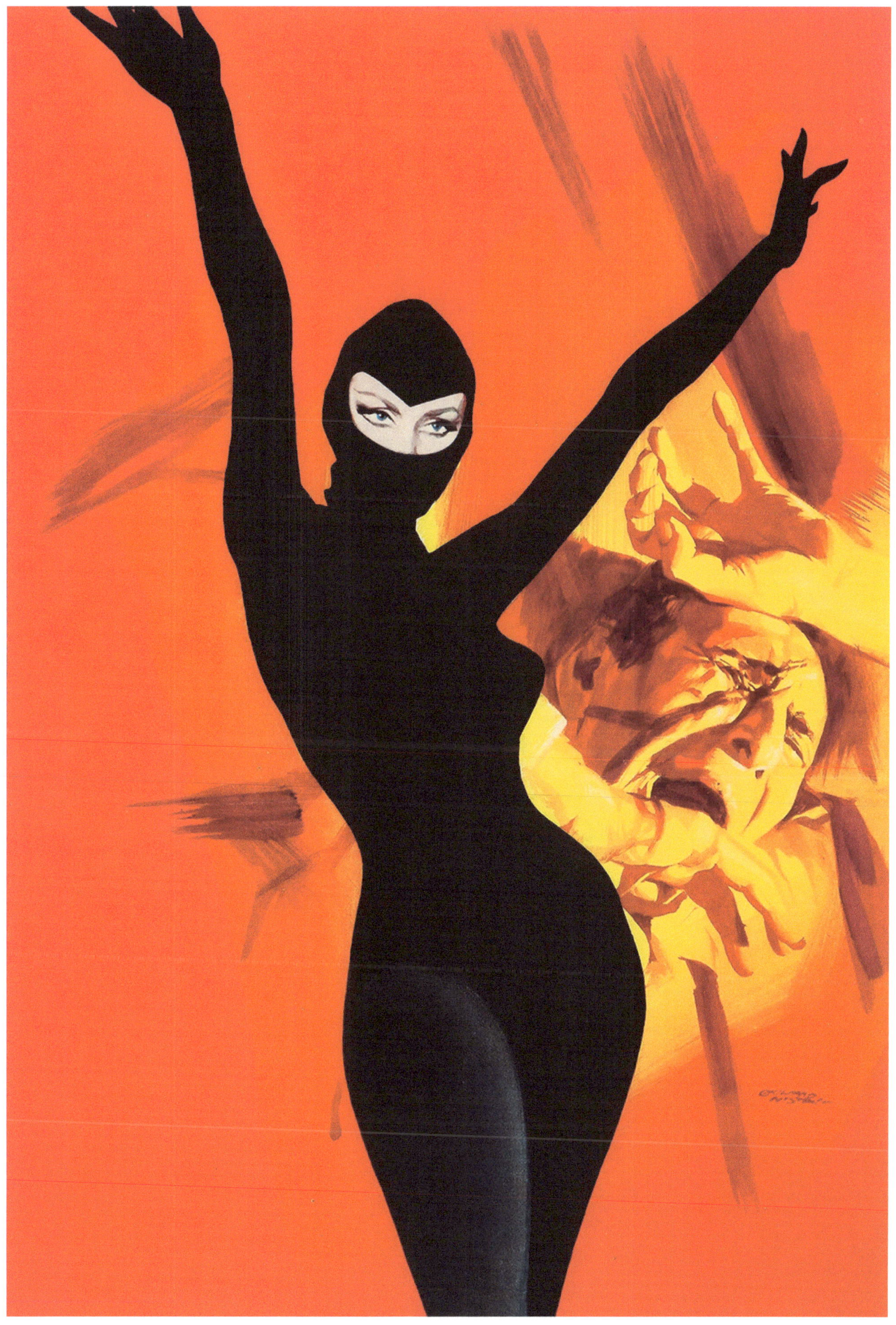

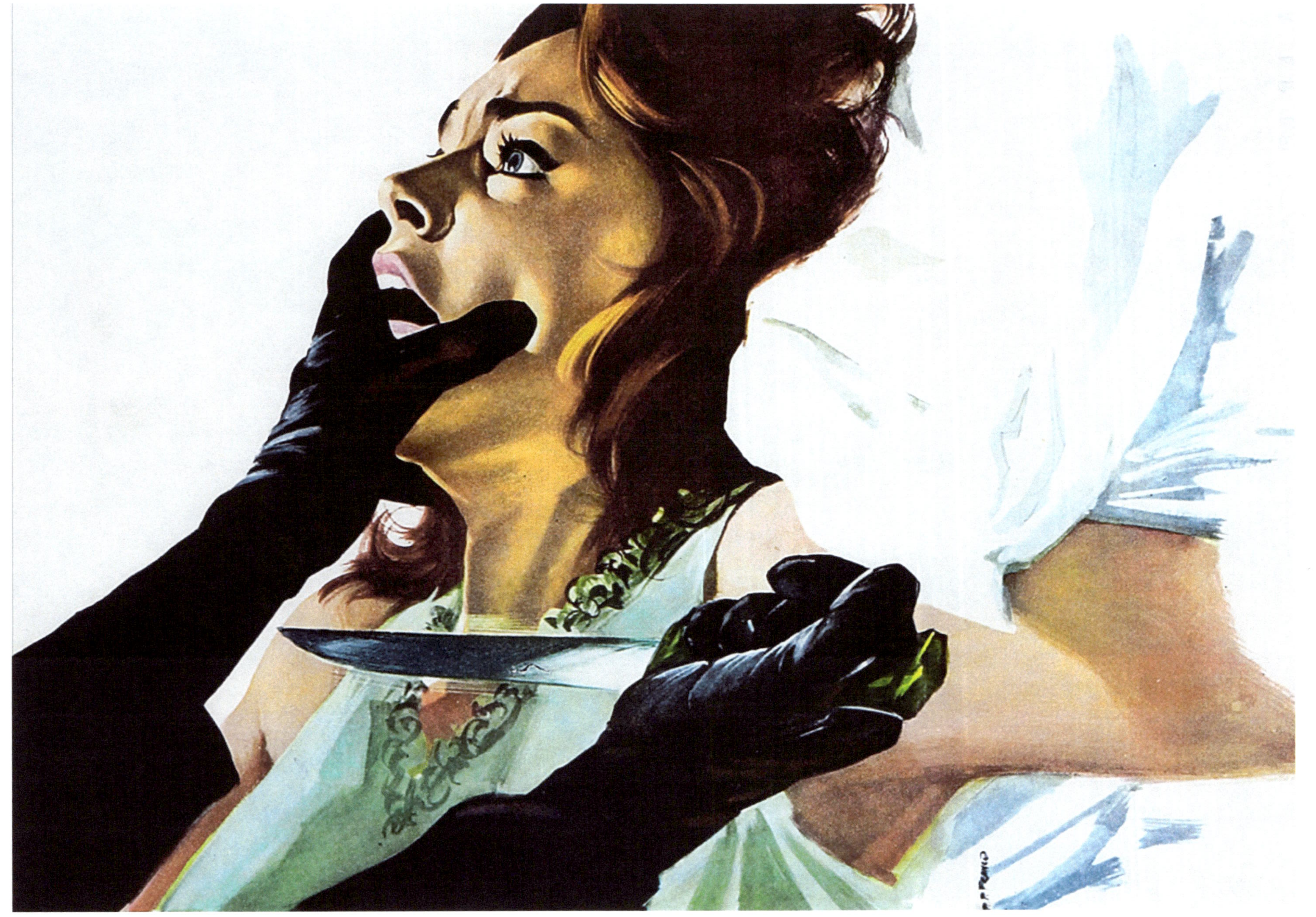

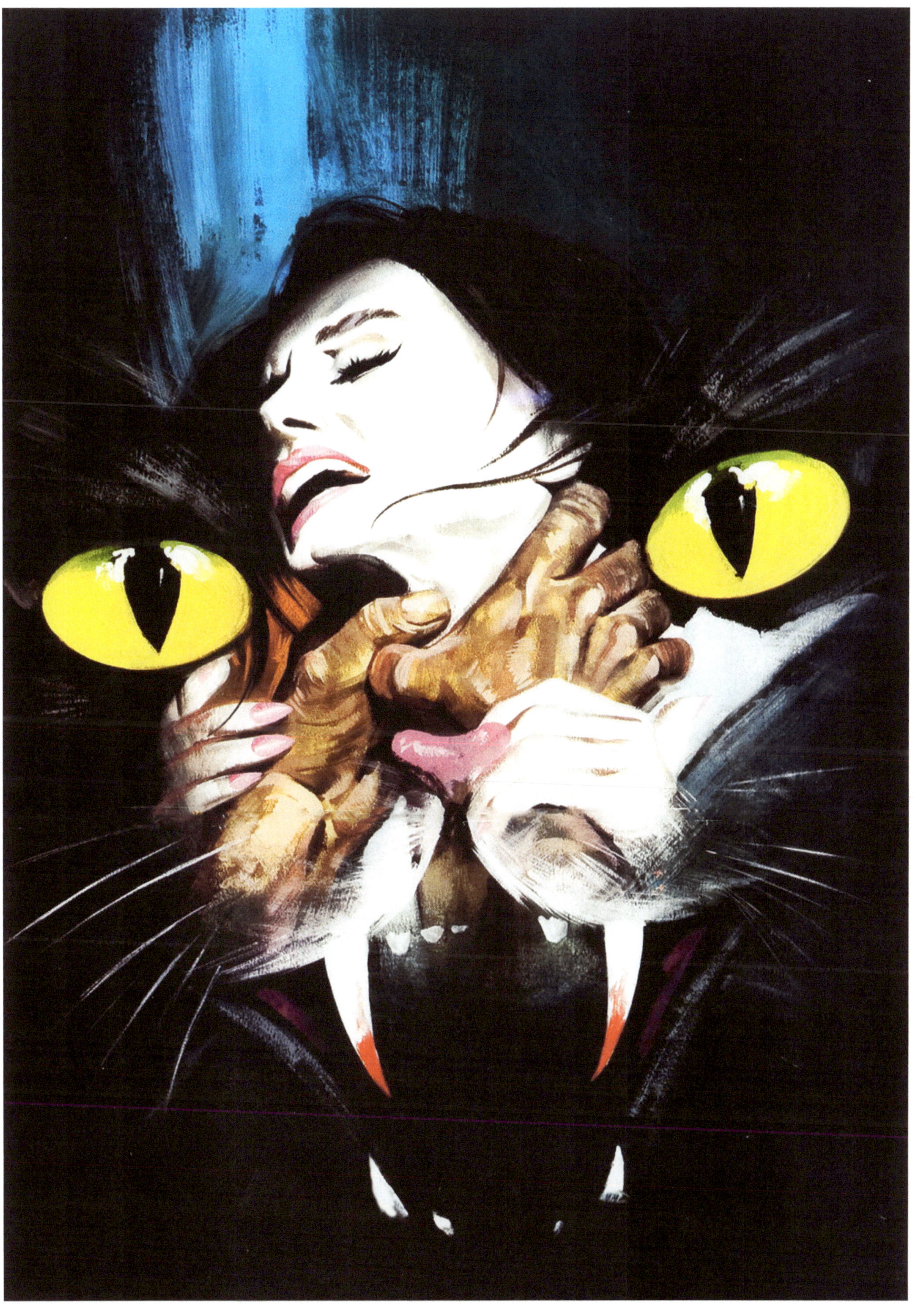

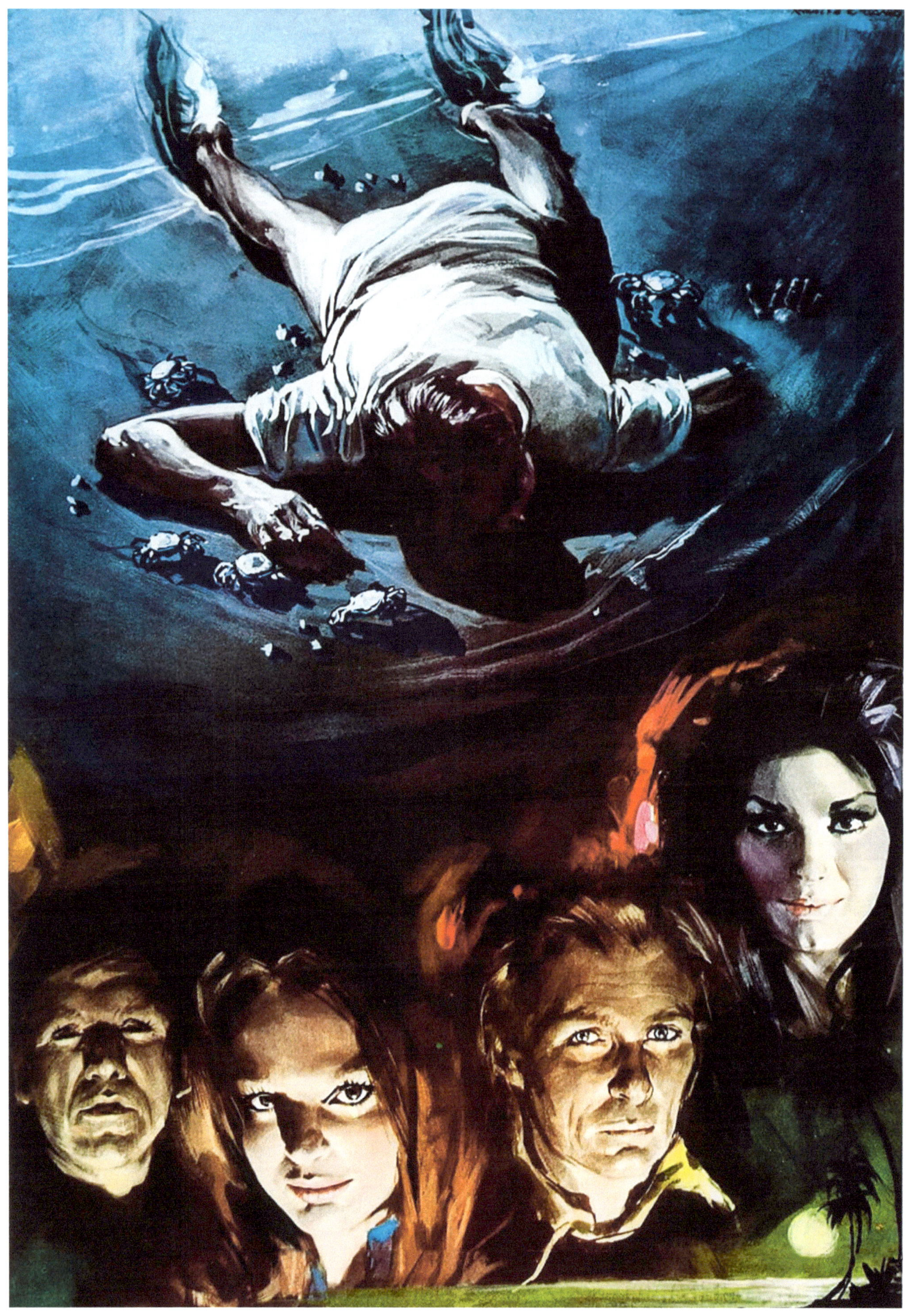

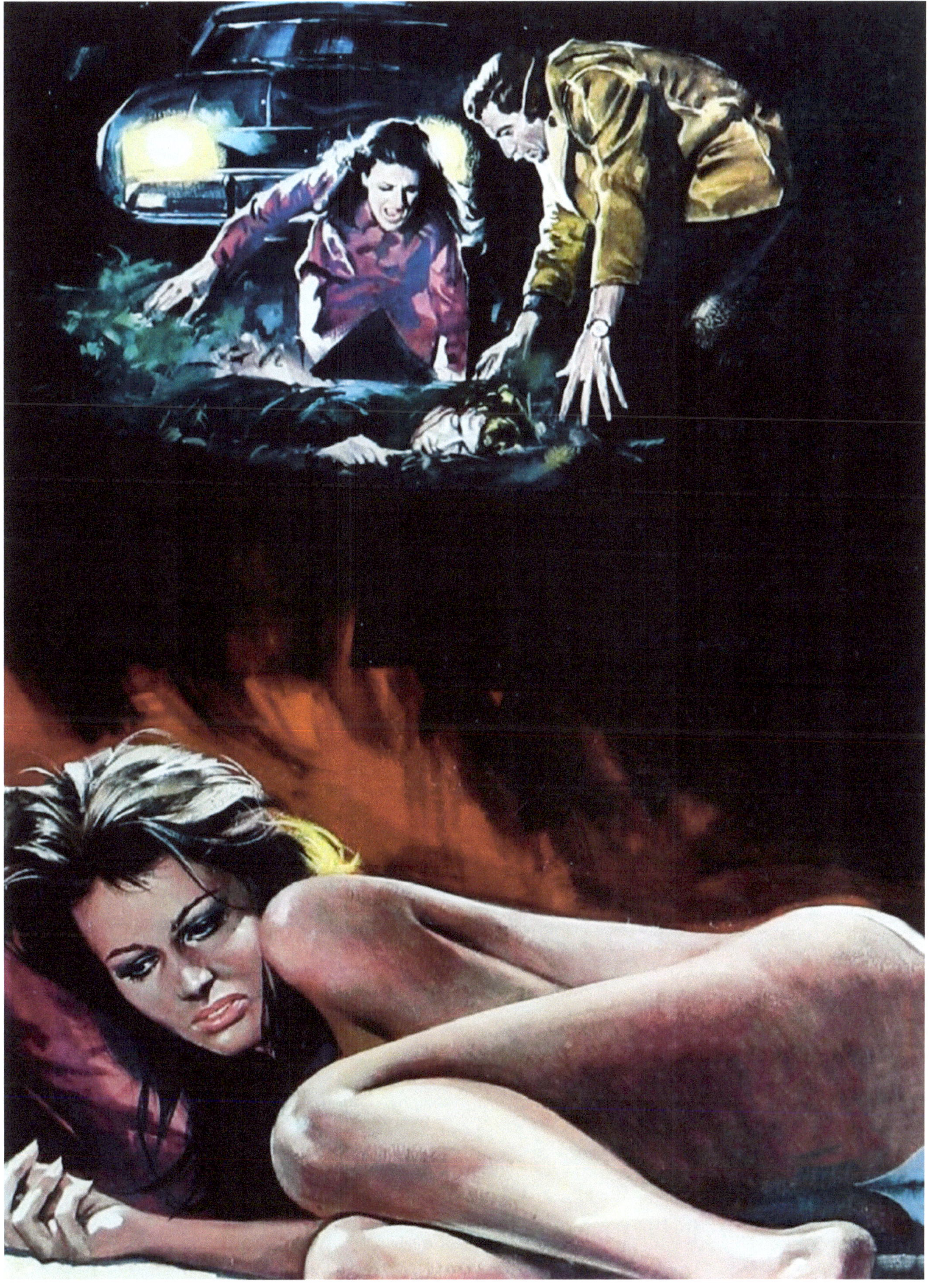

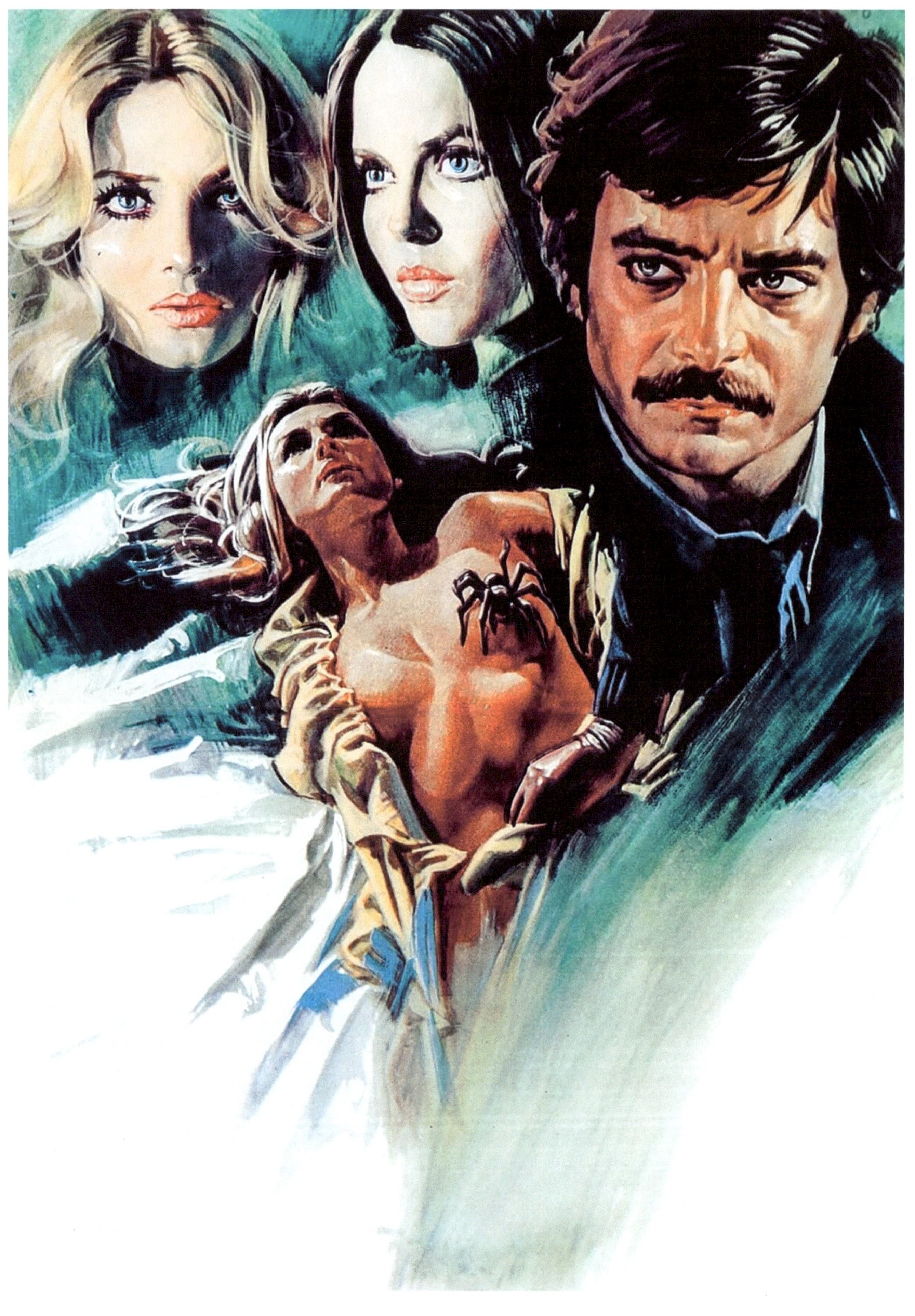

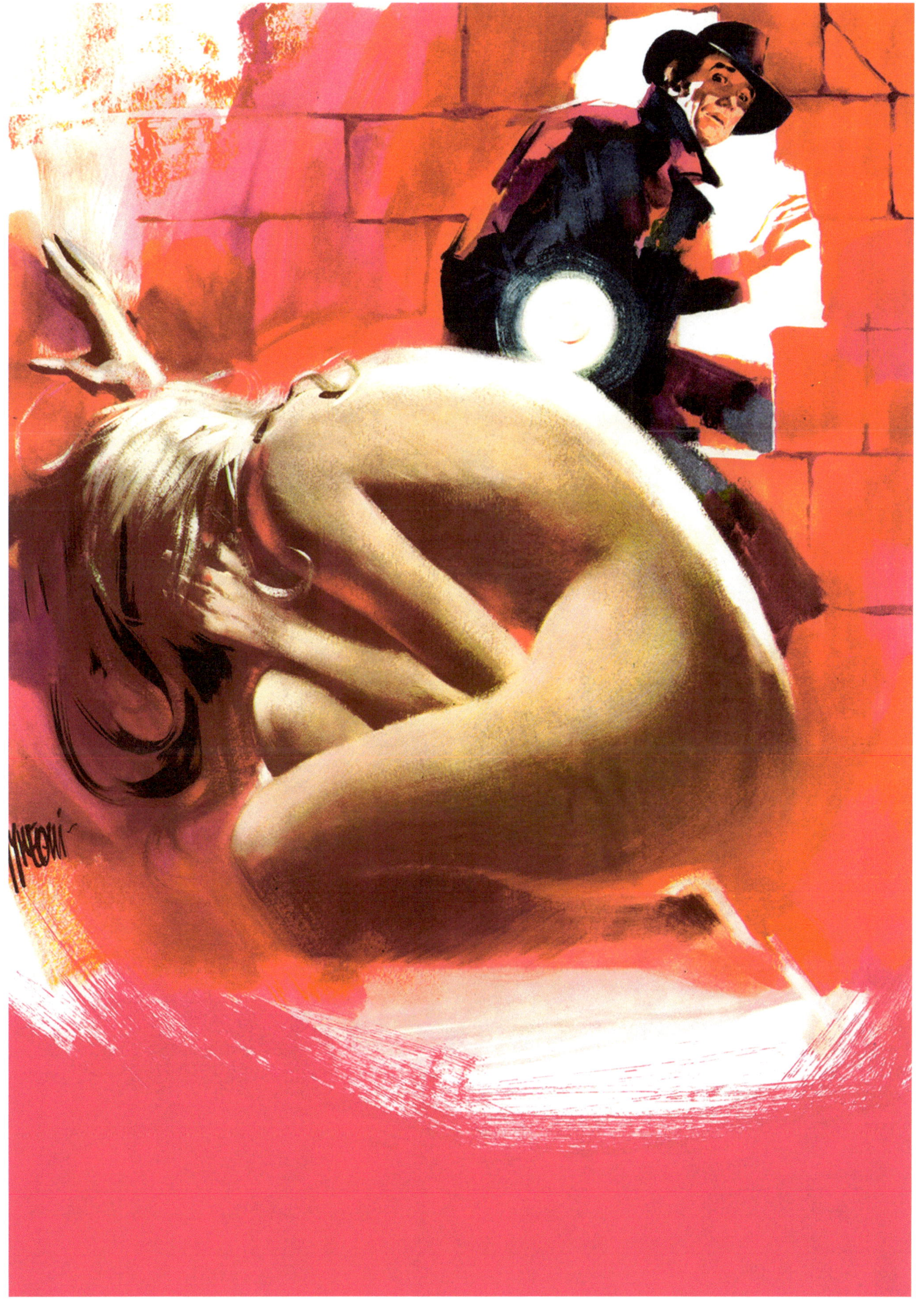

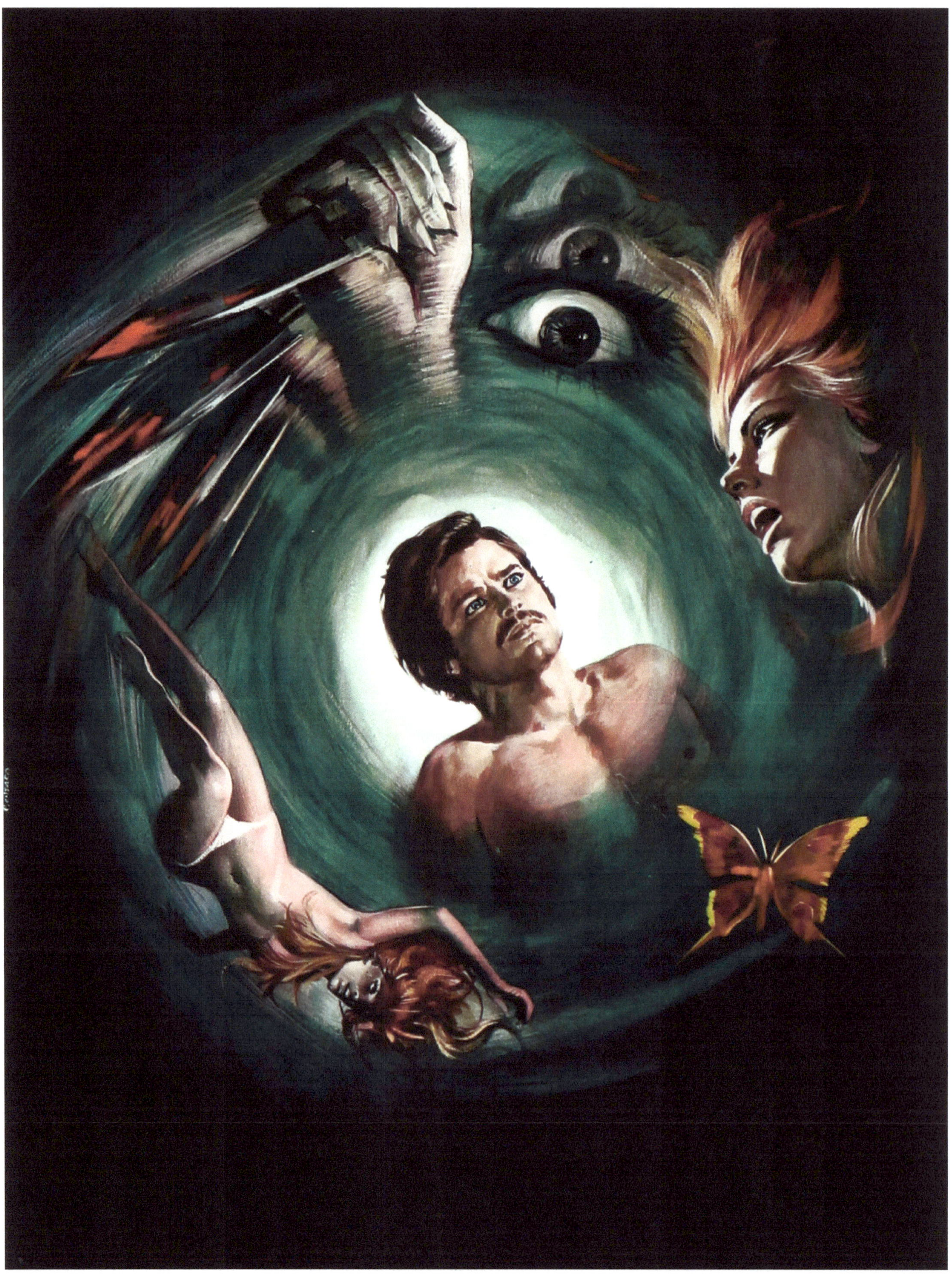

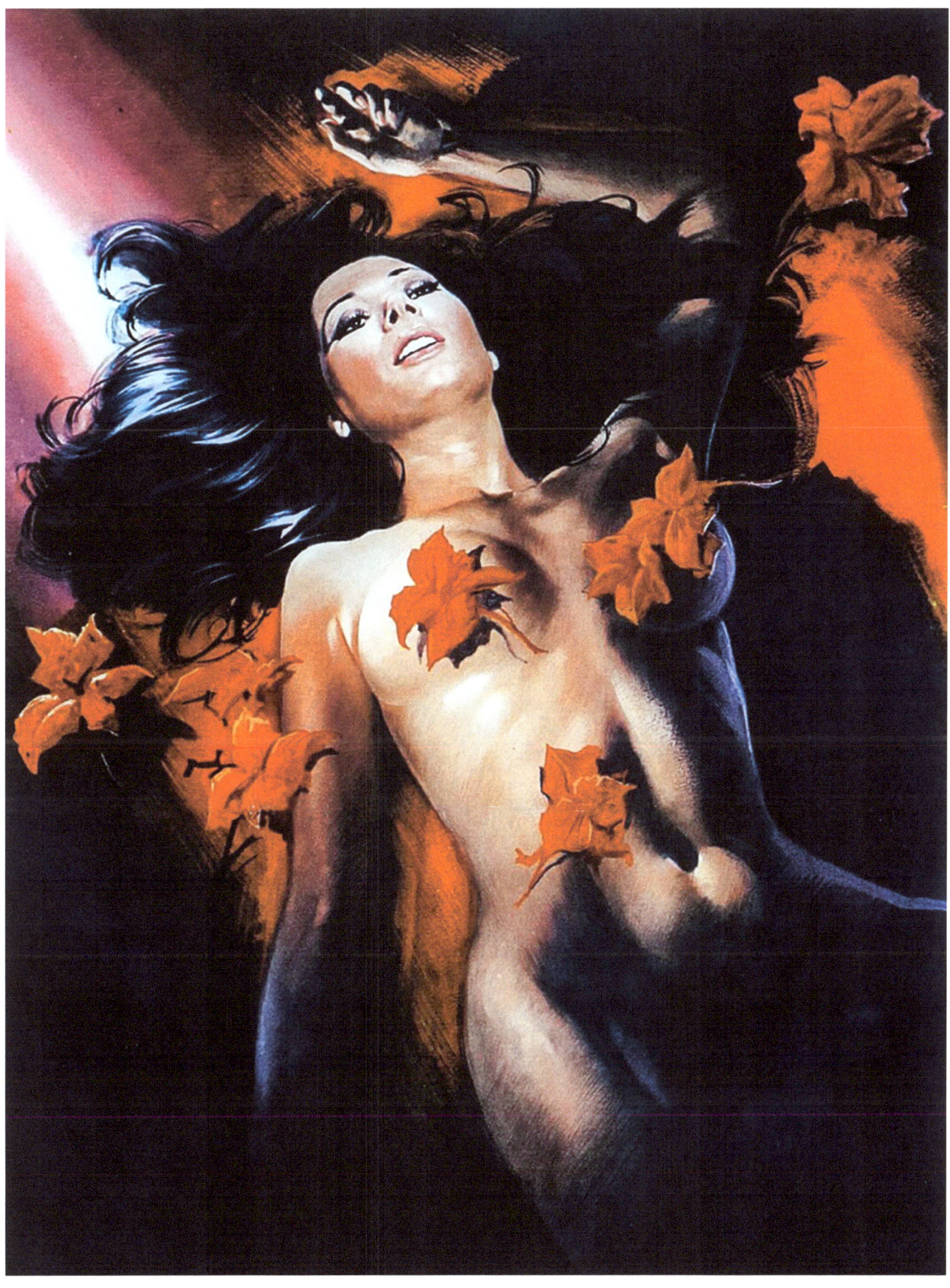

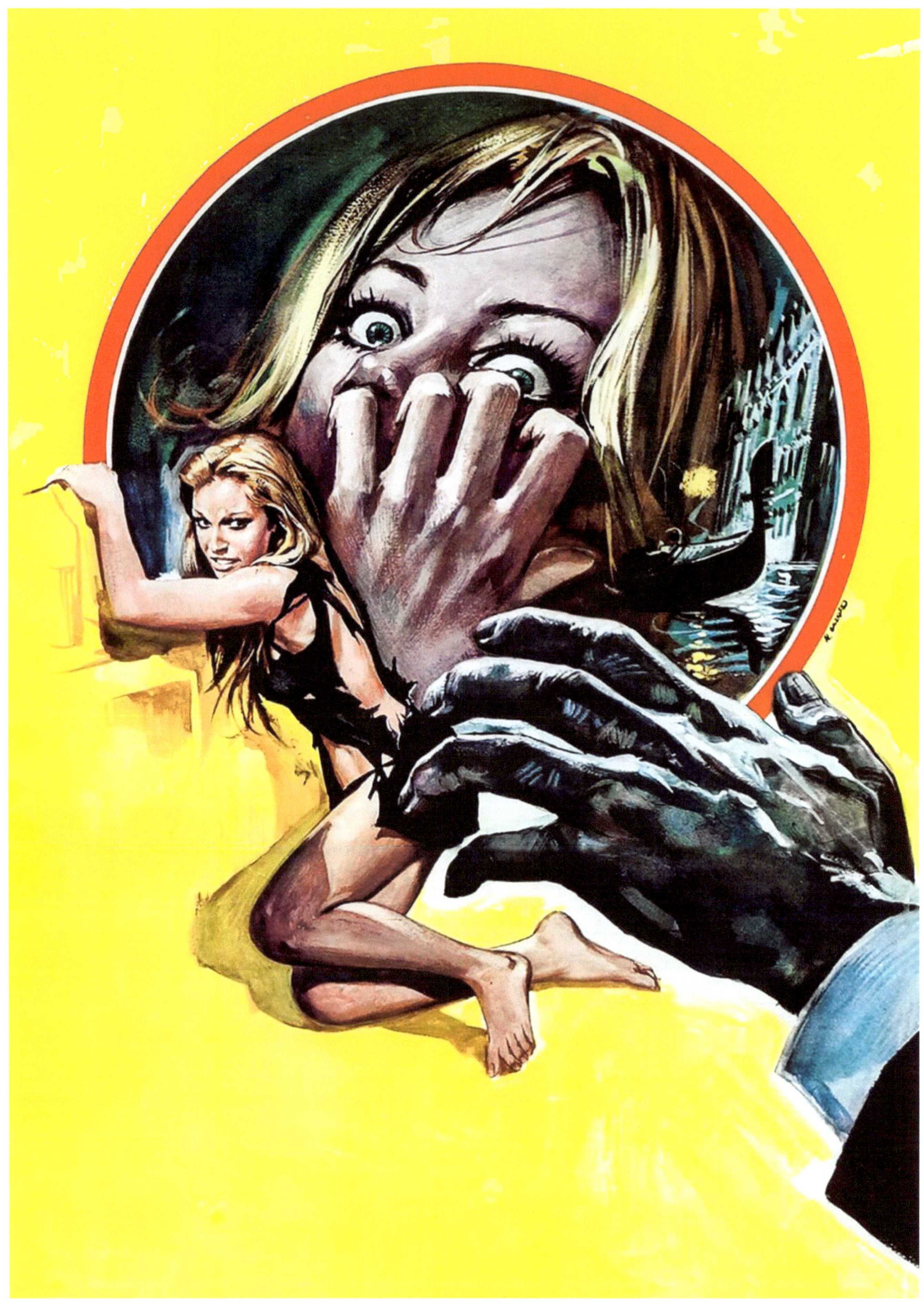

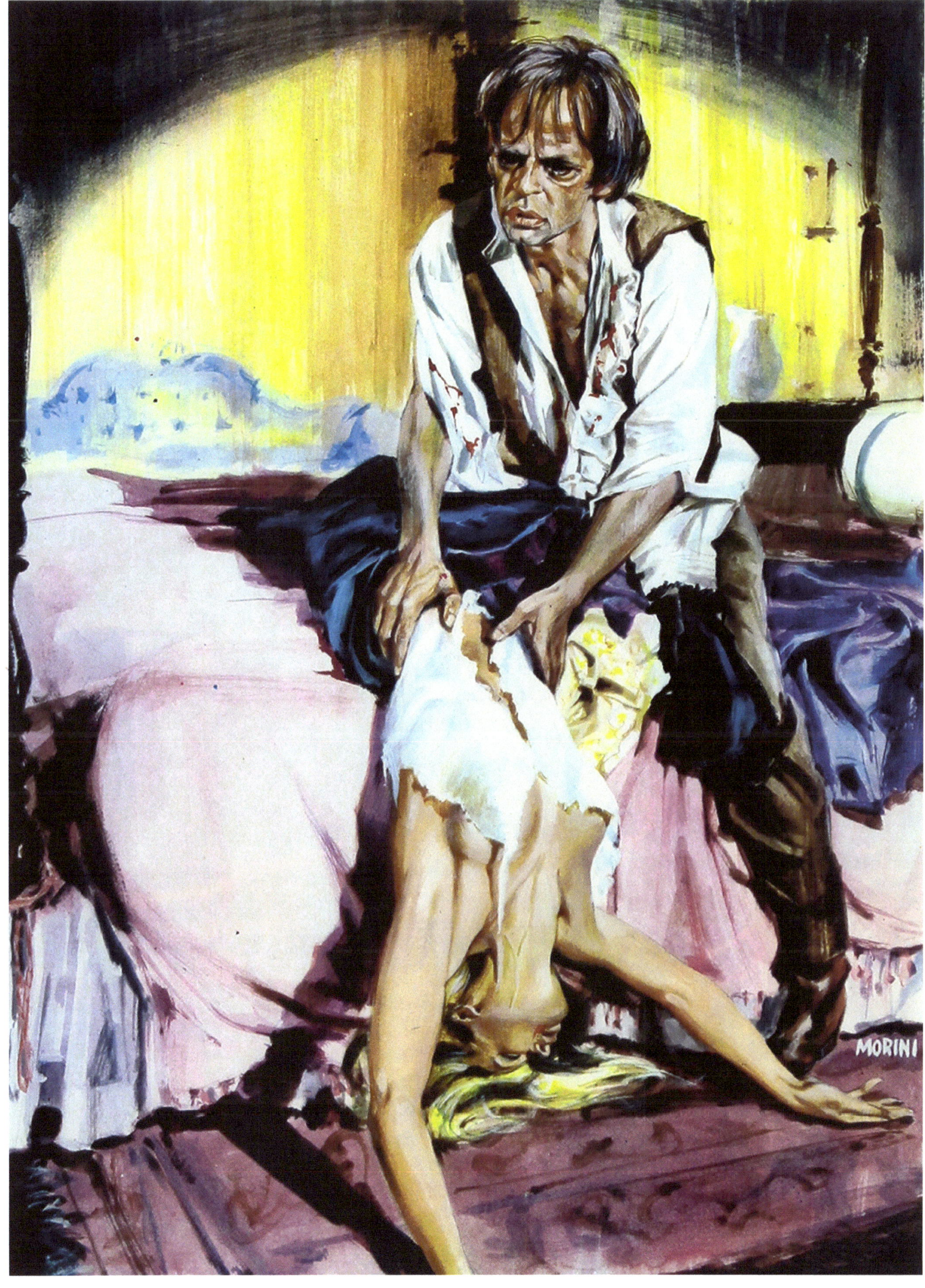
MORINI

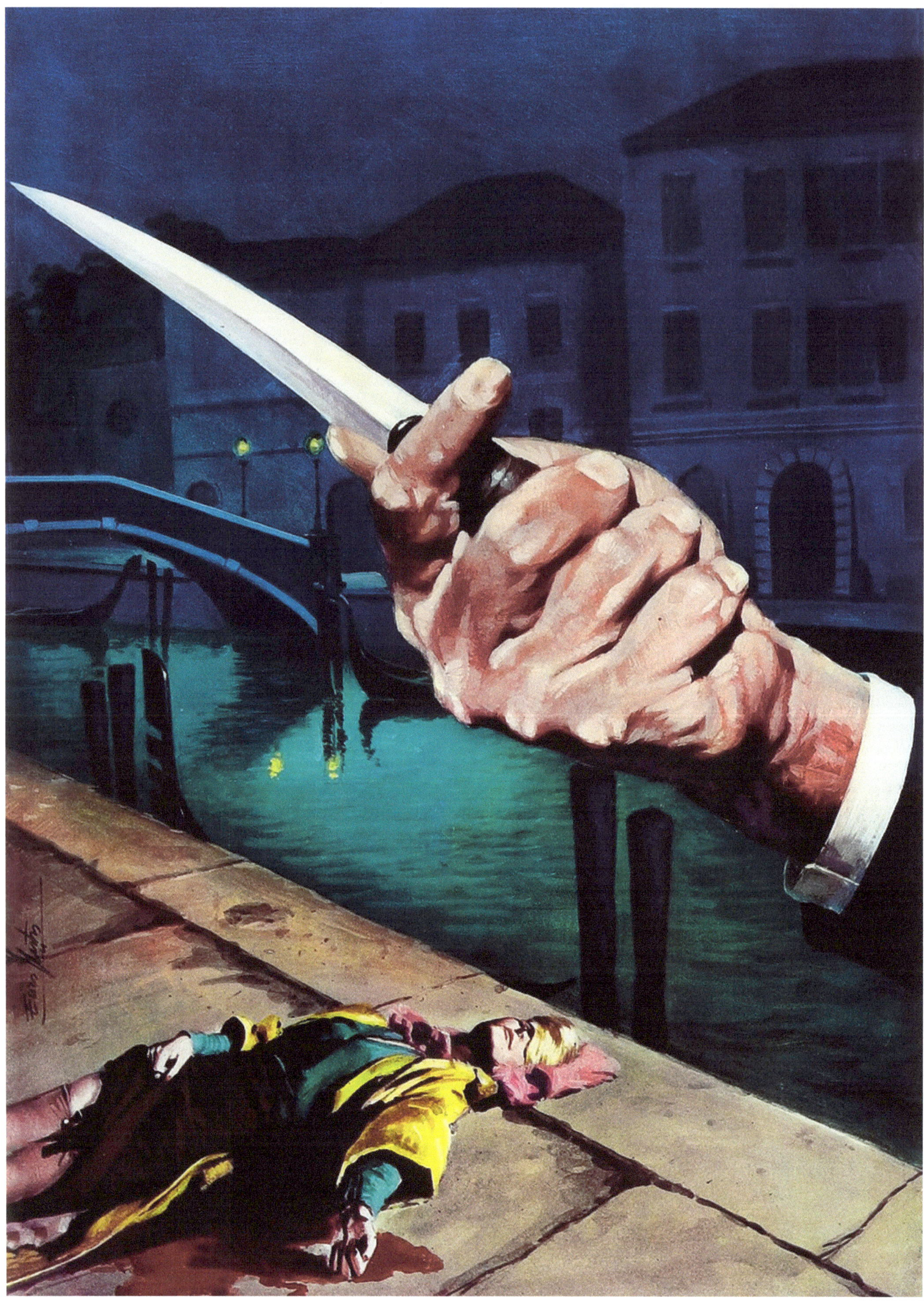

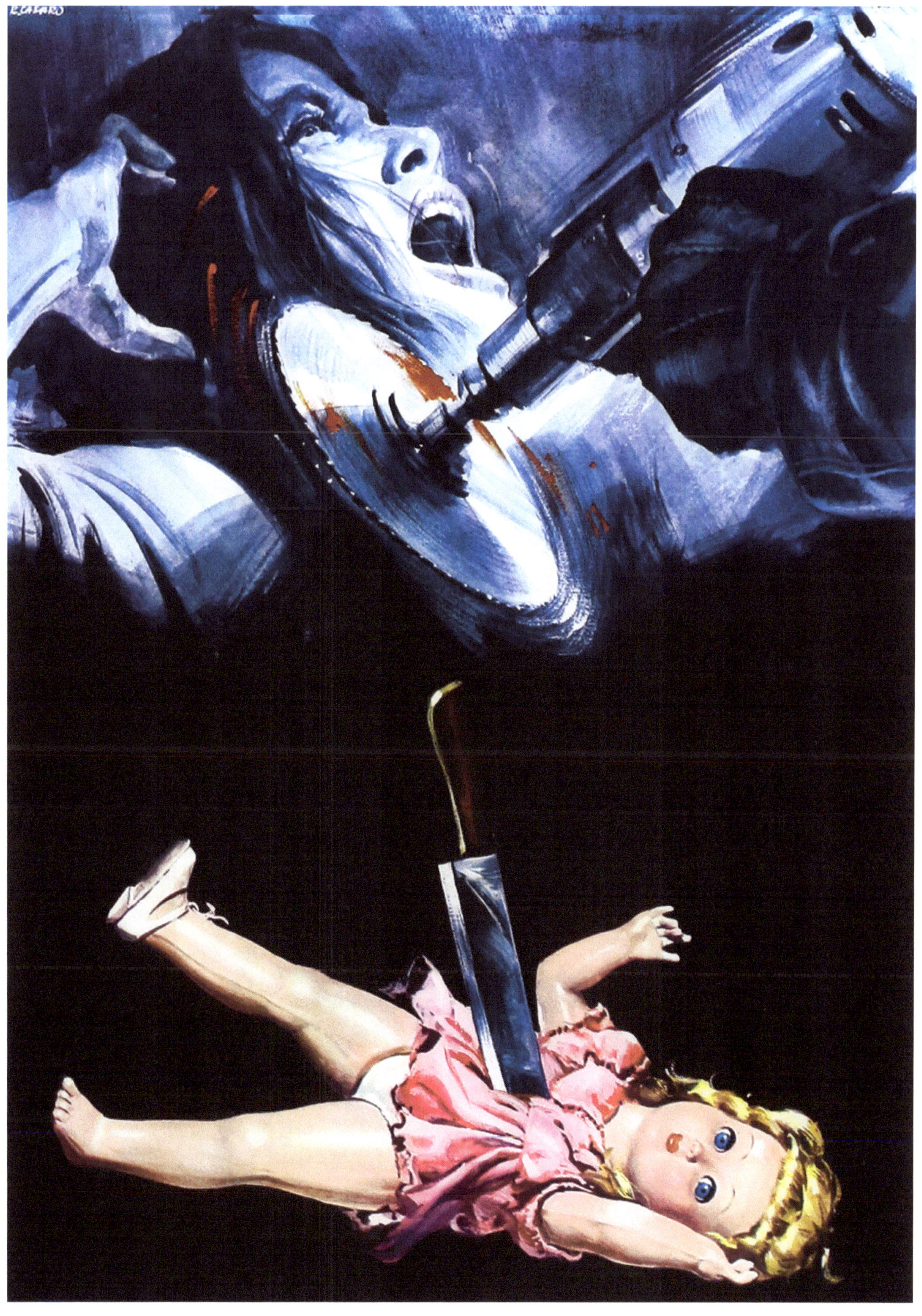

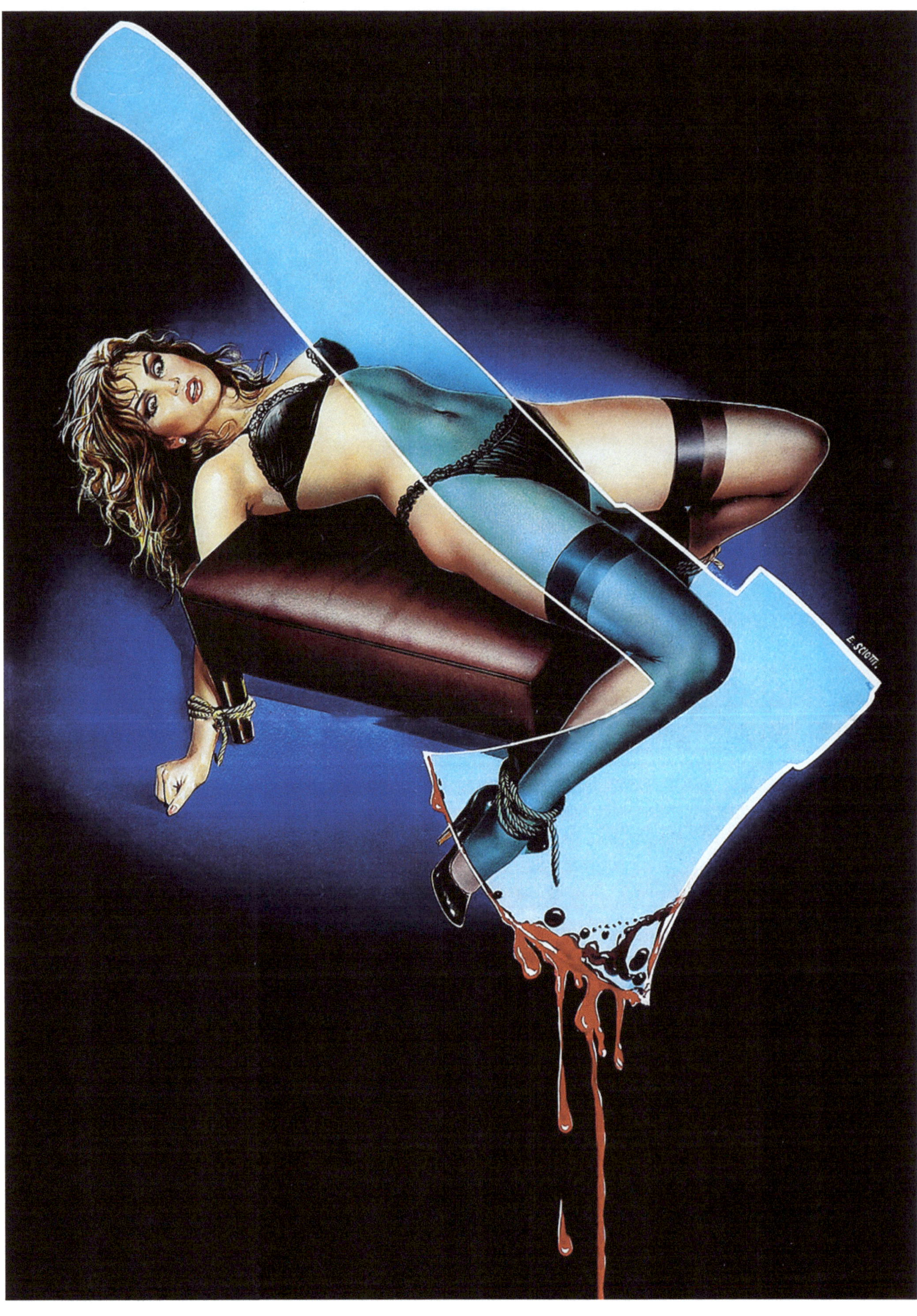

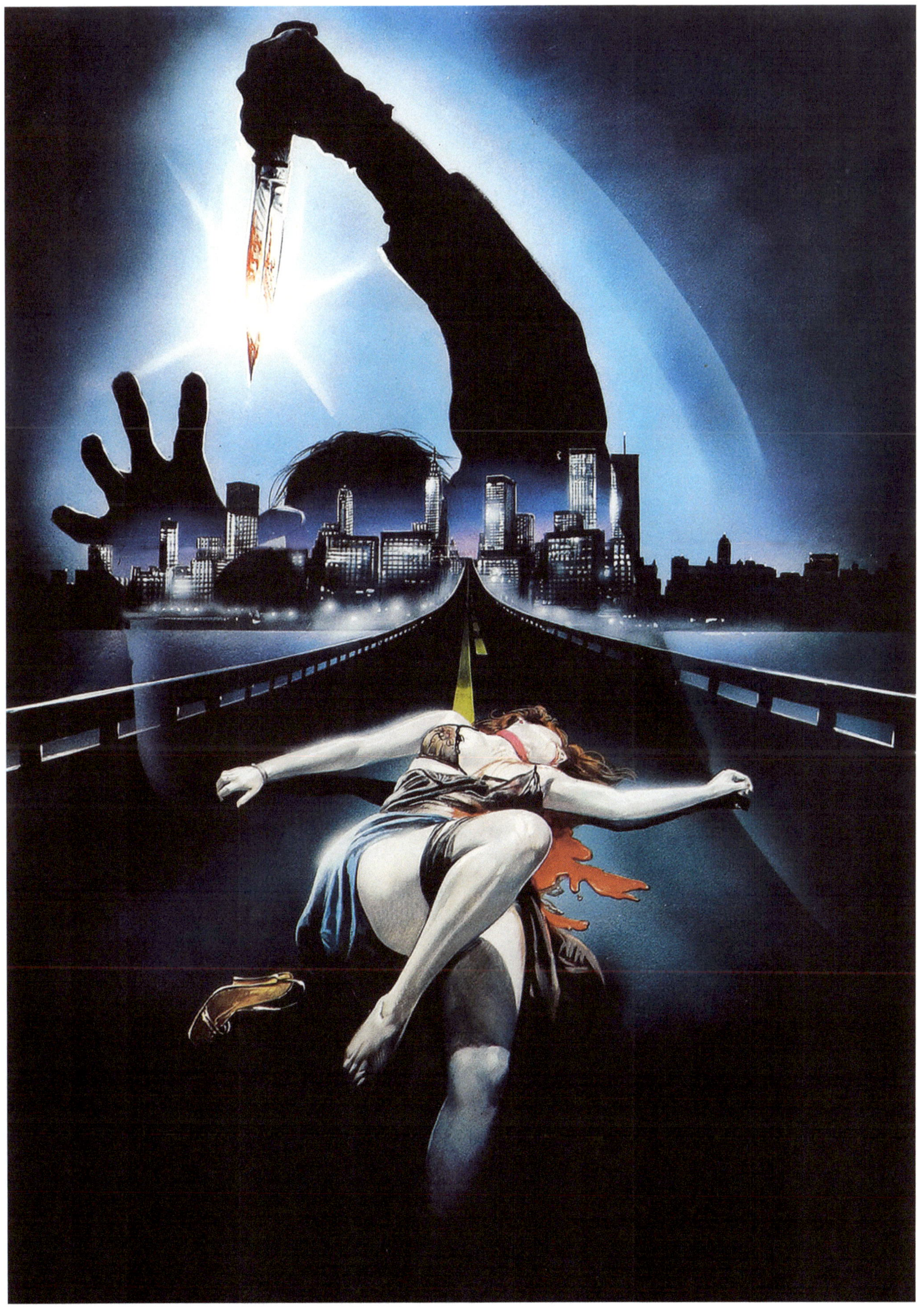

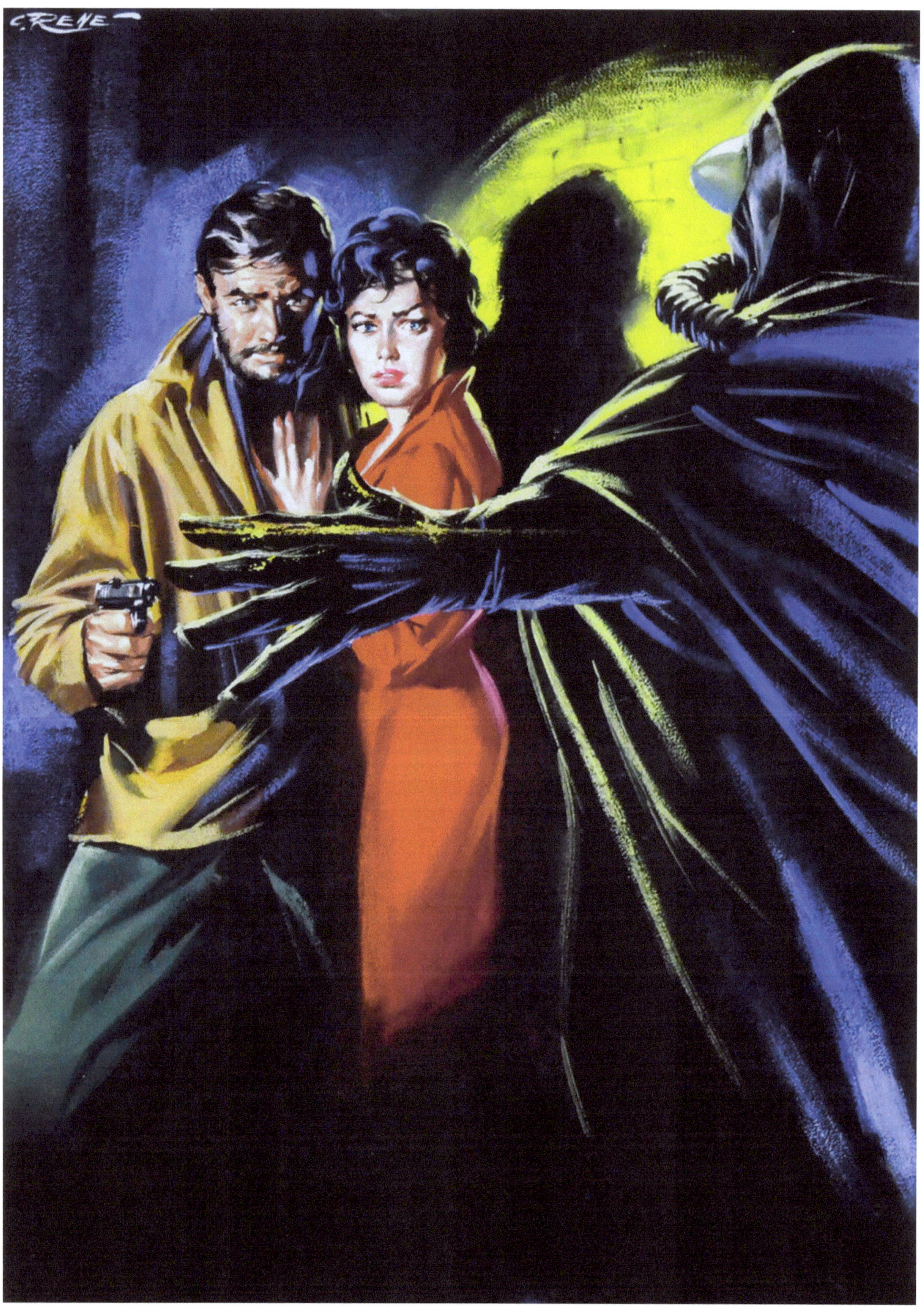

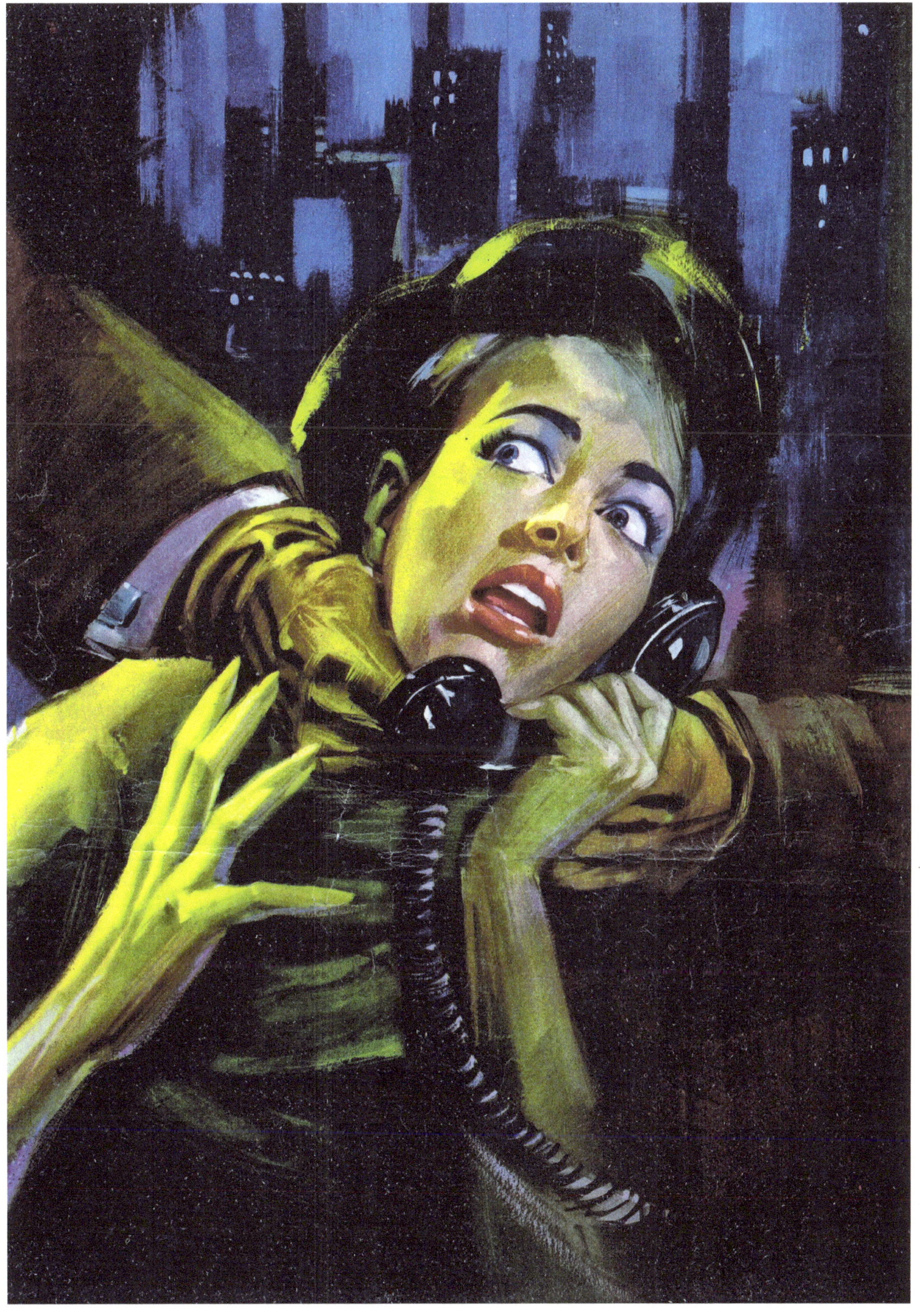

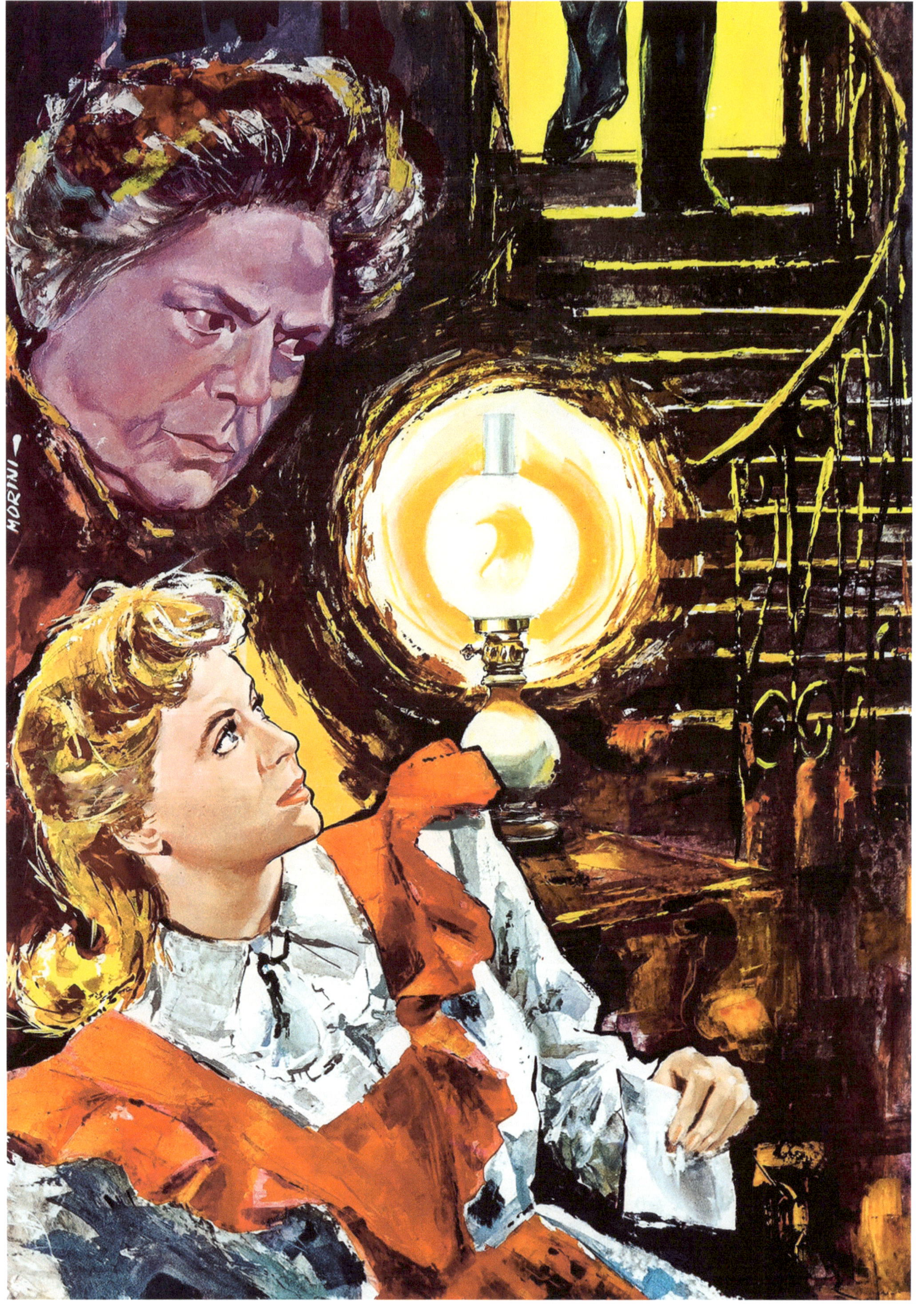

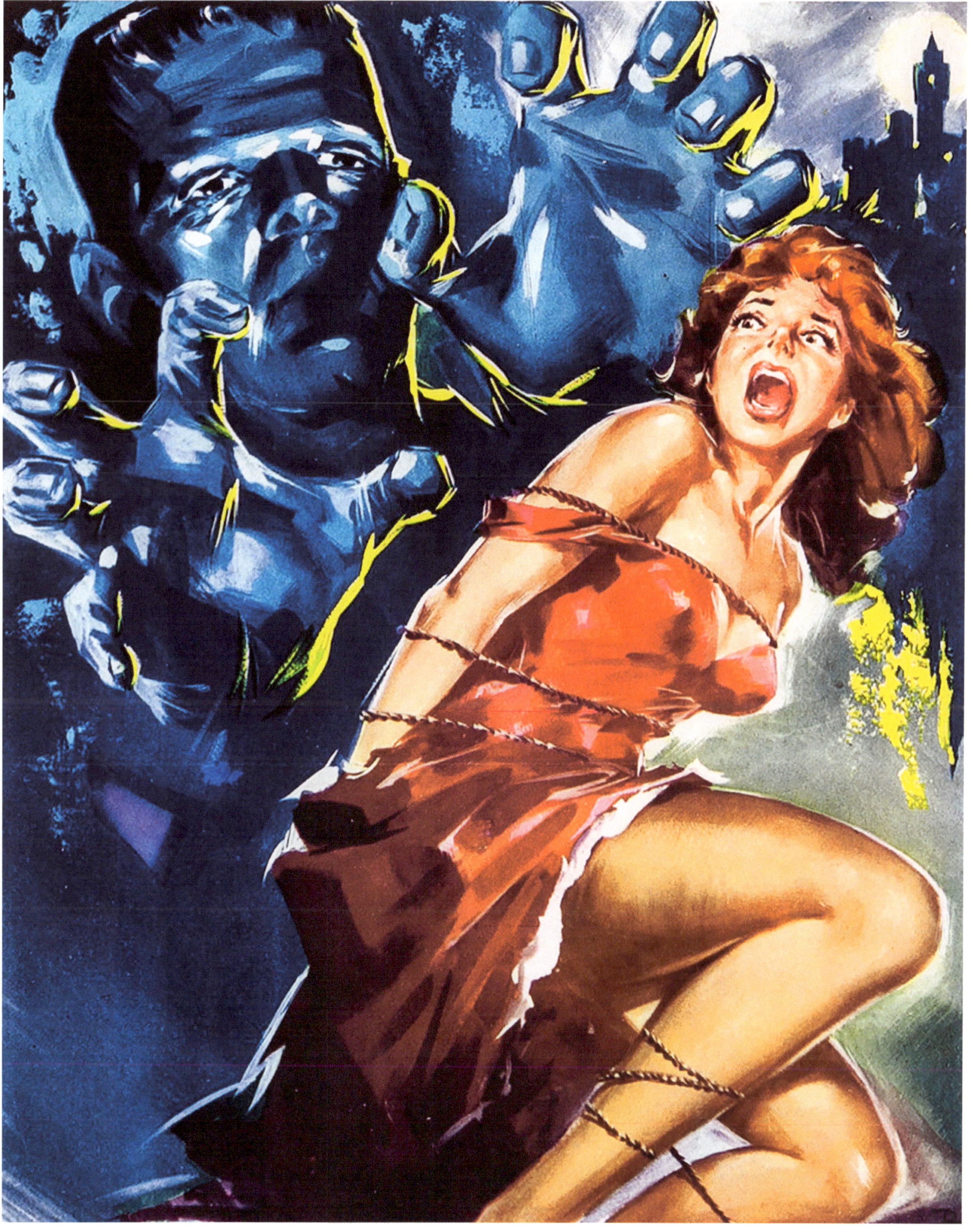

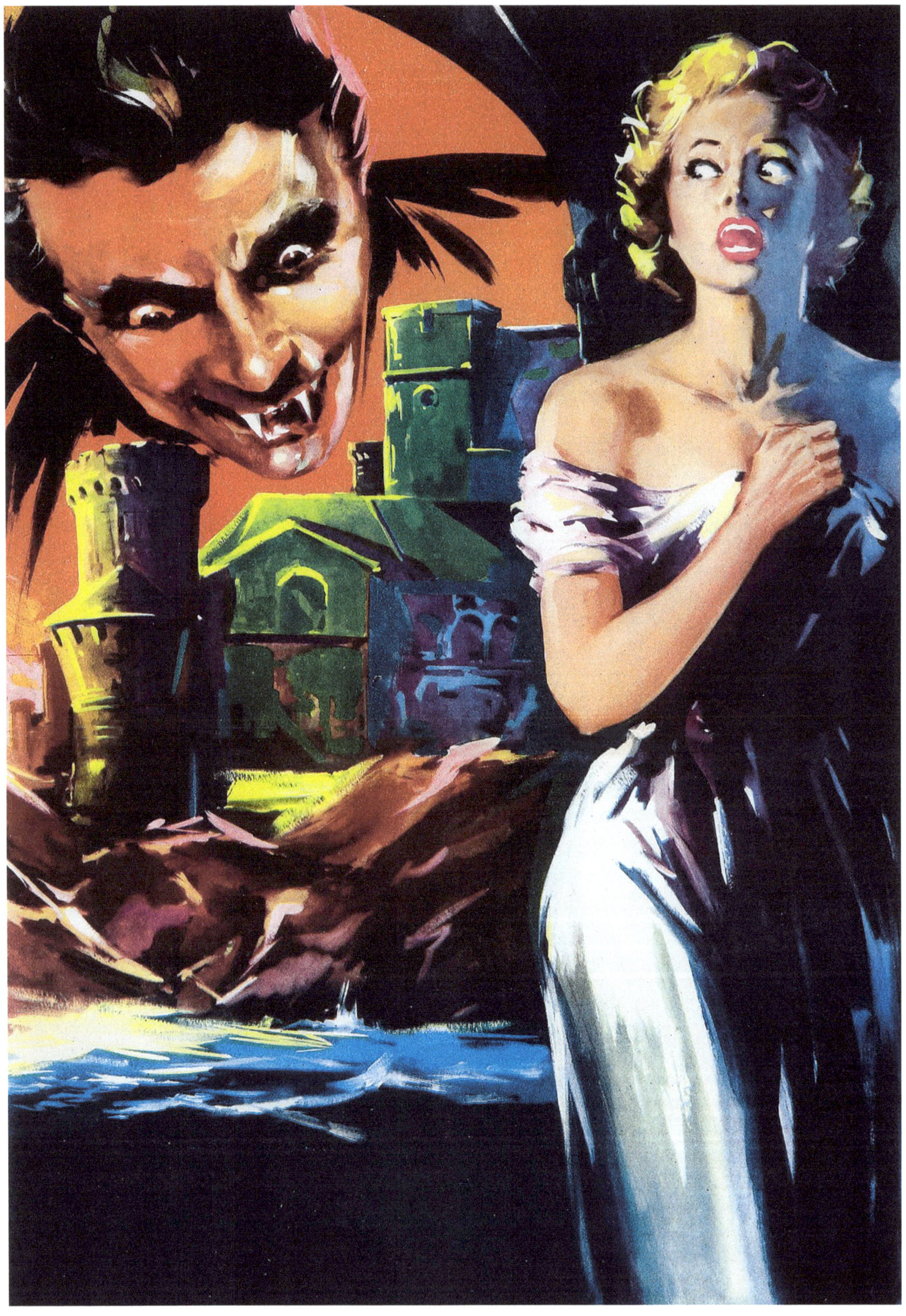

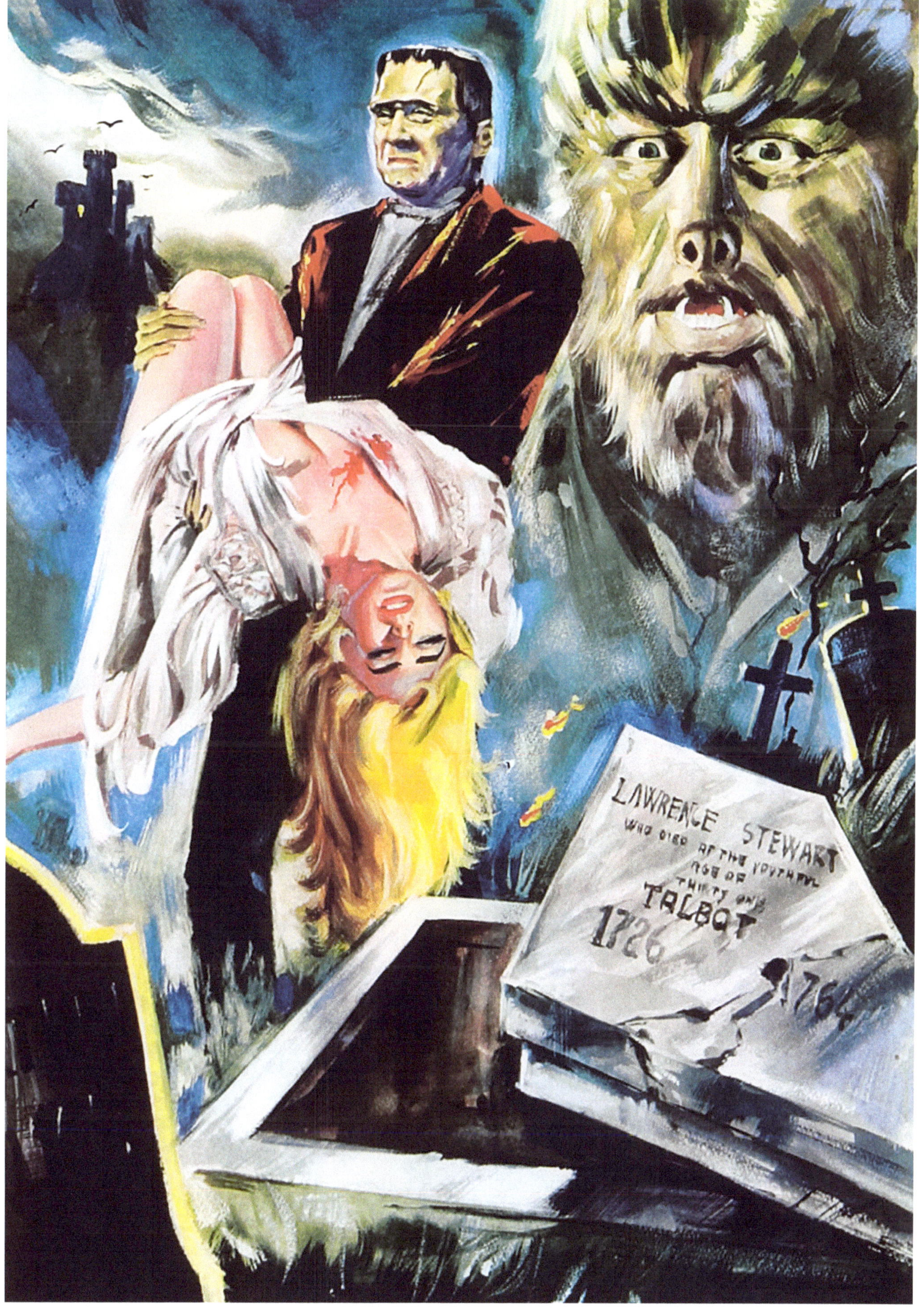

LAWRENCE STEWART
WHO DIED AT THE YOUTHFUL
AGE OF
THIRTY ONE
TALBOT
1726
1764

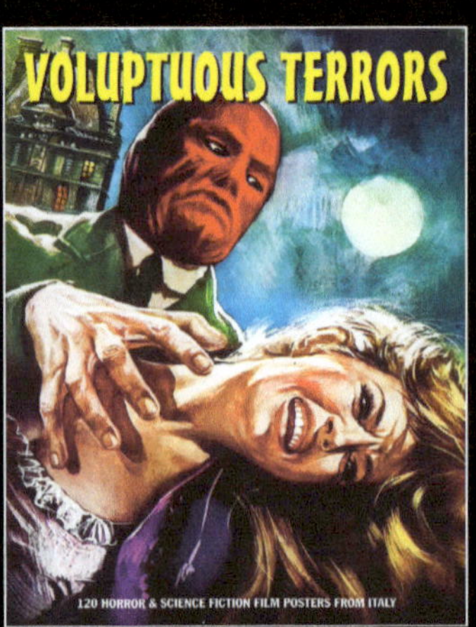
VOLUPTUOUS TERRORS
120 HORROR & SCIENCE FICTION FILM POSTERS FROM ITALY

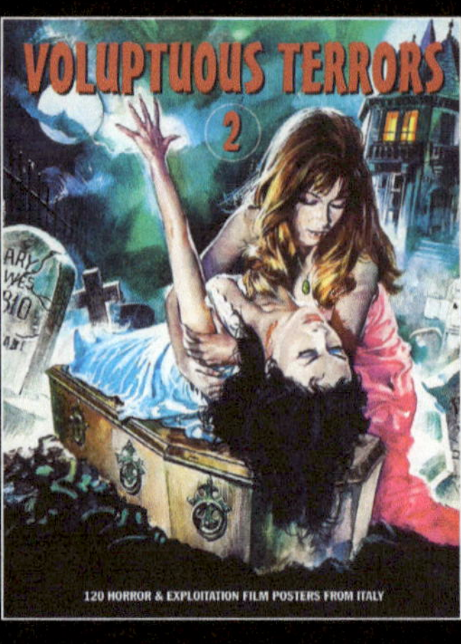
VOLUPTUOUS TERRORS
2
120 HORROR & EXPLOITATION FILM POSTERS FROM ITALY

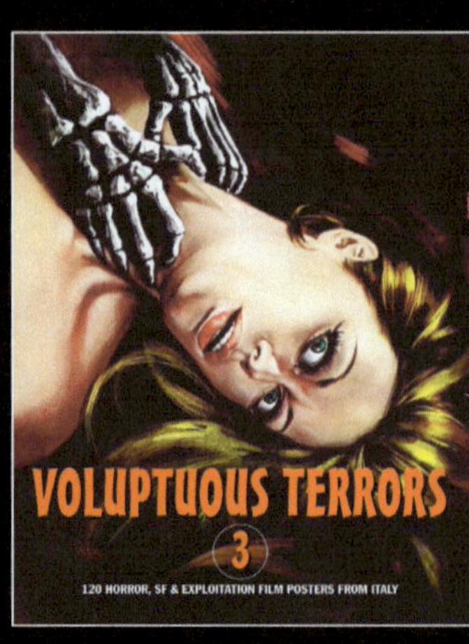
VOLUPTUOUS TERRORS
3
120 HORROR, SF & EXPLOITATION FILM POSTERS FROM ITALY

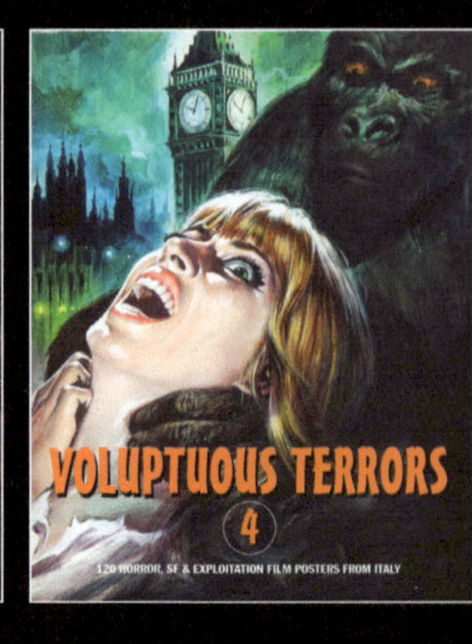
VOLUPTUOUS TERRORS
4
120 HORROR, SF & EXPLOITATION FILM POSTERS FROM ITALY

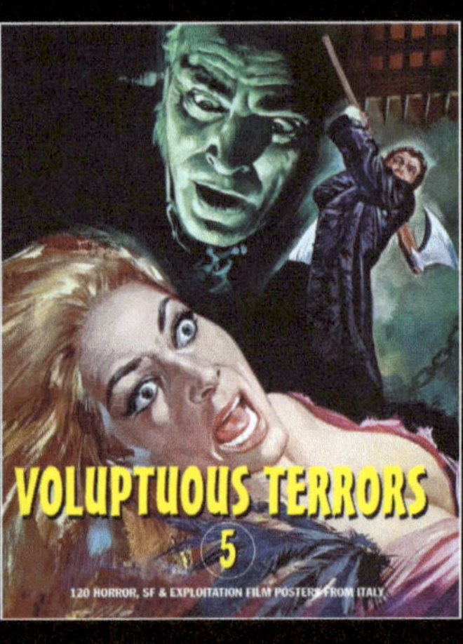
VOLUPTUOUS TERRORS
5
120 HORROR, SF & EXPLOITATION FILM POSTERS FROM ITALY

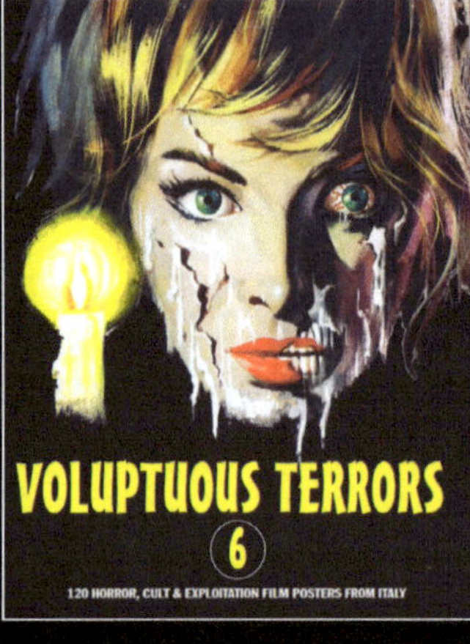
VOLUPTUOUS TERRORS
6
120 HORROR, CULT & EXPLOITATION FILM POSTERS FROM ITALY

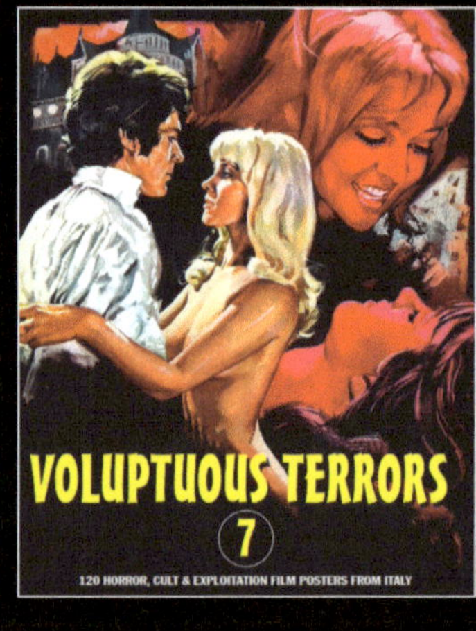
VOLUPTUOUS TERRORS
7
120 HORROR, CULT & EXPLOITATION FILM POSTERS FROM ITALY

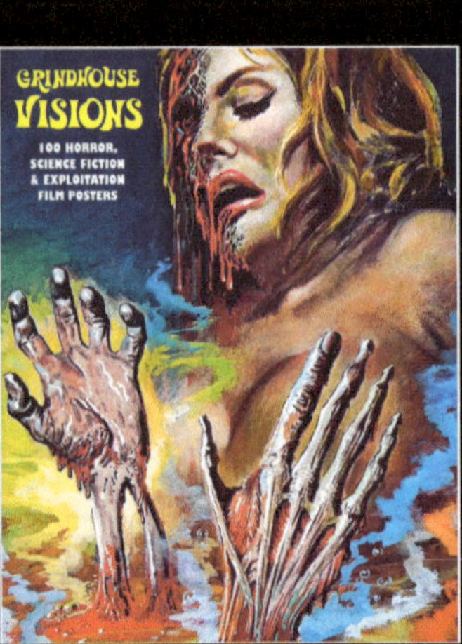
GRINDHOUSE
VISIONS
100 HORROR,
SCIENCE FICTION
& EXPLOITATION
FILM POSTERS

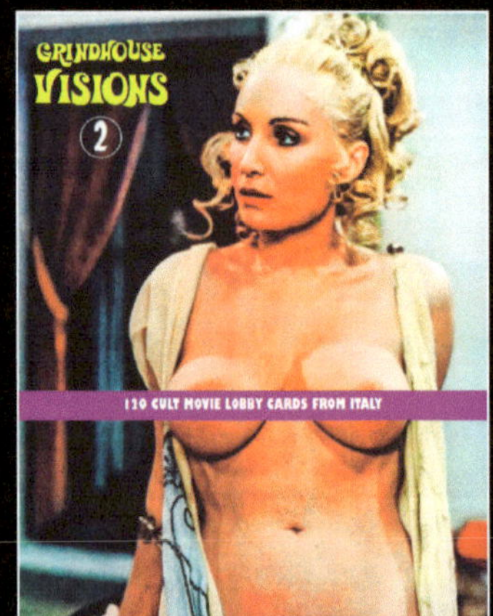
GRINDHOUSE
VISIONS
2
110 CULT MOVIE LOBBY CARDS FROM ITALY

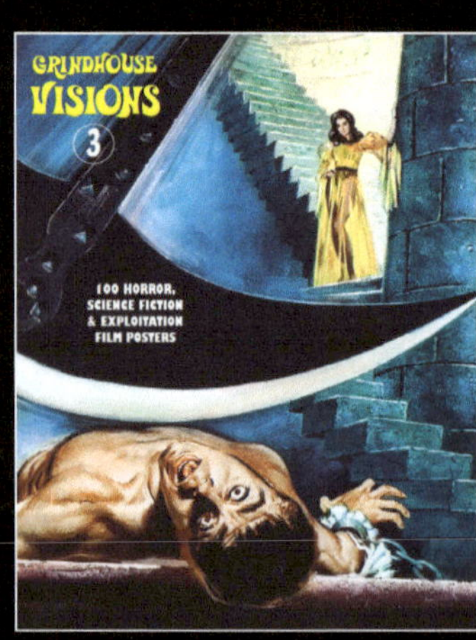
GRINDHOUSE
VISIONS
3
100 HORROR,
SCIENCE FICTION
& EXPLOITATION
FILM POSTERS

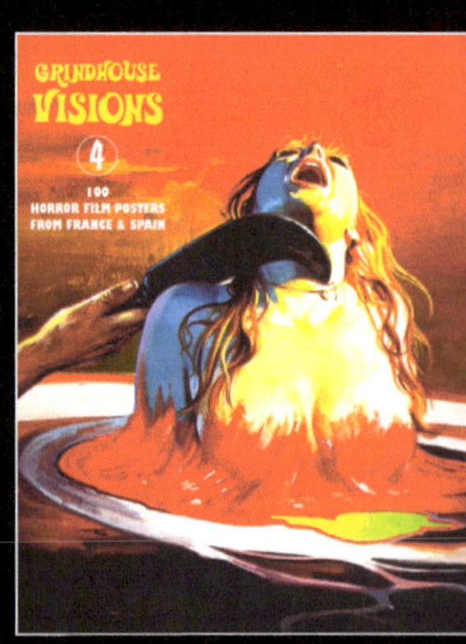
GRINDHOUSE
VISIONS
4
100
HORROR FILM POSTERS
FROM FRANCE & SPAIN

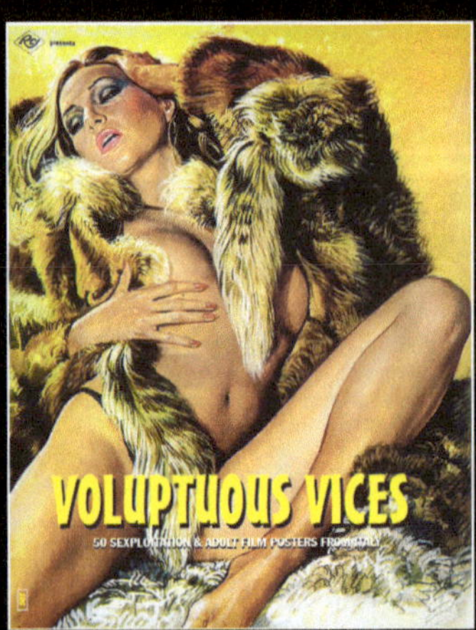
VOLUPTUOUS VICES
50 SEXPLOITATION & ADULT FILM POSTERS FROM ITALY

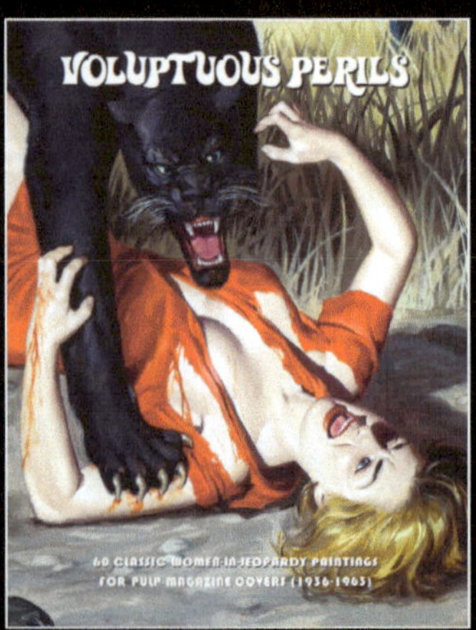
VOLUPTUOUS PERILS
60 CLASSIC WOMEN IN JEOPARDY PAINTINGS
FOR PULP MAGAZINE COVERS (1936-1963)

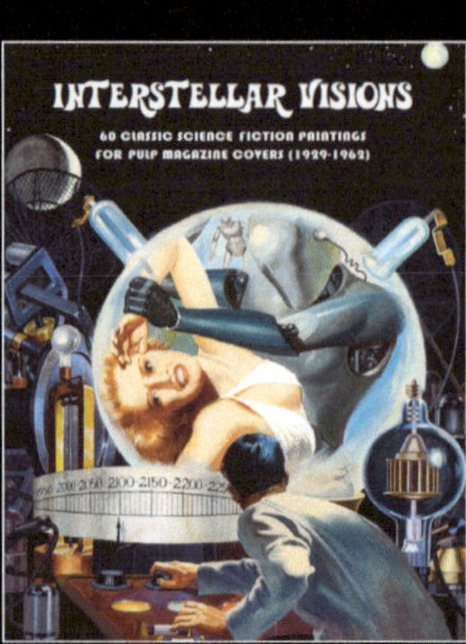
INTERSTELLAR VISIONS
60 CLASSIC SCIENCE FICTION PAINTINGS
FOR PULP MAGAZINE COVERS (1929-1962)